12th Workshop on Multiword Expressions (MWE 2016)

Held at ACL 2016

Berlin, Germany
11 August 2016

ISBN: 978-1-5108-2776-9

Printed by Curran Associates, Inc. (2016)

For permission requests, please contact the Association for Computational Linguistics
at the address below.

Association for Computational Linguistics
209 N. Eighth Street
Stroudsburg, Pennsylvania 18360

Phone: 1-570-476-8006
Fax: 1-570-476-0860

acl@aclweb.org

Additional copies of this publication are available from:

Curran Associates, Inc.
57 Morehouse Lane
Red Hook, NY 12571 USA
Phone: 845-758-0400
Fax: 845-758-2633
Email: curran@proceedings.com
Web: www.proceedings.com

ACL 2016

**The 54th Annual Meeting of the
Association for Computational Linguistics**

**Proceedings of the 12th Workshop on Multiword Expressions
(MWE'2016)**

August 11, 2016
Berlin, Germany

Introduction

The 12th Workshop on Multiword Expressions (MWE'2016) took place on August 11, 2016 in Berlin, Germany, in conjunction with the 54th Annual Meeting of the Association for Computational Linguistics (ACL'2016) and was endorsed by the Special Interest Group on the Lexicon of the Association for Computational Linguistics (SIGLEX), as well as by the SIGLEX Section dedicated to the study and research of Multiword Expressions (SIGLEX-MWE).

The workshop has been held almost every year since 2003, in conjunction with ACL, EACL, NAACL, COLING, and LREC. It is the main venue of the field for interaction, sharing of resources and tools and collaboration efforts for advancing the computational treatment of Multiword Expressions (MWEs), attracting the attention of an ever-growing community from all around the world working on a variety of languages and MWE types.

MWEs include idioms (*storm in a teacup, sweep under the rug*), fixed phrases (*in vitro, by and large*), noun compounds (*olive oil, laser printer*), compound verbs (*take a nap, bring about*), among others. These, while easily mastered by native speakers, are a key issue and a current weakness for natural language parsing and generation, as well as for real-life applications that require some degree of semantic interpretation, such as machine translation, just to name a prominent one among many. However, thanks to the joint efforts of researchers from several fields working on MWEs, significant progress has been made in recent years, especially concerning the construction of large-scale language resources. For instance, there is a large number of recent papers that focus on the acquisition of MWEs from corpora, and others that describe a variety of techniques to find paraphrases for MWEs. Current methods use a plethora of tools such as association measures, machine learning, syntactic patterns, web queries, etc.

In the call for papers, we solicited submissions about major challenges in the overall process of MWE treatment, both from a theoretical and a computational viewpoint, focusing on original research related (but not limited) to the following topics:

- Lexicon-grammar interface for MWEs
- Parsing techniques for MWEs
- Hybrid parsing of MWEs
- Annotating MWEs in treebanks
- MWEs in Machine Translation and Translation Technology
- Manually and automatically constructed resources
- Representation of MWEs in dictionaries and ontologies
- MWEs and user interaction
- Multilingual acquisition
- Multilingualism and MWE processing
- Models of first and second language acquisition of MWEs
- Crosslinguistic studies on MWEs
- The role of MWEs in the domain adaptation of parsers
- Integration of MWEs into NLP applications
- Evaluation of MWE treatment techniques
- Lexical, syntactic or semantic aspects of MWEs

Submission modalities included long papers and short papers. From a total of 49 submissions, we accepted 4 long papers for oral presentation. We further accepted 5 short papers for oral presentation and another 8 short papers as posters. Thus the total number of accepted papers is 18, or an overall acceptance rate of 37%.

Acknowledgements

We would like to thank the members of the Program Committee for the timely reviews and the authors for their valuable contributions.

Valia Kordoni, Kostadin Cholakov, Markus Egg, Stella Markantonatou, Preslav Nakov
Co-Organizers

Organizers:

Valia Kordoni, Humboldt Universität zu Berlin (Germany)
Kostadin Cholakov, Humboldt Universität zu Berlin (Germany)
Markus Egg, Humboldt Universität zu Berlin (Germany)
Stella Markantonatou, Institute for Language and Speech Processing (ILSP) - Athena Research Center (Greece)
Preslav Nakov, Qatar Computing Research Institute, HBKU (Qatar)

Program Committee:

Dimitra Anastasiou, LIST-Luxembourg Institute of Science and Technology (Luxembourg)
Tim Baldwin, The University of Melbourne (Australia)
Núria Bel, Pompeu Fabra University (Spain)
Lars Borin, University of Gothenburg (Sweden)
Jill Burstein, ETS (USA)
Aoife Cahill, ETS (USA)
Paul Cook, University of New Brunswick (Canada)
Anastasia Christofidou, Academy of Athens/National and Kapodistrian University of Athens (Greece)
Béatrice Daille, Nantes University (France)
Joaquim Ferreira da Silva, New University of Lisbon (Portugal)
Aggeliki Fotopoulou, Institute for Language and Speech Processing / Athena Research Center (Greece)
Voula Gotsoulia, National and Kapodistrian University of Athens (Greece)
Chikara Hashimoto, National Institute of Information and Communications Technology (Japan)
Kyo Kageura, University of Tokyo (Japan)
Dimitrios Kokkinakis, University of Gothenburg (Sweden)
Ioannis Korkontzelos, University of Manchester (UK)
Takuya Matsuzaki, Nagoya University (Japan)
Yusuke Miyao, National Institute of Informatics (Japan)
Joakim Nivre, University of Uppsala (Sweden)
Diarmuid Ó Séaghdha, University of Cambridge and VocalIQ (UK)
Haris Papageorgiou, Institute for Language and Speech Processing/Athena Research Center (Greece)
Yannick Parmentier, University of Orleans (France)
Pavel Pecina, Charles University in Prague (Czech Republic)
Scott Piao, Lancaster University (UK)
Barbara Plank, University of Groningen (The Netherlands)
Maja Popović, Humboldt Universität zu Berlin (Germany)
Prokopidis Prokopis, Institute for Language and Speech Processing/Athena Research Center (Greece)
Carlos Ramisch, Aix-Marseille University (France)
Martin Riedl, University of Darmstadt (Germany)
Will Roberts, Humboldt Universität zu Berlin (Germany)
Agata Savary, Université François Rabelais Tours (France)
Aline Villavicencio, Federal University of Rio Grande do Sul (Brazil)
Veronika Vincze, Hungarian Academy of Sciences (Hungary)

Table of Contents

Conference Program

Thursday, 11 August 2016

08:50–09:00 *Opening remarks*

Oral Session 1

09:00–09:30 *Learning Paraphrasing for Multiword Expressions*
Seid Muhie Yimam, Héctor Martínez Alonso, Martin Riedl and Chris Biemann

09:30–10:00 *Exploring Long-Term Temporal Trends in the Use of Multiword Expressions*
Tal Daniel and Mark Last

10:00–10:30 *Lexical Variability and Compositionality: Investigating Idiomaticity with Distributional Semantic Models*
Marco Silvio Giuseppe Senaldi, Gianluca E. Lebani and Alessandro Lenci

10:30–11:00 *Coffee Break*

Oral Session 2

11:00–11:20 *Filtering and Measuring the Intrinsic Quality of Human Compositionality Judgments*
Carlos Ramisch, Silvio Cordeiro and Aline Villavicencio

11:20–11:40 *Graph-based Clustering of Synonym Senses for German Particle Verbs*
Moritz Wittmann, Marion Weller-Di Marco and Sabine Schulte im Walde

11:40–12:00 *Accounting ngrams and multi-word terms can improve topic models*
Michael Nokel and Natalia Loukachevitch

12:00–13:00 *Invited Talk*

13:00–14:00 *Lunch*

Thursday, 11 August 2016 (continued)

14:00–14:40   Poster Booster Session (5 minutes per poster)

Top a Splitter: Using Distributional Semantics for Improving Compound Splitting
Patrick Ziering, Stefan Müller and Lonneke van der Plas

Using Word Embeddings for Improving Statistical Machine Translation of Phrasal Verbs
Kostadin Cholakov and Valia Kordoni

Modeling the Non-Substitutability of Multiword Expressions with Distributional Semantics and a Log-Linear Model
Meghdad Farahmand and James Henderson

Phrase Representations for Multiword Expressions
Joël Legrand and Ronan Collobert

Representing Support Verbs in FrameNet
Miriam R L Petruck and Michael Ellsworth

Inherently Pronominal Verbs in Czech: Description and Conversion Based on Treebank Annotation
Zdenka Uresova, Eduard Bejček and Jan Hajic

Using collocational features to improve automated scoring of EFL texts
Yves Bestgen

A study on the production of collocations by European Portuguese learners
Angela Costa, Luísa Coheur and Teresa Lino

Learning Paraphrasing for Multi-word Expressions

Seid Muhie Yimam[†] and **Héctor Martínez Alonso**[◇]
and **Martin Riedl**[†] and **Chris Biemann**[†]

[†]**FG Language Technology**
Computer Science Department
Technische Universität Darmstadt

[◇]**University of Paris 7**
The National Institute for Research
in Computer Science and Control – INRIA

Abstract

In this paper, we investigate the impact of context for the paraphrase ranking task, comparing and quantifying results for multi-word expressions and single words. We focus on systematic integration of existing paraphrase resources to produce paraphrase candidates and later ask human annotators to judge paraphrasability in context.

We first conduct a paraphrase-scoring annotation task with and without context for targets that are i) single- and multi-word expressions ii) verbs and nouns. We quantify how differently annotators score paraphrases when context information is provided. Furthermore, we report on experiments with automatic paraphrase ranking. If we regard the problem as a binary classification task, we obtain an F1–score of 81.56% and 79.87% for multi-word expressions and single words resp. using kNN classifier. Approaching the problem as a learning-to-rank task, we attain MAP scores up to 87.14% and 91.58% for multi-word expressions and single words resp. using LambdaMART, thus yielding high-quality contextualized paraphrased selection. Further, we provide the first dataset with paraphrase judgments for multi-word targets in context.

1 Introduction

In this work, we examine the influence of context for paraphrasing of multi-word expressions (MWEs). Paraphrases are alternative ways of writing texts while conveying the same information (Zhao et al., 2007; Burrows et al., 2013). There are several applications where an automatic text paraphrasing is desired such as text shortening (Burrows et al., 2013), text simplification, machine translation (Kauchak and Barzilay, 2006), or textual entailment.

Over the last decade, a large number of paraphrase resources have been released including PPDB (Pavlick et al., 2015), which is the largest in size. However, PPDB provides only paraphrases without context. This hampers the usage of such a resource in applications. In this paper, we tackle the research question on how we can automatically rank paraphrase candidates from abundantly available paraphrase resources. Most existing work on paraphrases focuses on lexical-, phrase-, sentence- and document level (Burrows et al., 2013). We primarily focus on contextualization of paraphrases based on existing paraphrase resources.

Furthermore, we target multi-worded paraphrases, since single-word replacements are covered well in lexical substitution datasets, such as (McCarthy and Navigli, 2007; Biemann, 2012). While these datasets contain multi-word substitution candidates, the substitution targets are strictly single words. Multi-word expressions are prevalent in text, constituting roughly as many entries as single words in a speaker's lexicon (Sag et al., 2002), and are important for a number of NLP applications. For example, the work by Finlayson and Kulkarni (2011) shows that detection of multi-word expressions improves the F-score of a word sense disambiguation task by 5 percent. In this paper, we experiment with both MWE and single words and investigate the difficulty of the paraphrasing task for single words vs. MWEs, using the same contextual features.

Our work, centered in assessing the effect of context for paraphrase ranking of humans and its automatic prediction, includes the following steps: 1) systematic combination of existing paraphrase

Proceedings of the 12th Workshop on Multiword Expressions, pages 1–10,
Berlin, Germany, August 7-12, 2016. ©2016 Association for Computational Linguistics

resources to produce paraphrase candidates for single- and multi-word expressions, 2) collection of dataset for paraphrase ranking/selection annotation task using crowdsourcing, and 3) investigating different machine learning approaches for an automatic paraphrase ranking.

2   Related Work

2.1   Paraphrase Resources and Machine Learning Approaches

Paraphrasing consists of mainly two tasks, paraphrase *generation* and paraphrase *identification*. Paraphrase generation is the task of obtaining candidate paraphrases for a given target. Paraphrase identification estimates whether a given paraphrase candidate can replace a paraphrase target without changing the meaning in context.

PPDB (Pavlick et al., 2015) is one of the largest collections of paraphrase resources collected from bilingual parallel corpora. PPDB2 has recently been released with revised ranking scores. It is based on human judgments for 26,455 paraphrase pairs sampled from PPDB1. They apply ridge regression to rank paraphrases, using the features from PPDB1 and include word embeddings.

The work of (Kozareva and Montoyo, 2006) uses a dataset of paraphrases that were generated using monolingual machine translation. In the dataset, sentence pairs are annotated as being paraphrases or not. For the binary classification, they use three machine learning algorithms (SVM, kNN and MaxEnt). As features they use word overlap features, n-grams ratios between targets and candidates, skip-grams longest common subsequences, POS tags and proper names.

Connor and Roth (2007) develop a global classifier that takes a word v and its context, along with a candidate word u, and determines whether u can replace v in the given context while maintaining the original meaning. Their work focuses on verb paraphrasing. Notions of context include: being either subject or object of the verb, named entities that appear as subject or object, all dependency links connected to the target, all noun phrases in sentences containing the target, or all of the above.

The work of Brockett and Dolan (2005) uses annotated datasets and Support Vector Machines (SVMs) to induce larger monolingual paraphrase corpora from a comparable corpus of news clusters found on the World Wide Web. Features include morphological variants, WordNet synonyms and hypernyms, log-likelihood-based based word pairings dynamically obtained from baseline sentence alignments, and string features such as word-based edit distance

Bouamor et al. (2011) introduce a targeted paraphrasing system, addressing the task of rewriting of subpart of a sentence to make the sentences easier for automatic translation. They report on experiments of rewriting sentences from Wikipedia edit history by contributors using existing paraphrase resources and web queries. An SVM classifier has been used for evaluation and an accuracy of 70% has been achieved.

Using a dependency-based context-sensitive vector-space approach, Thater et al. (2009) compute vector-space representations of predicate meaning in context for the task of paraphrase ranking. An evaluation on the subset of SemEval 2007 lexical substitution task produces a better result than the state-of-the-art systems at the time.

Zhao et al. (2007) address the problem of context-specific lexical paraphrasing using different approaches. First, similar sentences are extracted from the web and candidates are generated based on syntactic similarities. Candidate paraphrases are further filter using POS tagging. Second, candidate paraphrases are validated using different similarity measures such as co-occurrence similarity and syntactic similarity.

Our work is similar to previous approaches on all-words lexical substitution (Szarvas et al., 2013; Kremer et al., 2014; Hintz and Biemann, 2016) in the sense that we construct delexicalized classifiers for ranking paraphrases: targets, paraphrase candidates and context are represented without lexical information, which allows us to learn a single classifier/ranker for all potential paraphrasing candidates. However, these approaches are limited to single-word targets (Szarvas et al., 2013) resp. single-word substitutions (Kremer et al., 2014) only. In this paper, we extend these notions to MWE targets and substitutions, highlight the differences to single-word approaches, and report both on classification and ranking experiments.

2.2   Multi-word Expression Resources

While there are some works on the extraction of multi-word expressions and on investigation of their impact on different NLP applications, as far as we know, there is no single work dedicated on paraphrasing multi-word expressions. Various approaches exist for the extraction of MWEs: Tsvetkov and Wintner (2010) present an approach to extract MWEs from parallel corpora. They align the parallel corpus and focus on misalignment, which typically indicates expressions in the source language that are translated to the target in a non-compositional way. Frantzi et al. (2000) present a method to extract multi-word terms from English corpora, which combines linguistic and statistical information. The Multi-word Expression Toolkit (*MWEtoolkit*) extracts MWE candidates based on flat n-grams or specific morphosyntactic patterns (of surface forms, lemmas, POS tags) (Ramisch et al., 2010) and apply different fillters ranging form simple count thresholds to a more complex cases such as Association Measures (AMs). The tool further supports indexing and searching of MWEs, validation, and annotation facilities.

Schneider et al. (2014) developed a sequence-tagging-based supervised approach to MWE identification. A rich set of features has been used in a linguistically-driven evaluation of the identification of heterogeneous MWEs. The work by Vincze et al. (2011) constructs a multi-word expression corpus annotated with different types of MWEs such as compound, idiom, verb-particle constructions, light verb constructions, and others. In our work, we have used a combination of many MWEs resources from different sources for both MWE target detection and candidate generation (see Subsection 3.2).

3 Methods

In this section we describe our approach, which covers: the collection of training data, detection of multi-word paraphrases including annotating substitutes and learning a classifier in order to rank substitute candidates for a target paraphrase.

3.1 Impact of Context on Paraphrasing

In order to validate our intuitively plausible hypothesis that context has an impact on paraphrasing, we conduct experiments using the PPDB2 paraphrase database. PPDB2 is released with better paraphrase ranking than PPDB1 (Pavlick et al., 2015) but does not incorporate context information. Hence, we carry out different paraphrase ranking and selection annotation tasks using the Amazon Mechanical Turk crowdsourcing

	All (ρ)	MWE (ρ)	Single (ρ)
No context	0.35	0.25	0.36
Context	0.31	0.23	0.32

Table 1: Spearman correlation of human judgment with PPDB2 default rankings. The column *MWE* shows the result of only MWEs and the column *Single* shows the result of only single words.

platform.

In the first annotation task, a total of 171 sentences are selected from the British Academic Written English (BAWE) corpus[1] (Alsop and Nesi, 2009), with five paraphrase targets. The targets are selected in such a way that a) include MWEs as targets when it is possible (see Subection 3.2 how we select targets), b) the candidates could bear more than one contextual meaning and, c) workers can select up to three paraphrases and have to supply their own paraphrase if none of the candidates match. To satisfy condition b), we have used the JoBimText DT database API (Ruppert et al., 2015) to obtain single word candidates with multiple senses according to automatic sense induction.

We conduct this annotation setup twice, both with and without showing the original context (3–8 sentences). For both setups, a task is assigned to 5 workers. We incorporate control questions with invalid candidate paraphrases in order to reject unreliable workers. In addition to the control questions, JavaScript functions are embedded to ensure that workers select or supply at least one paraphrase. The results are aggregated by summing the number of workers that agreed on candidates, for scores between 0 and 5. Table 1 shows the Spearman correlation results. We can see that both single and MWE targets are context-dependent, as correlations are consistently lower when taking context into account. Further, we note that correlations are positive, but low, indicating that the PPDB2 ranking should not be used as-is for paraphrasing.

3.2 Paraphrase Dataset Collection using Crowdsourcing

In this subsection, we present the processes carried out to collect datasets for the paraphrase ranking task. This includes selection of documents,

---

identification of target paraphrases, and generation of candidate paraphrases from existing resources. We use 2.8k essay sentences from the ANC[2] and BAWE corpora for the annotation task.

Target detection and candidate generation: In order to explore the impact of contexts for paraphrasing, the first step is to determine possible targets for paraphrasing, as shown in Figure 1. As a matter of fact, every word or MWE in a sentence can be a target for paraphrasing. When prototyping the annotation setup, we found that five paraphrase targets are a reasonable amount to be completed in a single Human Intelligence Task (HIT), a single and self-contained unit of task to be completed and submitted by an annotator to receive a reward in a return[3].

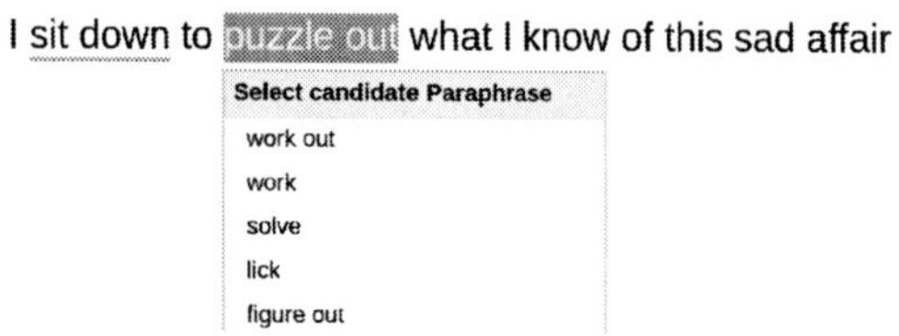

Figure 1: Paraphrase targets (a) and paraphrase candidates (b).

We select targets that have at least five candidates in our combined paraphrase resources. The paraphrase resources (S) for candidates generations are composed of collections from PPDB (Pavlick et al., 2015), WordNet and JoBimText distributional thesaurus (DT – only for single words).

For MWE paraphrase targets, we have used different MWE resources. A total of 79,349 MWE are collected from WordNet, STREUSLE (Schneider and Smith, 2015; Schneider et al., 2014)[4], Wiki50 (Vincze et al., 2011) and the MWE project (McCarthy et al., 2003; Baldwin and Villavicencio, 2002)[5]. We consider MWEs from this resources to be a paraphrase target when it is possible to generate paraphrase candidates from our paraphrase resources (S).

Candidates paraphrases for a target (both single and MWE) are generated as follows. For each paraphrase target, we retrieve candidates from the resources (S). When more than five candidates are collected: 1) for single words, we select the top candidates that bear different meanings in context using the automatic sense induction API by Ruppert et al. (2015), 2) for MWEs we select candidates that are collected from multiple resources in S. We present five candidates for the workers to select the suitable candidates in context. We also allow workers to provide their own alternative candidates when they found that none of the provided candidates are suitable in the current context. Figure 2 shows the Amazon Mechanical Turk user interface for the paraphrase candidate selection task. We discuss the different statistics and quality of annotations obtained in Section 5.2.

3.3 Machine Learning Approaches for Paraphrasing

In this work we investigate two types of machine-learning setups for paraphrase selection and ranking problems. In the first setup, we tackle the problem as a binary classification task, namely whether one candidate can be chosen to replace a target in context. All candidates annotated as possible paraphrases are considered a positive examples. We follow a 5-fold cross validation approach to train and evaluate our model.

In the second setup, we use a learning-to-rank algorithm to re-rank paraphrase candidates. There are different machine learning methods for the learning-to-ranking approach, such as *pointwise*, *pairwise* and *listwise* rankings. In the pointwise ranking, a model is trained to map candidate phrases to relevance scores, for example using a simple regression technique. Ranking is then performed by simply sorting predicted scores (Li et al., 2007). In the pairwise approach, the problem is regarded as a binary classification task where pairs are individually compared each other (Freund et al., 2003). Listwise ranking approaches learn a function by taking individual candidates as instances and optimizing a loss function defined on the predicted instances (Xia et al., 2008). We experiment with different learning-to-rank algorithms from the RankLib[6] Java package of the Lemur project[7]. In this paper, we present the results obtained using LambdaMART. LambdaMART (Burges, 2010) uses gradient boosting

---

[2]http://www.anc.org/
[3]https://www.mturk.com/mturk/help?helpPage=overview
[4]http://www.cs.cmu.edu/~ark/LexSem/
[5]http://mwe.stanford.edu
[6]https://people.cs.umass.edu/~vdang/ranklib.html
[7]http://sourceforge.net/projects/lemur/

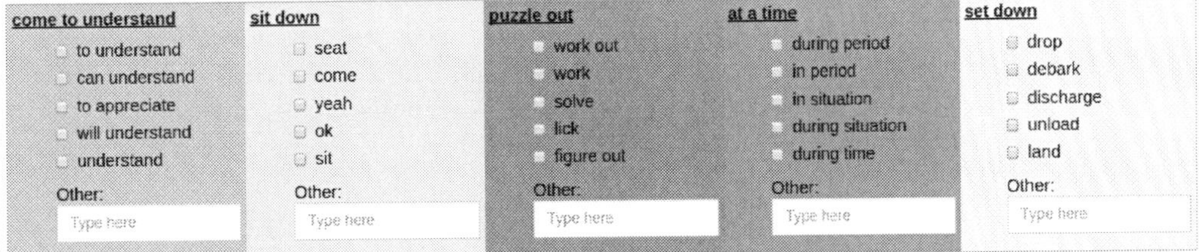

Figure 2: User-interface for paraphrase selection.

to directly optimize learning-to-rank specific cost functions such as Normalized Discounted Cumulative Gain (NDCG) and Mean Average Precision (MAP).

3.4 Features

We have modeled three types of features: a *resource-based* feature where feature values are taken from a lexical resource ($F0$), four features based on *global context* where we use word embeddings to characterize targets and candidates irrespectively of context ($F1, 2, 3, 4$) and four features based on *local context* that take the relation of target and candidate with the context into account ($F5, 6, 7, 8$).

PPDB2 score: We use the the PPDB2 score ($F0$) of each candidate as baseline feature. This score reflects a context-insensitive ranking as provided by the lexical resources.

First we describe features considering global context information:

Target and Candidate phrases: Note that we do not use word identity as a feature, and use the word embedding instead for the sake of robustness. We use the word2vec python implementation of Gensim (Řehůřek and Sojka, 2010)[8] to generate embeddings from BNC[9], Wikipedia, BAWE and ANC. We train embeddings with 200 dimensions using skip-gram training and a window size of 5. We approximate MWE embeddings

by averaging the embeddings of their parts. We use the word embeddings of the target ($F1$) and the candidate ($F2$) phrases.

Candidate-Target similarities: The dot product of the target and candidate embeddings ($F3$), as described in (Melamud et al., 2015).

Target-Sentence similarity: The dot product between a candidate and the sentence, i.e. the average embeddings of all words in the sentence ($F4$).

The following features use local context information:

Target-Close context similarity: The dot product between the candidate and the left and right 3-gram ($F5$) and 5-gram embedding ($F6$) resp..

Ngram features: A normalized frequency for a 2-5-gram context with the target and candidate phrases ($F7$) based on Google Web 1T 5-Grams[10].

Language model score: A normalized language model score using a sentence as context with the target and candidate phrases ($F8$). An n-gram language model (Pauls and Klein, 2011) is built using the BNC and Wikipedia corpora.

Also, we experimented with features that eventually did not improve results, such as the embeddings of the target's $n = 5$ most similar words, length and length ratios between target and candidate, most similar words and number of shared senses among target and candidate phrases based JoBimText DT (Ruppert et al., 2015), and N-gram POS sequences and dependency labels of the tar-

---

[8] https://radimrehurek.com/gensim/ models/word2vec.html

[9] http://www.natcorp.ox.ac.uk/

[10] https://catalog.ldc.upenn.edu/ LDC2009T25

<table>
<tr><td rowspan="2">Features</td><td colspan="3">kNN</td><td colspan="3">LambdaMART</td></tr>
<tr><td>P</td><td>R</td><td>F</td><td>P@1</td><td>NDCG
@5</td><td>MAP</td></tr>
<tr><td>All</td><td>69.27</td><td>90.41</td><td>78.41</td><td>90.53</td><td>89.03</td><td>91.35</td></tr>
<tr><td>F0+1+2+5</td><td>76.14</td><td>84.40</td><td>80.04</td><td>89.38</td><td>89.24</td><td>91.31</td></tr>
<tr><td>F1+2</td><td>75.28</td><td>85.05</td><td>79.85</td><td>88.13</td><td>88.98</td><td>90.88</td></tr>
<tr><td>F1+3</td><td>75.28</td><td>85.05</td><td>79.85</td><td>88.13</td><td>88.98</td><td>90.88</td></tr>
<tr><td>F1+5</td><td>74.42</td><td>86.69</td><td>80.07</td><td>88.11</td><td>88.76</td><td>90.82</td></tr>
<tr><td>F0+1+2+7</td><td>74.89</td><td>85.65</td><td>79.89</td><td>89.42</td><td>89.34</td><td>91.29</td></tr>
<tr><td>F3+7</td><td>70.28</td><td>79.82</td><td>74.61</td><td>82.31</td><td>84.08</td><td>86.34</td></tr>
<tr><td>F5+7</td><td>64.56</td><td>86.25</td><td>73.64</td><td>80.24</td><td>82.61</td><td>85.60</td></tr>
<tr><td>F0+3</td><td>68.87</td><td>81.39</td><td>74.43</td><td>87.04</td><td>86.37</td><td>88.78</td></tr>
<tr><td>F0+7</td><td>69.86</td><td>79.02</td><td>74.05</td><td>84.14</td><td>84.69</td><td>87.20</td></tr>
<tr><td>F6+7</td><td>65.20</td><td>79.49</td><td>71.34</td><td>80.03</td><td>84.98</td><td>85.54</td></tr>
<tr><td>F0+6</td><td>67.43</td><td>78.04</td><td>72.08</td><td>84.98</td><td>85.26</td><td>87.64</td></tr>
<tr><td>F0</td><td>72.49</td><td>79.84</td><td>75.18</td><td>84.12</td><td>84.51</td><td>87.15</td></tr>
</table>

(a) Performance on all datasets

<table>
<tr><td rowspan="2">Features</td><td colspan="3">kNN</td><td colspan="3">LambdaMART</td></tr>
<tr><td>P</td><td>R</td><td>F</td><td>P@1</td><td>NDCG
@5</td><td>MAP</td></tr>
<tr><td>All</td><td>76.74</td><td>82.99</td><td>79.71</td><td>89.72</td><td>88.82</td><td>91.58</td></tr>
<tr><td>F0+1+2+5</td><td>75.36</td><td>84.54</td><td>79.67</td><td>90.38</td><td>89.10</td><td>91.41</td></tr>
<tr><td>F1+2</td><td>75.74</td><td>83.66</td><td>79.49</td><td>88.28</td><td>88.82</td><td>90.98</td></tr>
<tr><td>F1+3</td><td>75.74</td><td>83.66</td><td>79.49</td><td>88.28</td><td>88.82</td><td>90.98</td></tr>
<tr><td>F1+5</td><td>74.95</td><td>85.52</td><td>79.87</td><td>87.50</td><td>88.51</td><td>90.76</td></tr>
<tr><td>F0+1+2+7</td><td>69.59</td><td>88.63</td><td>77.95</td><td>90.00</td><td>89.31</td><td>91.49</td></tr>
<tr><td>F3+7</td><td>70.25</td><td>78.71</td><td>74.09</td><td>81.92</td><td>83.78</td><td>86.03</td></tr>
<tr><td>F5+7</td><td>64.05</td><td>85.20</td><td>72.90</td><td>79.96</td><td>82.24</td><td>85.09</td></tr>
<tr><td>F0+3</td><td>68.89</td><td>80.52</td><td>74.05</td><td>86.41</td><td>86.46</td><td>88.64</td></tr>
<tr><td>F0+7</td><td>69.93</td><td>78.38</td><td>73.77</td><td>84.14</td><td>84.77</td><td>87.11</td></tr>
<tr><td>F6+7</td><td>64.67</td><td>78.80</td><td>70.71</td><td>78.97</td><td>82.06</td><td>84.98</td></tr>
<tr><td>F0+6</td><td>66.98</td><td>77.28</td><td>71.44</td><td>85.21</td><td>85.04</td><td>87.55</td></tr>
<tr><td>F0</td><td>74.08</td><td>72.18</td><td>71.47</td><td>84.81</td><td>84.60</td><td>87.29</td></tr>
</table>

(b) Performance on single words datasets

<table>
<tr><td rowspan="2">Features</td><td colspan="3">kNN</td><td colspan="3">LambdaMART</td></tr>
<tr><td>P</td><td>R</td><td>F</td><td>P@1</td><td>NDCG
@5</td><td>MAP</td></tr>
<tr><td>All</td><td>69.81</td><td>95.70</td><td>80.60</td><td>84.69</td><td>77.54</td><td>86.21</td></tr>
<tr><td>F0+1+2+5</td><td>73.66</td><td>91.25</td><td>81.56</td><td>81.76</td><td>76.40</td><td>85.43</td></tr>
<tr><td>F1+2</td><td>73.25</td><td>91.11</td><td>81.13</td><td>82.74</td><td>76.00</td><td>86.69</td></tr>
<tr><td>F1+3</td><td>73.25</td><td>91.11</td><td>81.13</td><td>82.74</td><td>76.00</td><td>86.69</td></tr>
<tr><td>F1+5</td><td>72.58</td><td>92.05</td><td>81.05</td><td>84.69</td><td>77.14</td><td>87.14</td></tr>
<tr><td>F0+1+2+7</td><td>72.85</td><td>91.14</td><td>80.89</td><td>83.71</td><td>75.95</td><td>84.97</td></tr>
<tr><td>F3+7</td><td>71.56</td><td>85.18</td><td>77.57</td><td>78.83</td><td>72.71</td><td>80.40</td></tr>
<tr><td>F5+7</td><td>68.03</td><td>89.72</td><td>77.18</td><td>72.31</td><td>67.27</td><td>80.66</td></tr>
<tr><td>F0+3</td><td>70.05</td><td>85.64</td><td>76.91</td><td>81.43</td><td>71.32</td><td>81.62</td></tr>
<tr><td>F0+7</td><td>70.28</td><td>84.56</td><td>76.56</td><td>71.34</td><td>67.76</td><td>77.35</td></tr>
<tr><td>F6+7</td><td>69.46</td><td>85.38</td><td>76.45</td><td>79.48</td><td>67.82</td><td>79.66</td></tr>
<tr><td>F0+6</td><td>71.49</td><td>82.35</td><td>76.39</td><td>80.78</td><td>69.16</td><td>82.37</td></tr>
<tr><td>F0</td><td>73.35</td><td>70.54</td><td>69.06</td><td>69.71</td><td>67.12</td><td>77.95</td></tr>
</table>

(c) Performance on MWEs datasets

Table 2: Binary classification vs. learning-to-rank results on baseline and 8 top-performing feature combinations.

4 Experimental Results

Now we discuss the different experimental results using the K-Nearest Neighbors (kNN)[11] from the scikit-learn[12] machine leaning framework (binary classification setup) and the LambdaMART learning to rank algorithm from the RankLib (learning to rank setup). We have used 5-fold cross validation on 17k data points (2k MWEs and 15k single) from the crowdsourcing annotation task for both approaches. The cross-validation is conducted in a way that there is no target overlap in in each split, so that our model is forced to learn a delexicalized function that can apply to all targets where substitution candidates are available, cf. (Szarvas et al., 2013).

As evaluation metrics, precision, recall, and F-score are used for the first setup. For the second setup we use P@1, Mean Average Precision (MAP), and Normalized Discounted Cumulative Gain (NDCG). P@1 measures the percentage of correct paraphrases at rank 1, thus gives the percentage of how often the best-ranked paraphrase is judged as correct. MAP provides a single-figure measure of quality across recall levels. NDCG is a ranking score that compares the optimal ranking to the system ranking, taking into account situations where many resp. very few candidates are relevant (Wang et al., 2013). In the following subsections, we will discuss the performance of the two machine learning setups.

4.1 Binary Classification

For paraphrase selection, we regard the problem as a binary classification task. If a given candidate is selected by at least one annotator, it is considered as possible substitute and taken as positive example. Otherwise it will be considered as a negative training example. For this experiment, kNN from the scikit-learn machine learning framework is used. Table 2 shows the evaluation result for the best subsets of feature combinations. The classification experiments obtain maximal F1s of 81.56% for MWEs and 79.77% for single words vs. a non-contextual baseline of 69.06% and 71.47% resp.

---

[11]Parameters: Number of neighbors (n_neighbors) = 20, weight function (weights) = distance
[12]http://scikit-learn.org/

4.2 Learning to Rank

Now we learn to rank paraphrase candidates, using the number of annotators agreeing on each candidate to assign relevance scores in the interval of [0–5].. The average evaluation result on the 5-fold splits is shown in Table 2. The baseline ranking given by $F0$ is consistently lower than our context-aware classifiers. The best scores are attained with all features enabled (P@1=89.72, NDCG@5=88.82 and MAP=91.58 for single words vs. P@1=84.69, NDCG@5=77.54 and MAP=86.21 for MWEs). A more detailed analysis between the ranking of single-worded targets and multi-worded paraphrases will be discussed in Section 5.3.

5 Analysis of the Result

In this section, we interpret the results obtained during the crowdsourcing annotation task and machine learning experimentation.

5.1 Correlation with PPDB2 Ranking

As it can be seen from Table 1, without contexts, a Spearman correlation of 0.36 and 0.25 is obtained by the workers against the PPDB2 default rankings for single and MWE annotations resp. However, when the contexts are provided to the workers, the ranking for the same items is lower with a Spearman correlation of 0.32 and 0.23 for single and MWE annotations resp. This indicates that the contexts provided has an impact on the ranking of paraphrases. Moreover, we observe that the correlation with PPDB2 ranking is considerably lower than the one reported by Pavlick et al. (2015) which is 0.71. Data analysis revealed a lot of inconsistent scores within the PPDB2. For example, the word pairs (*come in*, *sound*) and (*look at*, *okay*) have a high correlation score (3.2, 3.18 resp.). However, they do not seem to be related and are not considered as substitutable by our method. The perceived inconsistency is worse in the case of MWE scores hence the correlation is lower than for single words.

5.2 Annotation Agreement

According to Table 3, annotators agree more often on single words than on MWEs. This might be attributed to the fact that single word candidates are generated with different meanings using the automatic sense induction approach, provided by the JoBimText framework (Ruppert et al., 2015).

	#0	#1	#2	#3	#4	#5	Agreement
All	36.09	34.57	11.68	8.38	5.82	3.46	81.56
Single	36.54	34.47	11.48	8.24	5.79	3.48	81.76
MWE	32.39	35.43	13.35	9.47	6.06	3.30	76.97

Table 3: Score distributions and observed annotation agreement (in %). The columns #1 to #5 shows the percentage of scores the annotator give to each classes (0–5). The last column provides the observed agreements among 5 annotators.

Hence, when context is provided, it is much easier to discern the correct candidate paraphrase. On the other hand, in MWEs, their parts disambiguate each other to some extent, so there are less candidates with context mismatches. We can witness that from the individual class percentages (MWE candidates are on average scored higher than single word candidates, especially in the range of [2-4]) and from the overall observed agreements.

5.3 Machine Learning

According to the results shown in Table 2, we achieve higher scores for the binary classification for MWE than for single words. We found that this is due to the fact that we have more positive examples (67.6%) than the single words. Intuitively, it is much easier to have one of the five candidates to be a correct paraphrase as most of the MWE are not ambiguous in meaning (see recall (R) column in Table 2).

> **Example 1**: *this is the reason too that the reader disregards the duke 's **point of view** , and supports and sympathises with the duchess , acknowledging her innocence.*
> **Example 2**: *this list of verbs describes day-to-day occupations of the **young girl** , suggesting that she does n't distinguish the graveyard from other locations of her day .*
> **Example 3**: *this is apparent in the case of the priest who tries to vanquish **the devil** , who is infact mistaken for mouse slayer , the cat ...*

Error analysis of the classification result shows that some of the errors are due to annotation mistakes. In Example 1, the annotators do not select the candidate **stand** while the classifier predicts it correctly. We also found that the classifier wrongly picks antonyms from candidates. The classifier selected **younger man** and **heaven** for Example 2 and 3 resp. while the annotators do not

Target	Candidate	#Annotators	Ranker score
write about	write on	2	8.14
write about	write into	0	5.63
write about	discuss	1	2.81
write about	write in	1	1.20
write about	talk to	1	-1.82

Table 4: LambdaMART ranking scores

select them. Out of 91 MWE examples predicted by the classifier as positive, we found out that 24 of the examples have near synonym meaning while annotators fail to select them and also, 7 examples are antonyms.

The results for learning the ranking show a different trend. Once again, we can see that it is difficult to rank better when the candidates provided (in the case of MWEs) are less ambiguous. This could also be a consequence of the lower agreement on MWE candidate judgments. Analysis of the learn-to-rank result also revealed that the lower result is due to the fact that more often, the annotators do not agree on a single candidate, as it can be seen from Table 4.

Looking at the overall results, it becomes clear that our learning framework can substantially improve contextual paraphrase ranking over the PPDB2-resource-based baseline. The resource-based $F0$-feature, however, is still important for attaining the highest scores. While the global context features based on word embeddings (cf. $F1 + 2 + 3$ or $F1 + 3$) already show a very good performance, they are consistently improved by adding one or all feature that models local context ($F5, F6, F7, F8$). From this we conclude that all feature types (resource, global context, local context) are important.

6 Conclusion and Future Directions

In this paper we have quantified the impact of context on the paraphrase ranking scoring task. The direct annotation experiments show that paraphrasing is in fact a context-specific task: while the paraphrase ranking scores provided by PPDB2 were confirmed by a weak correlation with out-of-context judgments, the correlation between resource-provided rankings and judgments in context were consistently lower.

We conducted a classification experiment in a delexicalized setting, i.e. training and testing on disjoint sets of paraphrase targets. For a binary classification setting as well as for ranking, we im-

proved substantially over the non-contextualized baseline as provided by PPDB2. An F-score of 81.56% and 79.87% is attained for MWEs and Single words using kNN classifier from scikit-learn. A MAP score of 87.14% and 91.58% is obtained for MWEs and single words using the LambdaMART learn-to-rank algorithm from RankLib.

We recommend to use a learning-to-rank framework for utilizing features that characterize the paraphrase candidate not only with respect to the target, but also with respect to the context. The most successful features in these experiments are constructed from word embeddings, and the best performance is attained in combination of resource-based, global context and local context features.

Both experiments confirm the generally accepted intuition that paraphrasing, just like lexical substitution of single words, depends on context: while MWEs are less ambiguous than single words, it still does not hold that they can be replaced without taking the context into account. Here, we have quantified the amount of context dependence on a new set of contextualized paraphrase judgments, which is – to our knowledge – the first dataset with multi-word targets[13].

While our dataset seems of sufficient size to learn a high-quality context-aware paraphrase ranker, we would like to employ usage data from a semantic writing aid for further improving the quality, as well as for collecting domain- and user-specific paraphrase generation candidates.

References

Sian Alsop and Hilary Nesi. 2009. Issues in the development of the British Academic Written English (BAWE) corpus. *Corpora*, 4(1):71–83.

Timothy Baldwin and Aline Villavicencio. 2002. Extracting the unextractable: A case study on verb-particles. In *Proceedings of the 6th Conference on Natural Language Learning*, CoNLL-02, pages 1–7, Taipei, Taiwan.

Chris Biemann. 2012. Creating a System for Lexical Substitutions from Scratch using Crowdsourcing. *Language Resources and Evaluation: Special Issue on Collaboratively Constructed Language Resources*, 46(2):97–112.

---

[13]The AMT judgment datasets are provided as supplementary material and will be distributed under CC-BY.

Houda Bouamor, Aurélien Max, Gabriel Illouz, and Anne Vilnat. 2011. Web-based validation for contextual targeted paraphrasing. In *Proceedings of the Workshop on Monolingual Text-To-Text Generation*, MTTG '11, pages 10–19, Portland, OR, USA.

Chris Brockett and William B. Dolan. 2005. Support vector machines for paraphrase identification and corpus construction. In *Third International Workshop on Paraphrasing (IWP2005)*, pages 1–8, Jeju Island, South Korea.

Christopher J.C. Burges. 2010. From ranknet to lambdarank to lambdamart: An overview. Technical Report MSR-TR-2010-82, Microsoft Research.

Steven Burrows, Martin Potthast, and Benno Stein. 2013. Paraphrase acquisition via crowdsourcing and machine learning. *ACM Trans. Intell. Syst. Technol.*, pages 43:1–43:21.

Michael Connor and Dan Roth. 2007. Context sensitive paraphrasing with a single unsupervised classifier. In *18th European Conference on MAchine Learning (ECML)*, pages 289–295, Warsaw, Poland.

Mark Alan Finlayson and Nidhi Kulkarni. 2011. Detecting multi-word expressions improves word sense disambiguation. In *Proceedings of the Workshop on Multiword Expressions: From Parsing and Generation to the Real World*, MWE '11, pages 20–24, Portland, OR, USA.

Katerina Frantzi, Sophia Ananiadou, and Hideki Mima. 2000. Automatic recognition of multi-word terms: the C-value/NC-value method. *International Journal on Digital Libraries*, 3(2):115–130.

Yoav Freund, Raj Iyer, Robert E Schapire, and Yoram Singer. 2003. An efficient boosting algorithm for combining preferences. *The Journal of machine learning research*, 4:933–969.

Gerold Hintz and Chris Biemann. 2016. Language Transfer Learning for Supervised Lexical Substitution. In *The Annual Meeting of the Association for Computational Linguistics (ACL)*, page to apear, Berlin, Germany.

David Kauchak and Regina Barzilay. 2006. Paraphrasing for automatic evaluation. In *Proceedings of the Main Conference on Human Language Technology Conference of the North American Chapter of the Association of Computational Linguistics*, HLT-NAACL '06, pages 455–462, New York, NY, USA.

Zornitsa Kozareva and Andrés Montoyo. 2006. Paraphrase identification on the basis of supervised machine learning techniques. In *Advances in natural language processing*, pages 524–533, Turku, Finland.

Gerhard Kremer, Katrin Erk, Sebastian Padó, and Stefan Thater. 2014. What substitutes tell us - analysis of an "all-words" lexical substitution corpus. In *Proceedings of the 14th Conference of the European Chapter of the Association for Computational Linguistics*, pages 540–549, Gothenburg, Sweden.

Ping Li, Qiang Wu, and Christopher J Burges. 2007. Mcrank: Learning to rank using multiple classification and gradient boosting. In *Advances in neural information processing systems*, pages 897–904, Vancouver, BC, Canada.

Diana McCarthy and Roberto Navigli. 2007. Semeval-2007 task 10: English lexical substitution task. In *Proceedings of the Fourth International Workshop on Semantic Evaluations (SemEval-2007)*, pages 48–53, Prague, Czech Republic.

Diana McCarthy, Bill Keller, and John Carroll. 2003. Detecting a continuum of compositionality in phrasal verbs. In *Proceedings of the ACL 2003 Workshop on Multiword Expressions: Analysis, Acquisition and Treatment*, pages 73–80, Sapporo, Japan.

Oren Melamud, Omer Levy, and Ido Dagan. 2015. A simple word embedding model for lexical substitution. In *Proceedings of the 1st Workshop on Vector Space Modeling for Natural Language Processing*, pages 1–7, Denver, CO, USA.

Adam Pauls and Dan Klein. 2011. Faster and smaller n-gram language models. In *Proceedings of the 49th Annual Meeting of the Association for Computational Linguistics: Human Language Technologies - Volume 1*, HLT '11, pages 258–267, Portland, OR, USA.

Ellie Pavlick, Pushpendre Rastogi, Juri Ganitkevitch, Benjamin Van Durme, and Chris Callison-Burch. 2015. PPDB 2.0: Better paraphrase ranking, fine-grained entailment relations, word embeddings, and style classification. In *Proceedings of the 53rd Annual Meeting of the Association for Computational Linguistics and the 7th International Joint Conference on Natural Language Processing (Volume 2: Short Papers)*, pages 425–430, Beijing, China.

Carlos Ramisch, Aline Villavicencio, and Christian Boitet. 2010. MWEtoolkit: a Framework for Multiword Expression Identification. In *Proceedings of the Seventh International Conference on Language Resources and Evaluation (LREC'10)*, pages 134–136, Valletta, Malta.

Radim Řehůřek and Petr Sojka. 2010. Software Framework for Topic Modelling with Large Corpora. In *Proceedings of the LREC 2010 Workshop on New Challenges for NLP Frameworks*, pages 45–50, Valletta, Malta.

Eugen Ruppert, Manuel Kaufmann, Martin Riedl, and Chris Biemann. 2015. JOBIMVIZ: A Web-based Visualization for Graph-based Distributional Semantic Models. In *The Annual Meeting of the Association for Computational Linguistics (ACL) System Demonstrations*, pages 103–108, Beijing, China.

Ivan A. Sag, Timothy Baldwin, Francis Bond, Ann A. Copestake, and Dan Flickinger. 2002. Multiword expressions: A pain in the neck for nlp. In *Proceedings of the Third International Conference on Computational Linguistics and Intelligent Text Processing*, CICLing '02, pages 1–15, London, UK.

Nathan Schneider and Noah A. Smith. 2015. A corpus and model integrating multiword expressions and supersenses. In *Proceedings of the 2015 Conference of the North American Chapter of the Association for Computational Linguistics: Human Language Technologies*, pages 1537–1547, Denver, CO, USA.

Nathan Schneider, Emily Danchik, Chris Dyer, and Noah Smith. 2014. Discriminative Lexical Semantic Segmentation with Gaps: Running the MWE Gamut. *Transactions of the Association for Computational Linguistics*, 2:193–206.

György Szarvas, Róbert Busa-Fekete, and Eyke Hüllermeier. 2013. Learning to rank lexical substitutions. In *Proceedings of the 2013 Conference on Empirical Methods in Natural Language Processing, EMNLP 2013*, pages 1926–1932, Seattle, WA, USA.

Stefan Thater, Georgiana Dinu, and Manfred Pinkal. 2009. Ranking paraphrases in context. In *Proceedings of the 2009 Workshop on Applied Textual Inference*, TextInfer '09, pages 44–47, Suntec, Singapore.

Yulia Tsvetkov and Shuly Wintner. 2010. Extraction of multi-word expressions from small parallel corpora. In *Proceedings of the 23rd International Conference on Computational Linguistics: Posters*, COLING '10, pages 1256–1264, Beijing, China.

Veronika Vincze, István Nagy T., and Gábor Berend. 2011. Multiword Expressions and Named Entities in the Wiki50 Corpus. In *Proceedings of the International Conference Recent Advances in Natural Language Processing 2011*, pages 289–295, Hissar, Bulgaria.

Yining Wang, Liwei Wang, Yuanzhi Li, Di He, Wei Chen, and Tie-Yan Liu. 2013. A theoretical analysis of NDCG ranking measures. In *Proceedings of the 26th Annual Conference on Learning Theory (COLT 2013)*, Princeton, NJ, USA.

Fen Xia, Tie-Yan Liu, Jue Wang, Wensheng Zhang, and Hang Li. 2008. Listwise approach to learning to rank: theory and algorithm. In *Proceedings of the 25th international conference on Machine learning*, pages 1192–1199, New York, NY, USA.

Shiqi Zhao, Ting Liu, Xincheng Yuan, Sheng Li, and Yu Zhang. 2007. Automatic acquisition of context-specific lexical paraphrases. In *International Joint Conference on Artificial Intelligence*, Hyderabad, India.

Exploring Long-Term Temporal Trends in the Use of Multiword Expressions

Tal Daniel
Ben-Gurion University of the Negev
Beer-Sheva, Israel
dantal@post.bgu.ac.il

Mark Last
Ben-Gurion University of the Negev
Beer-Sheva, Israel
mlast@bgu.ac.il

Abstract

Differentiating between outdated expressions and current expressions is not a trivial task for foreign language learners, and could be beneficial for lexicographers, as they examine expressions. Assuming that the usage of expressions over time can be represented by a time-series of their periodic frequencies over a large lexicographic corpus, we test the hypothesis that there exists an old–new relationship between the time-series of some synonymous expressions, a hint that a later expression has replaced an earlier one. Another hypothesis we test is that Multiword Expressions (MWEs) can be characterized by sparsity & frequency thresholds.

Using a dataset of 1 million English books, we choose MWEs having the most positive or the most negative usage trends from a ready-made list of known MWEs. We identify synonyms of those expressions in a historical thesaurus and visualize the temporal relationships between the resulting expression pairs. Our empirical results indicate that old–new usage relationships do exist between some synonymous expressions, and that new candidate expressions, not found in dictionaries, can be found by analyzing usage trends.

1 Introduction

In this work, we explore Multiword Expressions (MWE) usage over a period of a few hundred years. Specifically, we focus on English MWEs of 2–3 words with long-term decreasing or increasing usage trends that exist in a ready-made list of MWEs. We do not focus on semantic change of these expressions, which is another research field.

From a list of MWEs with statistically significant trends, we try to identify a subset of expressions that have an inverse usage relationship with their near-synonymous expressions, replacing them, or being replaced by them over time.

Another objective of this work is to find potentially new candidate MWEs in a list of collocations that withstand certain sparsity & normalized frequency thresholds and have a statistically significant trend over the years. The normalized frequency threshold represents the minimum number of a collocation mentions, whereas the sparsity threshold represents the minimum number of years, or periods, a collocation is used (not necessarily in consecutive order), making a distinction between real MWEs and temporarily used multiword expressions.

2 Related Work

2.1 Multiword Expressions (MWEs)

Languages contain Multiword expressions (MWEs) that are compounded from a few words (lexemes). MWEs contain various types of expressions such as transparent collocations, fixed phrases, similes, catch phrases, proverbs, quotations, greetings, & phatic phrases (Atkins and Rundell, 2008). They are also used "to enhance fluency and understandability, or mark the register/genre of language use [...]. For example, MWEs can make language more or less informal/colloquial (c.f. *London Underground* vs. *Tube*, and *piss off* vs. *annoy*)." (Baldwin and Kim, 2010) Some MWEs are idiomatic expressions (e.g. *pull one's leg*), while others "[...] have the singularity of breaching general language rules" (Ramisch, 2013, p2) , such as *from now on*, *from time to time*, etc. They may be common names, e.g., *master key*, *vacuum cleaner*, and "sometimes the words [...] are collapsed and

Proceedings of the 12th Workshop on Multiword Expressions, pages 11–20,
Berlin, Germany, August 7-12, 2016. ©2016 Association for Computational Linguistics

form a single word" (Ramisch, 2013, p2), like *honeymoon*, and *firearm*.

Since MWEs are a mixed set with multiple phenomena, we adopt the broad and practical definition that Ramisch (2013) used, based on Calzolari et al. (2002): "[...] phenomena [that] can be described as a sequence of words that act as a single unit at some level of linguistic analysis" (Ramisch, 2013, p23). This definition emphasizes that MWEs are a single unit, which is especially important for translation, as Ramisch hints.

Several methods exist for finding, or extracting, MWEs from corpora. Often, researchers focus on a single kind of expressions, and length, e.g., Noun-Noun expressions of length two (Al-Haj and Wintner, 2010), or Verb-Noun idiom construction (Fazly et al., 2009). Focusing on a certain kind of expressions can be achieved by crafting a tailored-characterization of these MWEs, creating a model using a machine learning algorithm, and testing it. For example, Tsvetkov & Wintner (2011) suggested a method for any kind of MWEs, by training a system to learn a Bayesian model, based on characteristics such as the number of contexts the expression occurs in, how flexible it is to synonym word replacements, syntactic variability, or whether a translation of the expression appears in another language.

2.2 Trend Detection in Language Corpora

As new expressions become less, or more, frequently used, we can try to track these changes over the years by finding frequency trends. Identifying a trend involves a few tasks, though: One has to identify a statistically significant change in the data over time, to estimate the effect size of that change, while trying to pinpoint the exact time periods of these changes (Gray, 2007).

Buerki (2013) compared three methods for finding "ongoing change" in MWEs within Swiss Text Corpus, which he divided into 5 periods, or data points. He found that the Chi-square test was the most flexible, had an arbitrary cut-off frequency value when stating a statistically significant change in frequency, and could alert of a trend when it occurred in some periods, compared to other methods – not only to a continuous linear increase/decrease. Chi-square outperformed other methods as coefficient of difference (D) by Belica (1996) – the sum of squares of frequencies for each period, or coefficient of variance (CV) ,

which ranks the terms and uses an arbitrary cut-off point, e.g., the top third of the ranked list (Buerki, 2013). When the assumption of normal distribution is unrealistic or when the actual trend is nonlinear, Kendall's τ nonparametric statistic (Gray, 2007) can be used.

2.3 Synonymy

Synonymous expressions can replace each other to convey the same meaning. This claim is not accurate, though, since most synonyms are not semantically identical: "Synonymy, or more precisely near-synonymy, is the study of semantic relations between lexemes or constructions that possess a similar usage" (Glynn, 2010, p2). While Glynn's Cognitive Linguistics research investigated differences between *annoy*, *bother*, and *hassle*, Kalla (2006) studied differences between three Hebrew words that mean a friend: *yadid, rea, amit*.

Mahlow & Juska-Bacher (2011) created a German diachronic dictionary by finding variations of pre-selected expressions. Expression variations were found by using patterns and by assigning expressions to types (categories). Juska-Bacher & Mahlow (2012) elaborate more on their semi-automatic method to find structural and semantic changes in German phrasemes (idiomatic MWEs): First, they found candidate phrasemes by looking at nouns with at least 2% frequency, as well as other indicators. Then, they chose select phrasemes, after manually looking into old and contemporary dictionaries. These phrasemes were found in various corpora and manually analysed for changes. Above all, their work emphasizes the importance of manual examination, in addition to corpus-based approaches: "Fully automatic detection of phrasemes is not as yet possible, which is why lexicographers have to manually determine idiomaticity (Rothkegel, 2007)" (Juska-Bacher and Mahlow, 2012, p8).

Dagan & Schler (2013) used a semi-automatic iterative and interactive approach for creating a diachronic Hebrew thesaurus. They tried to automatically find synonym terms for a given list of terms by using second-order distributional similarity. Then they let a lexicographer to either select synonyms, or mark terms for query expansion. Kenter et al. (2015) presented an automatic algorithm that detects vocabulary change for specific input terms in Dutch, across a period of 40 years. They used distributional similarity to find time-stamped semantic spaces, and used the resulting graph to infer synonymous relationship.

3 Research Methods

3.1 Trend Detection & Analysis

To identify increasing and decreasing trends, we calculated the number of yearly mentions in the Google Syntactic Ngrams corpus for each MWE from the jMWE list. Then, we normalized the frequencies by dividing each yearly frequency by the number of words in the corpus for that year. Finally, we segmented the histograms into 7-year periods, summed-up the normalized frequencies in each period, and smoothed the histograms by using a simple moving average with a sliding window size of 5 periods.

Since we segmented and smoothed the time-series, the assumption of sample independence could not be assumed. Hence, we chose two non-parametric tests for trend existence: Kendall's τ correlation coefficient and Daniels test for trend. Kendall's τ correlation coefficient is often used when distributional assumptions of the residuals are violated or when there is a nonlinear association between two variables" (Gray, 2007, p29). The null hypothesis of Kendall's τ is that there is no trend ($H_0 : \tau = 0$), and the alternative hypothesis is that there is a trend ($H_1 : \tau \neq 0$).

Since the values in a time-series are ordered by time, let G_i be the number of data points after y_i that are greater than y_i. In the same manner, let L_i stand for the number of data points after y_i that are less than y_i. Given this, Kendall's τ coefficient is calculated as

$$\tau = 2S/n(n - 1) \qquad (1)$$

where S is the sum of differences between Gi and Li along the time-series:

$$S = \sum_{i=1}^{n-1} (Gi - Li) \qquad (2)$$

The test statistic z is calculated by

$$z = \frac{\tau}{\sqrt{2(2n + 5)/9n(n - 1)}} \qquad (3)$$

When n is large (e.g., $n > 30$), z has "approximately normal distribution", so a p-value can be based on the normal distribution table. For smaller n values, other tables can be used to get a p-value

(Gray, 2007). Daniels test for trend (1950, as mentioned in U.S. Environmental Protection Agency, 1974) uses Spearman's ρ rank correlation coefficient, which ranks each data point X_i in the time-series as $R(X_i)$. After ranking, ρ is calculated as

$$\rho = \frac{\sum_{i=1}^{n}[R(X_i) - i]^2}{n(n^2 - 1)} \qquad (4)$$

As with the Kendall's τ correlation test, Daniels test compares Spearman's ρ to a critical value, set by the sample size n: When $n < 30$, the critical value W_p for a desired p-value is set according to a dedicated table (U.S. Environmental Protection Agency, 1974). When $n \geq 30$, the critical value is calculated using X_p, which is the p quantile of a standard normal distribution:

$$W_p = \frac{X_p}{\sqrt{n - 1}} \qquad (5)$$

We ordered the list of computed trends by the statistic (Kendall's τ) and reviewed the top 30 expressions with the highest increasing trend and the 30 expressions with the lowest decreasing trend. The usage trends of these 60 expressions were tested again, using Daniels test for trend. Then, we looked up each expression in Oxford Historical Thesaurus[1], tried to find its synonymous expression, and compared the trends of both expressions to visualize an old–new relationship between them.

3.2 Finding New MWEs

We have tested the hypothesis that new MWEs can be detected in a collocations dataset by certain sparsity and normalized frequency thresholds. Using the Google Syntactic Ngrams corpus and the ready-made list of $65,450$ MWEs (Kulkarni and Finlayson, 2011), which is used by the jMWE library for detecting MWEs in text, we set the minimum normalized frequency threshold to that of the least mentioned MWE. In the same manner, we set the threshold of maximum sparsity to the sparsity of the MWE that was mentioned in the corpus across the smallest number of years. Next, we compared three criteria for selecting candidate expressions from Google Syntactic Ngrams (collocations) that are not part of the ready-made MWE list: (1) by their top trend statistic and normalized frequency, (2) by their top normalized frequency

---

[1]http://www.oed.com

only, or (3) by their lowest sparsity. For each criterion, we labeled the top k collocations as MWEs or not, according to our understanding, and calculated the *precision@k*. The trend statistic criterion was chosen based on the assumption that emerging MWEs are characterized by a positive usage trend until their common adoption.

The code we used, as well as the results can be found on Github[2].

4 Experimental Results

4.1 Dataset

We found the Google Books Syntactic-Ngrams dataset[3] suitable for our needs (Goldberg and Orwant, 2013), since it is a historical corpus containing data over hundreds of years. Specifically, we explored MWE usage using the 1 Million English subset of the dataset that was constructed from 1 Million English books corpus (Michel et al., 2011) published between 1520 and 2008 and originally contained 101.3 billion words. Each line in the dataset already contains 2–5 n-gram (words) collocations that were found in the 1M English corpus at least 10 times. Each collocation entry specifies its terms, part-of-speech tagging and syntactic dependency labels, total frequency, and a frequency histogram for the years where the n-gram was found. For example, here is how a line from the dataset looks like:

employed **more/JJR/dep/2 than/IN/prep/3** em-**ployed/VBN/ccomp/0** 12 1855,1 1856,2 1936,2 1941,1 1982,1 1986,1

For our research, we only used the "arcs" files of the dataset, which contain trigrams – two content words and optionally their functional markers. Content words are meaningful elements whereas functional-markers "[...] add polarity, modality or definiteness information to the meaningful elements, but do not carry semantic meaning of their own." (Goldberg and Orwant, 2013, p3). These phrases were checked against jMWE's predefined MWE list (Kulkarni and Finlayson, 2011), which is described later. Although one can explore files with single-word terms as well, tracking their usage should be problematic as they may be polysemous, i.e. their meaning may vary depending on context and language changes. We assume that polysemy of multi-word expressions is so rare that it can be ignored. Since the jMWE parser relies on part-of-speech tagging to find MWEs, we did not differentiate collocations by their syntactic dependency, and summed histograms with similar part-of-speech (POS) in the dataset into a single histogram, even though they could have different syntactic dependencies.

In order to bring the words to their stem form before sending the trigrams to jMWE expression detector, we lemmatized the terms with Stanford CoreNLP Toolkit (Manning et al., 2014). In addition, due to the special function underscores ("_") have in jMWE, we converted them to dashes ("-"). If that was the only character of the token/term, it was ignored. The total counts of the number of tokens in the corpus were taken from the Google Books 1M English Corpus (Google, 2009).

4.2 Usage Analysis of Multiword Expressions

For the Google Syntactic Ngrams dataset, we created expression histograms for the years 1701-2008, since only from 1701 there is more than 1 book per year. As a result, histograms spanned 309 years instead of 489 years, before segmentation, and 44 periods, or bins, in the final histograms.

We found 45,759 MWEs (out of 65,450 entries in the MWE index) in the arcs, or trigram files of the dataset (see research methods, above, for details). 41,366 MWEs of them had a statistically significant trend – an increase or decrease in counts – over the years (Kendall's $\tau|z| > 3$ or Daniels Test for trend, where Spearman's $|\rho| > 0.392; \alpha = .01$).

The most frequently used expressions were *of which* and *in case* (5% frequency, or 50,000/Million words, over a total of 30 periods – 210 years), while the least frequently used expressions were *bunker buster* and *qassam brigades* (0.122/Million words, over a total of 28 years). Figure 1 plots the normalized frequency versus rank of each expression that was found, and shows that Zipf's law (Estoup, 1916, as mentioned in Manning & Schutze, 1999), which states that there is a constant relationship between word frequencies and their rank, fits most of the expressions we have explored.

93% of expressions had a sparse histogram, meaning they were used during a rather short period in the dataset (i.e. 90% sparsity corresponds

[2]https://github.com/Tal-Daniel/daniel-last-MWEs
[3]http://commondatastorage.googleapis.com/books
/syntactic-ngrams/index.html, Version 20130501.

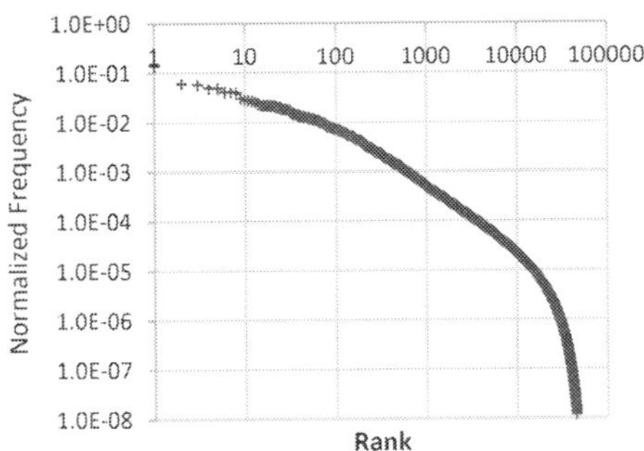

Figure 1: Rank versus Normalized frequency, using logarithmic scales.

to usage during 4 periods – 28 years). These MWEs were mostly named entities, as *Georgia O'Keef*, though some of them were rarely used MWEs (e.g., *Sheath pile*), or new expressions such as *web log*. In order to overcome these problems, we selected only MWEs with a trend that were used for at least 30% of 7–year periods. That step left us with 15,895 MWEs (907 of them with negative trends) that were frequently used across most periods of the dataset, so we could clearly see change in their usage and focus on prevalent expressions. Table 1 shows the 30 expressions with the most increasing usage trends, and Table 2 shows the 30 expressions with the most decreasing usage trends that were found in the dataset.

4.3 Finding Candidate MWEs

In addition to ready-made MWEs found in the dataset, collocations that were not included in the ready-made MWEs list [24] were considered candidate expressions if they passed two thresholds. We set the normalized frequency threshold to 1.22E-08, which equals the normalized frequency of the least mentioned MWE that was found in the MWE list (Kulkarni and Finlayson, 2011). This threshold represents 0.122 mentions per million words, or 1,359 mentions across the 111 Billion words in the Google Syntactic n-gram dataset (between the years 1701–2008). We also set the sparsity threshold to 4 periods – the shortest period an MWE spans, which equals to 28 years. In order to find only newer expressions, we looked for candidate expressions that started to appear since 1904.

Using these thresholds, we found 4,153 candidate expressions. 2,881 of them had a statistically significant trend ($\alpha = .01$), of which, only 13 showed a decreasing trend. 24 (80%) of the 30 candidate expressions with the most increasing usage trend have MWE characteristics, though some of them are actually professional terms used only in a very specific domain, such as *acoustic energy*, *learning environment*, and *control subject*; However, seven of the candidate expressions were not found in dictionaries[4], while showing characteristics of a multi-word expression as *Diary entry*, *older adult*, *entry into force*, *emergency entrance*, etc. This may suggest that the two thresholds can be used to find candidate multiword expressions in a multi-year corpus of collocations, as a complement to other existing methods for finding MWEs.

We have also evaluated two other methods that select candidate expressions by taking into account (1) only the normalized frequency values, or (2) only the sparsity values, without taking into account the trend value. We compared the three methods using *precision@k* measure, which allows to track the precision over a range of candidate expressions (collocations) list sizes. As Figure 2 shows, it seems that the best method is to select candidate expressions by sparsity alone while leaving-out proper name expressions.

4.4 Trend Analysis

Before looking at expressions with trends, we looked how expressions with no statistically significant trend behave. We chose expressions that have nearly constant mean number of mentions, and their Kendall's τ test statistic and Spearman's ρ are relatively far from statistically significant values.

Two expressions (*collect call* and *lift up*) had no trend and behaved almost as straight lines; other expressions did not behave as a straight horizontal line, as one expects when no trend is reported, however, this fits our expectations from Kendall's τ and Spearman's ρ to identify a statistically significant trend only with high confidence ($\alpha = .01$): Expressions with high frequency peak fluctuations (e.g., *white wine*, or *tribes of Israel*) had a trend canceling effect by previous or future fluctuations, in Kendall's τ equation 2, which is based on the sum of differences. Expressions with a peak in frequency towards the end, as *natural language*, had no trend too since the trend is rather short (the last 48 years of over a period 300 years).

---

[4]Merriam-Webster dictionary (http://www.merriam-webster.com/dictionary/) and Oxford English Dictionary (http://www.oed.com/).

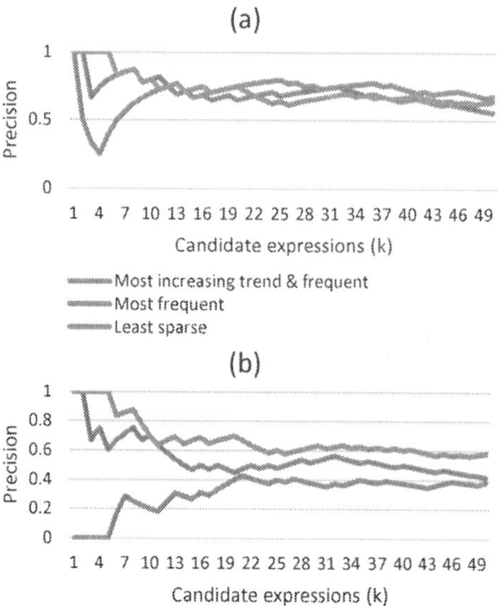

Figure 2: Comparison of the three methods to find candidate expressions, using *Precision@k* measure. In (a), precision was calculated for all candidate expressions. In (b), precision was calculated after leaving-out proper name expressions (marking them as non-valid expressions).

These results have confirmed the robustness of our tests.

It is noteworthy that some expressions with the most decreasing trends in Table 2 are related to religion (e.g., *revealed religion, god almighty, Church of Rome, St. Peter,* and *high church*). Though our work does not explain language changes, this may be an interesting finding for sociolinguistic researchers, which may indicate a secularization process.

4.5 Top Increasing trends

In order to find old–new relationships between the time-series of some synonymous expressions, we chose the top 30 expressions with the most increasing usage trend, and looked for their historical synonymous expressions in a thesaurus. By visualizing the trends of the synonymous expressions, we could find evidence that later expressions replaced earlier ones. We found synonymous expressions in a thesaurus for 8 out of the 30 expressions in Table 1: *in practice, better off, talk about, go wrong, In fact, for instance, police officer* and *on and off*. However, we did not find

Increasing trends	Kendall's τ	Spearman's ρ
in turn (r)	9.568	1.000
in practice (r)	9.528	1.000
better off (j)	9.528	1.000
think about (v)	9.507	1.000
work through (v)	9.497	0.999
white woman (n)	9.497	1.000
human being (n)	9.487	0.999
talk about (v)	9.487	0.999
written record (n)	9.447	0.999
united kingdom (n)	9.437	0.999
rule of law (n)	9.406	0.999
take into account (v)	9.406	0.998
two dozen (n)	9.396	0.998
rather than (r)	9.386	0.998
go wrong (v)	9.386	0.998
human activity (n)	9.376	0.998
in fact (r)	9.366	0.997
Cambridge university (n)	9.366	0.999
bring together (v)	9.346	0.997
san Antonio (n)	9.335	0.998
critical analysis (n)	9.335	0.998
for instance (r)	9.325	0.995
end on (r)	9.325	0.997
life form (n)	9.325	0.997
police officer (n)	9.325	0.997
medical history (n)	9.315	0.998
run by (v)	9.305	0.997
conflict of interest (n)	9.305	0.998
per year (r)	9.295	0.996
on and off (r)	9.295	0.997

Table 1: 30 expressions with the highest increasing usage trend. (*n* – noun phrase; *v* – verb phrase; *j* – adjective; *r* – adverb; *o* – other).

synonymous expressions in our ready-made MWE list for *in practice* and *better off*. None of the synonymous expressions for the remaining 6 expressions had a statistically significant decreasing usage trend. Here are some detailed examples:

Talk about is "[...] often used colloq. to contrast something already mentioned with something still more striking; [...]" (Talk, v., 2015). Its synonym expressions are *talk of*, as well as *speak of* – a synonym not mentioned in Oxford English Dictionary. Figure 3 shows that *speak of* is more widely used than *talk about* since it may have additional meanings, as stating another example to the discussion, where *talk about* and *talk of* are used only

Decreasing trends	Kendall's τ	Spearman's ρ
take notice (v)	-9.184	-0.994
no more (r)	-9.164	-0.991
as much (o)	-9.143	-0.993
king James (n)	-9.103	-0.989
ill nature (n)	-9.062	-0.990
according as (j)	-9.062	-0.988
root out (v)	-8.941	-0.985
think piece (n)	-8.799	-0.987
high church (n)	-8.718	-0.979
of it (r)	-8.718	-0.976
make happy (v)	-8.658	-0.979
fourth part (n)	-8.658	-0.965
St. peter (n)	-8.638	-0.979
church of rome (n)	-8.597	-0.973
ought to (v)	-8.557	-0.972
good nature (n)	-8.557	-0.971
god almighty (n)	-8.536	-0.975
give ear (v)	-8.476	-0.974
law of nature (n)	-8.476	-0.948
let fly (v)	-8.415	-0.973
bring forth (v)	-8.415	-0.968
build upon (v)	-8.354	-0.969
perpetual motion (n)	-8.334	-0.971
revealed religion (n)	-8.334	-0.940
many a (j)	-8.314	-0.968
states general (n)	-8.314	-0.966
take care (v)	-8.294	-0.951
as many [as] (j)	-8.273	-0.956
take pains (v)	-8.273	-0.940
nemine contradicente (r)	-8.253	-0.957

Table 2: 30 expressions with the most decreasing usage trend. (*n* – noun phrase; *v* – verb phrase; *j* – adjective; *r* – adverb; *o* – other).

to contradict a point in the discussion. Though *talk of* has no significant decreasing trend, it shows a decline along the 20th century.

The expression *[to] go wrong* has several meanings: It could mean to take a wrong way, either literally, in mistake, or morally. It could also mean that an event "[...] can happen amiss or unfortunately[, when something broke-down, or when food [...] get[s] into bad or unsound condition [...]" (Wrong, adj. and adv., 2015). It has many synonym expressions; in Figure 4 we compare it with synonyms we found in the ready-made MWE list (Kulkarni and Finlayson, 2011): *break down* (1837), *go bad* (1799) and *go off* (1695).

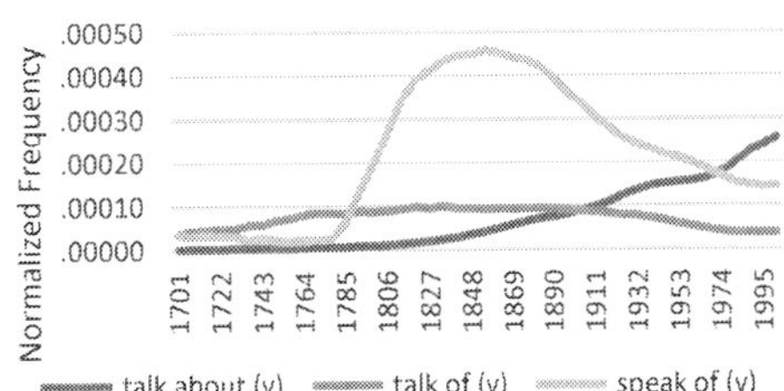

Figure 3: Comparison between *talk about*, *talk of* and *speak of*.

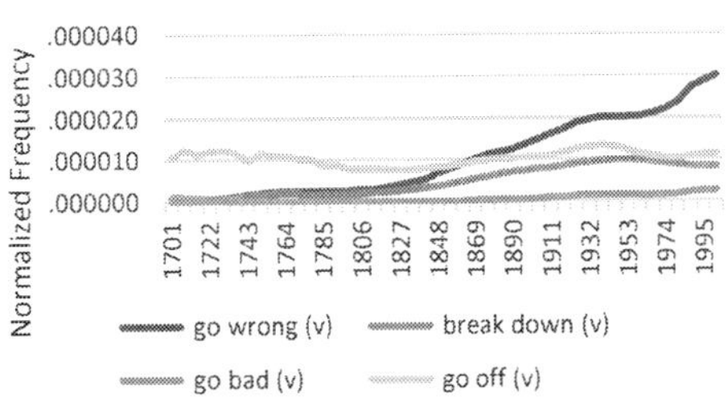

Figure 4: Comparison of *go wrong* with its synonymous expressions.

In fact (dated 1592) is defined as "in reality, actually, as a matter of fact. Now often used parenthetically as an additional explanation or to correct a falsehood or misunderstanding (cf. in point of fact at Phrases 3)" (Fact, n., int., and adv. [P2], 2015). In Figure 5 we compare it with synonyms we found in the ready-made MWE list (Kulkarni and Finlayson, 2011): *'smatter of fact* (1922), *in effect*, *in truth* (1548), *in esse[nce]*, and *de facto* (Really or actually [adverb], 2015).

The expression *on and off* has an earlier synonym expression: *off and on* (On and off, adv., adj., and n., 2015), as shown in Figure 6. Both expressions have statistically significant increase trends, while *on and off* exceeds *off and on* since around 1921.

4.6 Top Decreasing trends

Similar to the previous section 4.5, we chose the top 30 expressions with the most decreasing usage trend, and looked for their historical synonymous expressions in a thesaurus. Again, we saw evidence that later expressions replace earlier ones.

In total, we found synonymous expressions in a thesaurus for 7 out of the 30 expressions in Ta-

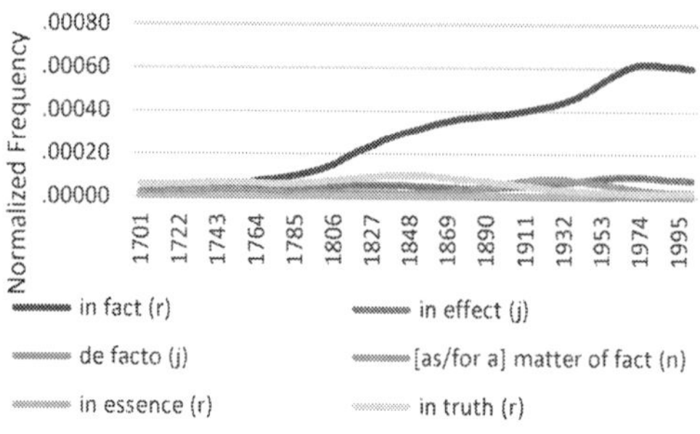

Figure 5: Comparison of *in fact* with its synonymous expressions.

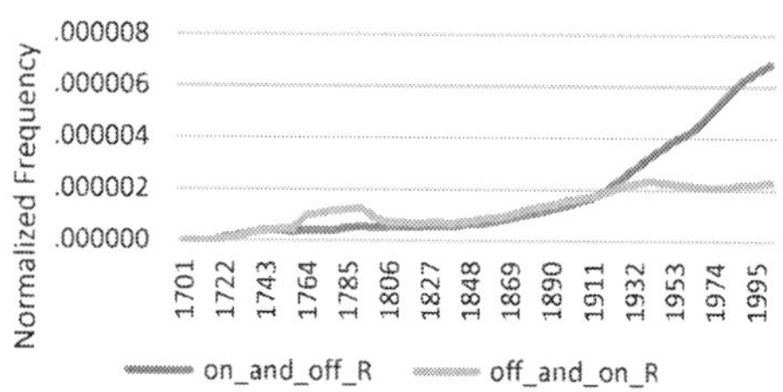

Figure 6: Comparison between *on and off* and *off and on*.

ble 2: *Let fly, take notice, give ear, law of nature, good nature, ought to* and *no more*. However, we did not find synonymous expressions for *good nature* in our ready-made MWE list, to compare with. All of the synonymous expressions for the remaining 6 expressions had a statistically significant increasing usage trend, hinting that old–new relationships exist between them. In addition, expressions with decreasing trends were often found in Oxford Online Dictionary[5] as an obsolete, rare, or poetic expressions. Here are two examples:

The expressions *take notice* and *give ear* could also be phrased as *pay attention* or *take heed* (Notice, n., 2015). The expression *pay attention* has an increasing trend, and may partially explain the decrease of *take notice*, as shown in Figure 7. The drastic decrease in usage of the expression *take notice* could also be explained by single-word synonyms as *note, notice,* and *listen,* which we did not compare to.

Though *no more* has several meanings, we found in the MWE list (Kulkarni and Finlayson,

[5]http://www.oed.com/

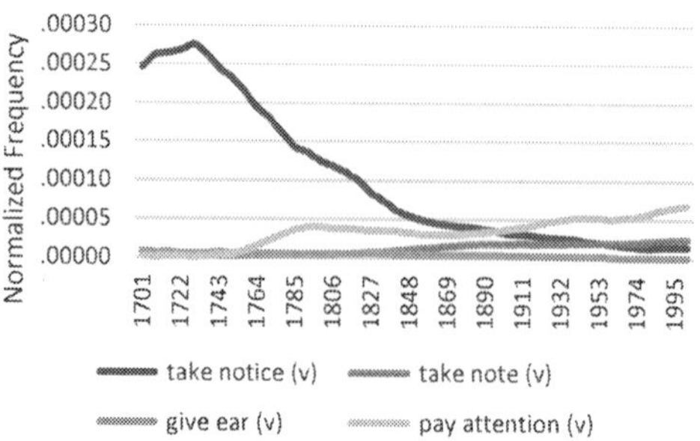

Figure 7: Comparison of expressions *take notice, take note, give ear* and *pay attention*.

2011) only synonyms in the sense of never again or nevermore: *never again* and *no longer* (Never again, 2015):

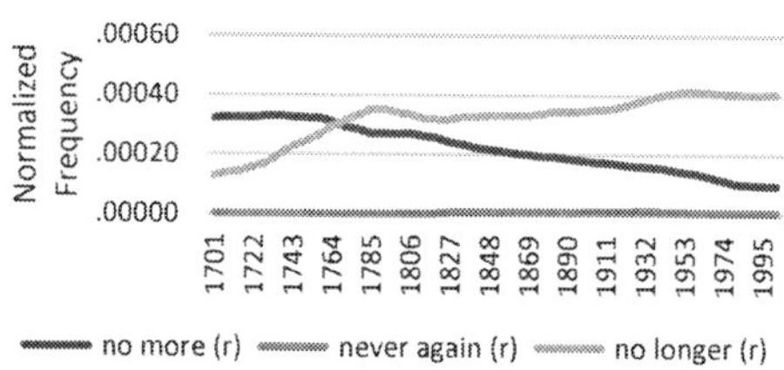

Figure 8: Comparison of *no more, no longer,* and *never again*.

5 Discussion & Conclusions

We explored the change in Multiword expressions (MWEs) usage, or functionality over the years. By visualizing the trends of synonymous expressions, we found evidence to our hypothesis that old–new relationship exists between some expressions: We found synonymous expressions with an increasing usage trend for all 6 expressions with decreasing usage trends, though we did not find decreasing usage trends for synonymous expressions of expressions with increasing usage trends. We found that some expressions with the most decreasing trends are related to religion, which might interest sociolinguists.

We showed that it is possible to find new MWEs in a historical collocations corpus using either normalized frequency or sparsity thresholds, as seven of the 24 candidate expressions were found to be metaphoric phrases not included in dictionaries[6]. Using normalized frequency was better, on average, as a criterion to find any type of candidate expressions, whereas using sparsity was better if one is not interested in proper name expressions. Expressions in the MWE list (Kulkarni and Finlayson, 2011) were mentioned in the Google Syntactic-Ngrams dataset for at least 28 years in a row. This may suggest a minimum period lexicographers can test an expression against before entering it into a dictionary or thesaurus.

In the future, it is possible to tweak Kendall's τ coefficient, especially equation 2, so a short-term trend towards the end of the time-series would also be recognized as statistically significant. Future work may also improve the methods for finding MWEs by introducing flexibility in the expression structure, and by using synonym words replacement. These would assist lexicographers to track the evolution of human language. A usage trend may also be used as a feature by an MWE extraction algorithm; the historical perspective of an expression usage may be valuable for identifying stable expressions, while filtering out short–term collocations.

References

U.S. Environmental Protection Agency. 1974. Guideline for the evaluation of air quality trends: Guideline series (oaqps no. 1.2-014). Technical report, U.S. environmental Protection Agency, Office of Air Quality Planning and Standards, Monitoring and Data Analysis Division. Available from: http://nepis.epa.gov/Exe/ZyPURL.cgi ?Dockey=9100FOJ5.txt.

H. Al-Haj and Shuli Wintner. 2010. Identifying multi-word expressions by leveraging morphological and syntactic idiosyncrasy. In *Proceedings of the 23rd International Conference on Computational Linguistics (COLING 2010)*, pages 10–18, Beijing, Aug 2010.

B. T. S. Atkins and M. Rundell. 2008. *The oxford guide to practical lexicography*. Oxford University Press, Oxford.

T. Baldwin and S. N. Kim, 2010. *Handbook of Natural Language Processing*, chapter Multiword Expressions, pages 267–292. CRC Press, Boca Raton, USA, 2nd edition. N. Indurkhya, F. J. Damerau, editors; DOI: 10.1038/nbt1267.

A. Buerki. 2013. Automatically identifying instances of change in diachronic corpus data. Presentation at the Corpus Linguistics 2013 conference, Jul 22-26.

Nicoletta Calzolari, Charles J. Fillmore, Ralph Grishman, Nancy Ide, Alessandro Lenci, Catherine MacLeod, and Antonio Zampolli. 2002. Towards best practice for multiword expressions in computational lexicons. In *Proceedings of the third LREC (LREC 2002)*, pages 1934–1940, Las Palmas, Canary Islands, Spain.

H. E. Daniels. 1950. Rank correlation and population models. *Journal of the Royal Statistical Society. Series B (Methodological)*, 12(2):171–191.

J. B. Estoup. 1916. *Gammes Stenographiques*. Institut Stenographique de France, Paris, 4th edition.

Fact, n., int., and adv. [P2]. 2015. In *Oxford English Dictionary*. Oxford University Press. [cited 2015 Mar 10]. Available from: http://www.oed.com/view/Entry/67478.

A. Fazly, P. Cook, and S. Stevenson. 2009. Unsupervised type and token identification of idiomatic expressions. *Computational Linguistics*, 35(1):61–103.

Dylan Glynn. 2010. Synonymy, lexical fields, and grammatical constructions: Developing usage-based methodology for cognitive semantics. In H. J. Schmid and S. Handl, editors, *Cognitive Foundations of Linguistic Usage Patterns*, pages 89–118. Mouton de Gruyter, Berlin.

Yoav Goldberg and Jon Orwant. 2013. A dataset of syntactic-ngrams over time from a very large corpus of english books. In *Proceedings of the 2nd Joint Conference on Lexical and Computational Semantics (*SEM 2013)*.

Google. 2009. Google ngram viewer, total counts file for english one million corpus, version 20090715. Available from: http://storage.googleapis.com/books/ngrams/books /googlebooks-eng-1M-totalcounts-20090715.txt [Accessed: Aug 27, 2014].

K. L. Gray. 2007. *Comparison of Trend Detection Methods*. Ph.D. thesis, University of Montana, Department of Mathematical Sciences, Missoula, MT. 86 pages.

B. Juska-Bacher and C. Mahlow. 2012. Phraseological change – a book with seven seals? tracing back diachronic development of german proverbs and idioms. In M. Durell, S. Scheible, and R. J. Whitt, editors, *Volume of Corpus linguistics and Interdisciplinary perspectives on language*. Gunter Narr, Tbingen, Germany.

M. Kalla. 2006. A diachronic semiotic analysis of words signifying 'friendship' in hebrew. Master's thesis, Ben-Gurion Univ. of the Negev, Dept. of Foreign Languages and Literatures, Beer-Sheva, Israel. 96 pages.

---

[6]Merriam-Webster dictionary (http://www.merriam-webster.com/dictionary/) and Oxford English Dictionary (http://www.oed.com/).

Tom Kenter, Pim Huijnen, Melvin Wevers, and Maarten de Rijke. 2015. Ad hoc monitoring of vocabulary shifts over time. In *CIKM 2015: 24th ACM Conference on Information and Knowledge Management*. ACM, October.

N. Kulkarni and M. A. Finlayson. 2011. jmwe: A java toolkit for detecting multi-word expressions. In *Proceedings of the 2011 Workshop on Multiword Expressions (ACL 2011)*, pages 122–124, Portland, OR.

C. Liebeskin, Ido Dagan, and J. Schler. 2013. Semi-automatic construction of cross-period thesaurus. In *Proceedings of the 7th Workshop on Language Technology for Cultural Heritage, Social Sciences, and Humanities (LaTeCH 2013)*, pages 29–35, Sofia, Bulgaria, Aug 8. The Association for Computational Linguistics.

C. Mahlow and B. Juska-Bacher. 2011. Exploring new high german texts for evidence of phrasemes. *Journal for Language Technology and Computational Linguistics*, 26(2):117–128.

C. D. Manning and H. Schütze, 1999. *Foundations of Statistical Natural Language Processing*, chapter Introduction, pages 23–29. The MIT Press, Cambridge, Massachusetts; London, England.

C. D. Manning, M. Surdeanu, J. Bauer, J. Finkel, S. J. Bethard, and D. McClosky. 2014. The stanford corenlp natural language processing toolkit. In *Proceedings of 52nd Annual Meeting of the Association for Computational Linguistics: System Demonstrations*, pages 55–60.

Jean-Baptiste Michel, Yuan Kui Shen, Aviva Presser Aiden, Adrian Veres, Matthew K. Gray, The Google Books Team, Joseph P. Pickett, Dale Hoiberg, Dan Clancy, Peter Norvig, Jon Orwant, Steven Pinker, Martin A. Nowak, and Erez Lieberman Aiden. 2011. Quantitative analysis of culture using millions of digitized books. *Science*, 331(6014):176–182. DOI: 10.1126/science.1199644.

Never again. 2015. In *Oxford English Dictionary*. Oxford University Press. [cited 2015 Feb]. Available from: http://www.oed.com/view/th/class/96637.

Notice, n. 2015. In *Oxford English Dictionary*. Oxford University Press. [cited 2015 Mar 10]. Available from: http://www.oed.com/view/Entry /128591#eid933873046.

On and off, adv., adj., and n. 2015. In *Oxford English Dictionary*. Oxford University Press. [cited 2015 Mar 10]. Available from: http://www.oed.com/view/Entry/131310.

C. Ramisch. 2013. *A Generic open framework for multiword expressions treatment: from acquisition to applications*. Ph.D. thesis, Universidade Federal do Rio Grande do Sul, Porto Alegre, Brazil & Grenoble, France.

Really or actually [adverb]. 2015. In *Oxford English Dictionary*. Oxford University Press. [cited 2015 Mar 10]. Available from: http://www.oed.com/view/th/class/82683.

Talk, v. 2015. In *Oxford English Dictionary*. Oxford University Press. [cited 2015 Mar 10]. Available from: http://www.oed.com/view/Entry/197246.

Yulia Tsvetkov and Shuli Wintner. 2011. Identication of multi-word expressions by combining multiple linguistic info sources. In *Proceedings of the 2011 Conference on Empirical Methods in Natural Language Processing (EMNLP 2011)*, pages 836–845, Edinburgh, Scotland, UK, Jul 27–31. Association for Computational Linguistics.

Wrong, adj. and adv. 2015. In *Oxford English Dictionary*. Oxford University Press. [cited 2015 Mar 10]. Available from: http://www.oed.com/view/Entry/230802.

Lexical Variability and Compositionality: Investigating Idiomaticity with Distributional Semantic Models

Marco S. G. Senaldi
Laboratorio di Linguistica
Scuola Normale Superiore
Pisa, Italy
marco.senaldi@sns.it

Gianluca E. Lebani and **Alessandro Lenci**
Computational Linguistics Laboratory
Department of Philology, Literature, and Linguistics
University of Pisa, Italy
gianluca.lebani@for.unipi.it
alessandro.lenci@unipi.it

Abstract

In this work we carried out an *idiom type identification* task on a set of 90 Italian V-NP and V-PP constructions comprising both idioms and non-idioms. Lexical variants were generated from these expressions by replacing their components with semantically related words extracted distributionally and from the Italian section of MultiWordNet. Idiomatic phrases turned out to be less similar to their lexical variants with respect to non-idiomatic ones in distributional semantic spaces. Different variant-based distributional measures of idiomaticity were tested. Our indices proved reliable in identifying also those idioms whose lexical variants are poorly or not at all attested in our corpus.

1 Introduction

Extensive corpus studies have provided support to Sinclair (1991)'s claim that speakers tend to favor an *idiom principle* over an *open-choice principle* in linguistic production, resorting, where possible, to (semi-)preconstructed phrases rather than using compositional combinatorial expressions. These *multiword expressions* (MWEs) and *idioms* in particular (Nunberg et al., 1994; Sag et al., 2002; Cacciari, 2014; Siyanova-Chanturia and Martinez, 2014) exhibit an idiosyncratic behavior that makes their account troublesome for most grammar models (Chomsky, 1980; Jackendoff, 1997; Hoffmann and Trousdale, 2013), including restricted semantic compositionality and transparency, low morphosyntactic versatility and, crucially for the study at hand, a considerable degree of lexical fixedness. The existence of such prefabricated patterns ties in well with the basic tenets of constructionist approaches (Goldberg, 1995; Hoffmann and Trous-

dale, 2013), that view the lexicon and the grammar as a network of form-meaning correspondences spanning from abstract and complex syntactic schemata to single words and morphemes.

Idioms show a gradient behavior according to the lexicosyntactic variation that each of them can undergo. It has indeed been traditionally argued that while replacing the constituents of a literal combination like *to watch a movie* with synonymous or semantically related words (e.g. *to watch a film*) does not result in a significant change in meaning, modifying an idiomatic string like *to spill the beans* into something like *to spill the peas* entails the loss of the figurative interpretation (Cacciari and Glucksberg, 1991; Sag et al., 2002; Fazly and Stevenson, 2008). Actually, psycholinguistic studies investigating the comprehension of idiom lexical variants have found such alternative forms to be more acceptable when the idiom parts independently contribute to the idiomatic meaning (e.g. *burst the ice* from *break the ice*) than when they don't (e.g. *boot the bucket* from *kick the bucket*) (Gibbs et al., 1989) or when the idioms are more familiar to the speakers (McGlone et al., 1994). Anyway, while contributions of this kind are useful to assess whether potentially occurring variants can be understood by speakers or not, it is looking at corpus analyses that we can gain an insight into the actual occurrence of such lexical alternatives in real text. Moon (1998) and Duffley (2013) have found all kinds of idioms to be used sometimes in an altered form with the idiomatic reading preserved (e.g. *kick the pail* and *kick the can* for *kick the bucket*), with Moon (1998) positing the existence of *idiom schemas* that subsume alternative lexical realizations of idiomatic strings (e.g. *shake/quake/quiver in one's shoes/boots*). Nonetheless, this kind of lexical flexibility does not turn out to be so widespread, systematic and predictable as in literal constructions.

Proceedings of the 12th Workshop on Multiword Expressions, pages 21–31,
Berlin, Germany, August 7-12, 2016. ©2016 Association for Computational Linguistics

As we will briefly outline in Section 2, previous computational researches took advantage of the restricted formal variability exhibited by idioms to devise indices that automatically separate them from more literal combinations. Some of them have accomplished it by comparing the different collocational association between the canonical form of an expression and the lexical variants of that construction obtained by replacing its parts with semantically related words (Lin, 1999; Fazly et al., 2009). Others exploited the difference in cosine similarity between an entire phrase and its components that is observed in idioms and non-idioms in Distributional Semantics Models (DSMs) (Baldwin et al., 2003; Venkatapathy and Joshi, 2005; Fazly and Stevenson, 2008). Here, we combined insights from both the aforementioned approaches, using the generation of lexical variants as the departure point for a distributional semantic analysis. Compositional expressions exhibit systematicity (Fodor and Lepore, 2002) in that if a speaker can comprehend *spill the beans* as taken literally and *drop the peas*, he/she will also be able to understand *spill the peas* and *drop the beans*, but this does not happen if we read *spill the beans* as an idiom. The restricted lexical substitutability of a given construction could thus be regarded as a clue of its semantic non-compositionality and idiomatic status. To implement this idea, we generated a series of lexical variants from a set of target Italian V-NP and V-PP constructions, including both idioms and literals, but instead of measuring differences in the association scores between a given target and its variants, we computed the cosine similarities between them. Idiomatic expressions are expected to result less similar to their lexical variants with respect to literal ones.

2   Related work

Existing computational research on idiomaticity mainly splits into studies aimed at *idiom type identification* (i.e. separating potentially idiomatic constructions like *spill the beans* from only literal ones like *write a book*) and studies aimed at *idiom token identification* (i.e. distinguishing the idiomatic vs. literal usage of a given expression in context, e.g. *The interrogated man finally spilled the beans* vs. *The cook spilled the beans all over the kitchen floor*). Since in this paper we focus on the former issue, we only review related researches on idiom type identification.

Various techniques have been employed to separate idioms and non-idioms. McCarthy et al. (2003), for instance, focus on verb-particles constructions and find that thesaurus-based measures of the overlap between the neighbors of a phrasal verb and those of its simplex verb strongly correlate with human-elicited compositionality judgments given to the same expressions. Fixedness in the word order is exploited by Widdows and Dorow (2005), who observe that asymmetric lexicosyntactic patterns such as 'A and/or B' which never occur in the reversed order 'B and/or A' very often appear to represent idiomatic combinations. Bannard (2007) devises measures of determiner variability, adjectival modification and passivization to distinguish idiomatic and non-idiomatic VPs, resorting to conditional Pointwise Mutual Information (Church and Hanks, 1991) to calculate how the syntactic variation of a given V-N pair differs from what would be expected considering the variation of the single lexemes. In a similar way, Fazly et al. (2009) devise a syntactic flexibility index to single out V-NP idiomatic pairs that compares the behavior of a given pair to that of a typical V-N schema as regards the definiteness and the number of the noun and verbal voice. Muzny and Zettlemoyer (2013) propose a supervised technique for identifying idioms among the Wiktionary lexical entries with lexical and graph-based features extracted from Wiktionary and WordNet, while Graliński (2012) bases on metalinguistic markers such as *proverbially* or *literally* to retrieve idioms from the Web. Crucially for the present experiment, a series of studies have more precisely focused on lexical flexibility to identify non-compositional constructions. Among them, Lin (1999) classifies a phrase as non-compositional if the PMI between its components is significantly different from the PMI between the components of all its lexical variants. These variant forms are obtained by replacing the words in the original phrase with semantic neighbours. Fazly and Stevenson (2008) and Fazly et al. (2009) further elaborate on Lin's formula, regarding a certain V-N combination as lexically fixed and more likely to be idiomatic if its PMI highly differs from the mean PMI of its variants. Other contributions have employed distributional measures to determine the similarity between a given phrase and its components, observing that idiomatic phrase vectors appear to be less similar to their component vectors than literal phrase vectors (Baldwin et al., 2003; Venkatapathy and Joshi, 2005; Fazly and Stevenson, 2008).

3 Measuring compositionality with variant-based distributional similarity

In the present work we propose a method for idiom type classification that starts from a set of V-NP and V-PP constructions, generates a series of lexical variants for each target by replacing the verb and the argument with semantically related words and then compares the semantic similarity between the initial constructions and their respective variants. For the sake of clarity, henceforth we will refer to the initial idiomatic and non-idiomatic expressions as *target* expressions, while the lexical alternatives that were generated for each target will be simply called *variants*. Since idiomatic expressions are supposed to exhibit a greater degree of non-compositionality and lexical fixedness than literal ones, with the substitution of their component words resulting in the impossibility of an idiomatic reading (e.g. *spill the beans* vs. *spill the peas*), we expected them to be less similar to their variants with respect to literal constructions. Starting from the assumption that we can study the semantics of a given word or expression by inspecting the linguistic contexts in which it occurs (Harris, 1954; Firth, 1957; Sahlgren, 2008), Distributional Semantic Models (DSMs) provide a viable solution for representing the content of our target and variant constructions with vectors recording their distributional association with linguistic contexts (Turney and Pantel, 2010). The semantic similarity between a given target and its variants is therefore implemented as the cosine similarity between them. Similarly to Lin (1999) and Fazly et al. (2009), we used lexical variants for each target expression, but instead of contrasting their associational scores, we used vector-based measures to grasp their degree of semantic compositionality.

3.1 Extraction of the target and variant constructions

45 Italian V-NP and V-PP idioms were selected from an Italian idiom dictionary (Quartu, 1993) and extracted from the itWaC corpus (Baroni et al., 2009), which consists of about 1,909M tokens. Their corpus frequency spanned from 364 (*ingannare il tempo* 'to while away the time') to

8294 (*andare in giro* 'to get about'). A set of 45 non-idioms (e.g. *leggere un libro* 'to read a book', *uscire da una stanza* 'to get out of a room') of comparable frequencies were then extracted from the corpus, ending up with 90 target constructions. Two different methods were explored for generating lexical variants from our targets:

DSM variants. For both the verb and argument component of each target construction, we extracted its 10 nearest neighbours (NNs) in terms of cosine similarity in a DSM created from the La Repubblica corpus (Baroni et al., 2004) (about 331M tokens); this space used all the content words (nouns, verbs, adjectives and adverbs) with token frequency > 100 as target vectors and the top 10,000 content words as contexts; the co-occurrence matrix, generated from a context window of ± 2 content words from each target word, was weighted by Positive Pointwise Mutual Information (PPMI) (Evert, 2008), a statistical association measure that assesses whether two elements x and y co-occur more frequently than expected by chance and sets to zero all the negative values:

$$PPMI(x, y) = max(0, log\frac{P(x, y)}{P(x)P(y)})$$

The matrix was reduced to 300 latent dimensions via Singular Value Decomposition (SVD) (Deerwester et al., 1990). The variants were finally obtained by combining the verb with each of the 10 NNs of the argument, the argument with each of the 10 NNs of the verb and every NN of the verb with every NN of the argument. This resulted in 120 potential variants for each target expression, which were then extracted from itWaC.

iMWN variants. For both the verb and argument component of each target construction, the words occurring in same synsets and its co-hyponyms were extracted from the Italian section of MultiWordNet (iMWN) (Pianta et al., 2002). For each verbal head, we extracted 5.9 synonyms/co-hyponyms on average (SD = 5.41), while for the noun arguments we extracted 25.18 synonyms/co-hyponyms on average (SD = 27.45). The variants of the targets were then generated with the same procedure described for the distributionally derived variants and extracted from itWaC.

3.2 Collecting idiomaticity judgments

To provide the variant-based distributional measures with a gold standard, we collected idiomaticity judgments for our 90 target expressions from Linguistics students. Nine undergraduate and graduate students were presented with a list of our targets and asked to evaluate how idiomatic each expression was on a 1-7 Likert scale. More specifically, we split our initial list into three sublists of 30 targets, each one being compiled by three subjects. Intercoder agreement, computed via Krippendorff's α (Krippendorff, 2012), was 0.83 for the first sublist and 0.75 for the other two. Following common practice, we interpreted these values as an evidence of reliability for the collected judgments (Artstein and Poesio, 2008).

4 Experiment 1

In the first experiment, we wanted to verify our predictions on a subset of our 90 target constructions that had a considerable number of variants represented in the corpus, so as to create reliable vector representations for them. We therefore selected those constructions that had at least 5 DSM and 5 iMWN variants occurring more than 100 times in itWaC. This selection resulted in a final set of 26 targets (13 idioms + 13 non-idioms).

4.1 Data extraction and method

Two DSMs were then built on the itWaC corpus, the first one representing the 26 targets and their DSM variants with token frequency > 100 as vectors, and the second one representing as vectors the 26 targets and their iMWN variants with token frequency > 100. Co-occurrences were recorded by counting how many times each target or variant construction occurred in the same sentence with each of the 30,000 top content words in the corpus. The two matrices were weighted with PPMI and reduced to 300 dimensions via SVD.

Four different measures were tested to compute how much the vector representations of the targets differed from those of their respective variants:

Mean. The mean of the cosine similarities between the vector of a target construction and the vectors of its variants.

Max. The maximum value among the cosine similarities between the vector of a target construction and the vectors of its variants.

Min. The minimum value among the cosine similarities between the vector of a target construction and the vectors of its variants.

Centroid. The cosine similarity between the vector of a target expression and the centroid of the vectors of its variants.

In both the DSMs, each of these four measures was computed for each of our 26 targets. We then sorted the targets in ascending order for each of the four scores, creating a ranking in which we expected idioms (our positives) to be placed at the top and non-idioms (our negatives) to be placed at the bottom, since idioms are expected to be less similar to the vectors of their lexical variants.

4.2 Results and discussion

The main goal of this study was to assess whether our variant-based method was suitable for identifying idiom types. Hence we evaluated the goodness of our four measures (Mean, Max, Min and Centroid) in placing idioms before non-idioms in the rankings generated by our idiomaticity indices.

Figures 1 and 2 plot the Interpolated Precision-Recall curves for the four measures in the two trained DSMs plus a random baseline. In the DSM variants model, Max, Mean and Centroid performed better than Min and the baseline. Max showed high precision at low levels of recall ($<$ 40%), but it dropped as far as higher recall levels were reached, while Mean and Centroid kept higher precision at higher levels of recall. Min initially performed comparably to Mean, but it drastically dropped after 50% of recall.

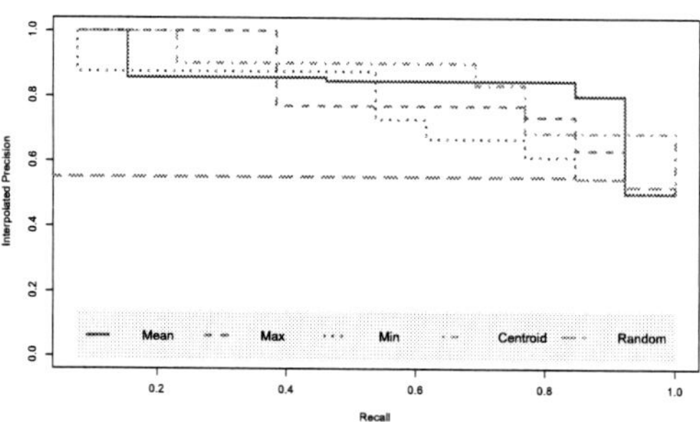

Figure 1: Interpolated Precision-Recall curve for Mean, Max, Min, Centroid and the baseline in the DSM variants space with 26 targets.

In the iMWN variants space both Mean and Centroid performed better than the other measures, with the baseline being the worst one. Both Max and Min exhibited the same pattern, with high precision at low recall levels and a subsequent drop in performance around 50% of recall.

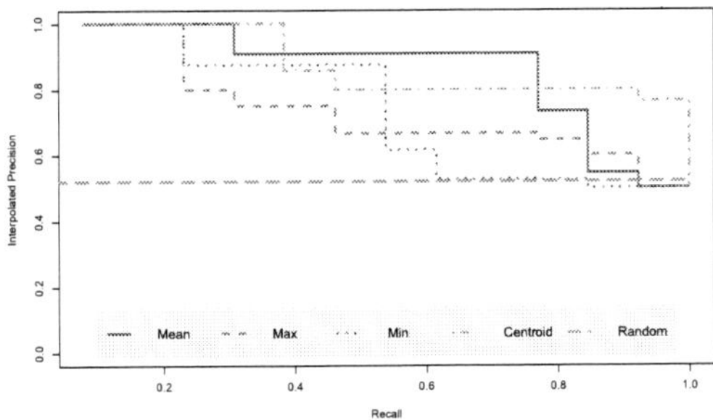

Figure 2: Interpolated Precision-Recall curve for Mean, Max, Min, Centroid and the baseline in the iMWN variants space with 26 targets.

Model	IAP	F	ρ
DSM Centroid	.83	.77	**-.66*****
iMWN Centroid	**.87**	.77	-.59**
DSM Mean	.80	**.85**	-.63***
iMWN Mean	.80	.77	-.58**
DSM Max	.74	.77	-.60**
iMWN Max	.68	.62	-.30
DSM Min	.69	.62	-.37
iMWN Min	.65	.62	-.28
Random	.53	.46	.30

Table 1: Interpolated Average Precision, F-measure at the median and Spearman's ρ correlation with the speaker judgments for the models with 26 targets ($^{**} = p < .01$, $^{***} = p < .001$).

The first two columns of Table 1 show the Interpolated Average Precision (IAP) and the F-measure of all the models employed in this first experiment. Interpolated Average Precision consists in the average of the interpolated precisions at recall levels of 20%, 50% and 80%, while F-measure is computed for the median. Both iMWN and DSM Mean and Centroid, together with DSM Max, had the highest IAPs, therefore standing out as the models the suceeded the most in placing idioms before non-idioms in the obtained rankings and exhibited the best trade-off between precision and recall, as shown by the F-measure values. The third column in Table 1 shows Spearman's ρ correlation between our models and the speaker-elicited idiomaticity judgments we described in Section 3.2. The Mean and the Centroid similarity in both the DSM and the iMWN variants spaces and the Max similarity in the DSM variants spaces showed a significant strong negative correlation with the speaker-collected ratings: the less the vector of a given expression resulted similar to the vectors of its lexical variants, the more the subjects perceived the expression as idiomatic. iMWN Min, DSM Min and iMWN Max exhibited a weak, non-significant, negative correlation, while the baseline showed a non-significant weak positive correlation score. All in all, Centroid and Mean turned out as the best measures in separating idioms from non-idioms, while there was no clear advantage of one variant type (DSM or iMWN) over the other.

5 Experiment 2

The first experiment proved our variant-based distributional measures to be suitable for telling apart idioms and non-idioms that had a fair number of lexical variants occurring in our corpus with con- siderable frequency, with the Mean and the Centroid measures performing the best. The research question at the root of the following experiment was whether such measures could be extended to all the 90 target constructions in our dataset (45 idioms + 45 non-idioms), including expressions whose lexical variants were poorly represented or not at all found in itWaC. Such negative evidence, in our reasoning, should be taken into account as an additional clue of the restricted lexical transformability of the expressions at hand and, consequently, of their idiosyncratic and idiomatic status.

5.1 Data extraction and method

As in the first experiment, two kinds of DSMs were built from itWaC, the former comprising the 90 initial idiomatic and non-idiomatic expressions and their DSM variants as target vectors and the latter considering the 90 expressions and their iMWN variants as target vectors. The parameters of these vector spaces are identical to those used in Experiment 1. The vectors of the targets were compared to the vectors of their variants by means of the four measures described in Section 4.1 (Mean, Max, Min, Centroid). Aside from the method chosen to extract the variants (DSM vs. iMWN), the parameter space explored in constructing the DSMs for the second experiment further comprised the following options:

Number of variants per target. For both the variants that were extracted distributionally and those that were chosen from iMWN, we built different DSMs, each time setting a fixed number of alternative forms for each target expression. As for the DSM-generated variants, we kept the alternative expressions that were generated by combining the top 3, 4, 5 and 6 cosine neighbours of each verb and argument component of the initial 90 targets. As a result, we obtained 4 types of spaces, in which each target had respectively 15, 24, 35 and 48 variants represented as vectors. As for the spaces built with the iMWN variants, we experimented with eight types of DSMs. In the first four, we kept the variants that were created by combining the top 3, 4, 5 and 6 synonyms and co-hyponyms of each component of the initial 90 targets in terms of cosine similarity. These cosine similarities were extracted from a DSM trained on the La Repubblica corpus that had the same parameters as the space used to extract the DSM variants and described in Section 3.1. In the other four, we used the top 3, 4, 5 and 6 synonyms and co-hyponyms that were most frequent in itWaC.

Encoding of non-occurring variants. In each of the DSMs obtained above, every target was associated with a fixed number of lexical variants, some of them not occurring in our corpus. We experimented with two different ways of addressing this problem. In the first case, we simply did not take them into account, thus focusing only on the positive evidence in our corpus. In the second case, we represented them as orthogonal vectors to the vectors of their target. For the Mean, Max and Min measures, this merely consisted in automatically setting to 0.0 the cosine similarity between a target and a non-attested variant. For the Centroid measure, we first computed the cosine similarity between the vector of a target expression and the centroid of its attested variants and then hypothesized that each zero variant contributed by a costant factor k in tilting this centroid similarity towards 0.0. Preliminary investigations have proved a k-value of 0.01 to give reliable results. We leave to future contributions the tuning of this parameter, limiting ourselves to propose and test this centroid-based measure for the present work. Concretely, from the centroid similarity computed with the attested variants (cs_a), we subtracted the product of k and cs_a multiplied by the number of non-attested variants (n) for the construction under consideration, obtaining a final centroid similarity that also includes non-attested variants:

$$Centroid = cs_a - (cs_a \cdot k \cdot n)$$

Crucially, the rationale behind multiplying k by

the original centroid similarity lies in the fact that non-attested variants were not expected to contribute in modifying the original cosine value towards zero always in the same way, but depending on the specific target construction at hand and on the positive evidence available for it.

Table 2 summarizes the parameters explored in building the DSMs for the second experiment. In each model resulting from the combination of these parameters, we ranked our 90 targets in ascending order according to the idiomaticity scores given by the four variant-based distributional measures (Mean, Max, Min, and Centroid).

Parameter	Values
Variants source	DSM, iMWN
Variants filter	cosine (DSM, iMWN), raw frequency (iMWN)
Variants per target	15, 24, 35, 48
Non-attested variants	not considered (*no*), orthogonal vectors (*orth*)
Measures	Mean, Max, Min, Centroid

Table 2: Parameters explored in creating the DSMs for Experiment 2.

5.2 Results and discussion

All the 96 models obtained by combining the parameters in Table 2 had higher IAP and F-measure scores than the random baseline, with the exception of two models displaying lower (iMWN$_{cos}$ 35$_{var}$ Centroid$_{orth}$) or comparable (iMWN$_{freq}$ 15$_{var}$ Centroid$_{orth}$) F scores. All the models had significant correlational scores with the human-elicited ratings save 7 non significant models.

Table 3 reports the 5 best models for IAP, F-measure at the median and Spearman's ρ correlation with our gold standard idiomaticity judgments respectively. All the best models predictably employed the Centroid measure, which already turned out to perform better than the other indices in the first part of our study. The best performance in placing idioms before non-idioms (IAP) and the best trade-off between precision and recall (F-measure) were exhibited both by models that considered (*orth*) and not considered (*no*) non-attested variants, with a prevalence of the latter models. Moreover, the top IAP and top F-measure models used both DSM and iMWN variants. On the other hand, the models correlating the best with the judgments all took non-occurring variants into account as orthogonal vectors and all made use of iMWN variants. There seemed not to be an effect of the number of variants per target across all the three evaluation measures.

Top IAP Models	IAP	F	ρ
iMWN$_{cos}$ 15$_{var}$ Centroid$_{no}$	.91	.80	-.58***
iMWN$_{cos}$ 24$_{var}$ Centroid$_{no}$	.91	.78	-.62***
iMWN$_{cos}$ 35$_{var}$ Centroid$_{no}$	.91	.82	-.60***
DSM 48$_{var}$ Centroid$_{no}$	.89	.82	-.64***
DSM 48$_{var}$ Centroid$_{orth}$	.89	.82	-.60***
Top F-measure Models	**IAP**	**F**	ρ
iMWN$_{cos}$ 35$_{var}$ Centroid$_{no}$	.91	.82	-.60***
DSM 48$_{var}$ Centroid$_{no}$	.89	.82	-.64***
DSM 48$_{var}$ Centroid$_{orth}$	.89	.82	-.60***
iMWN$_{cos}$ 15$_{var}$ Centroid$_{no}$	.91	.80	-.58***
DSM 24$_{var}$ Centroid$_{no}$	.89	.80	-.60***
Top ρ Models	**IAP**	**F**	ρ
iMWN$_{cos}$ 48$_{var}$ Centroid$_{orth}$	.86	.80	-.67***
iMWN$_{cos}$ 35$_{var}$ Centroid$_{orth}$	.72	.44	-.66***
iMWN$_{cos}$ 24$_{var}$ Centroid$_{orth}$	.85	.78	-.66***
iMWN$_{cos}$ 15$_{var}$ Centroid$_{orth}$	.88	.80	-.65***
iMWN$_{freq}$ 15$_{var}$ Centroid$_{orth}$	.66	.51	-.65***
Random	.55	.51	.05

Table 3: Best 5 models with 90 targets for IAP (top), F-measure at the median (middle) and Spearman's ρ correlation with the speaker judgments (bottom) against the random baseline (*** = $p < .001$).

After listing the best overall models for each evaluation measure, we resorted to linear regression to assess the influence of the parameter settings on the performance of our models, following the methodology proposed by Lapesa and Evert (2014). As for the IAP and correlation with human judgments, our linear models achieved adjusted R^2 of 0.90 and 0.94 respectively, therefore explaining the influence of our parameters and their interactions on these two evaluation measures very well. In predicting F-measure, our linear model reported an adjusted R^2 of 0.52. Figure 3 depicts the rankings of our parameters according to their importance in a feature ablation setting. The ΔR^2 values can be understood as a measure of the importance of a parameter, and it is calculated as the difference in fit that is registered by removing the target parameter together with all the pairwise interactions involving it from our full models.

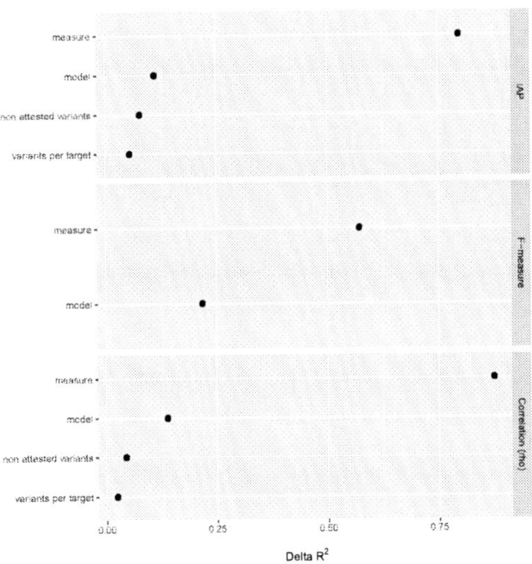

Figure 3: Parameters and feature ablation for IAP, F-measure and correlation with the human ratings.

The parameters we refer to are the same listed in Table 2, with the exception of the parameter *model*, which merges the *variants source* and the *variants filter* parameters. For all our three evaluation measures, *measure* (i.e. Mean, Max, Min vs. Centroid) turned out to be the most influential parameter, followed by *model* (i.e. DSM, iMWN$_{cos}$ vs. iMWN$_{freq}$). As for the *measure* parameter, both in the IAP and in the ρ models the best performing setting is Centroid, followed by Mean, Max and Min, all being significantly different from each other. In the F-measure model, only Min, i.e. the worst performing model, was significantly different from the other settings. As for *model*, the iMWN$_{freq}$ setting was significantly worse than DSM and iMWN$_{cos}$ in the IAP and in the ρ models, but not in the F-measure one.

Table 4 reports all the significant pariwise interactions and their ΔR^2. In line with results reported in Figure 3, almost all the interactions involved the *model* parameter.

Interaction	ΔR^2		
	IAP	F	ρ
model:measure	.03	.13	.08
model:non-attested var	.01	*n.s.*	.02
non-attested var:measure	.02	*n.s.*	.01
model:variants per target	.02	*n.s.*	*n.s.*

Table 4: Significant interactions and ΔR^2 for IAP, F-measure and correlation with the human ratings.

Figure 4 displays the interaction between *measure* and *model* when modeling IAP. The best models, DSM and iMWN$_{cos}$, had a different performance on the worst measure (Min) but converged on the two best ones (Mean and Centroid). On the other side, iMWN$_{freq}$ showed a less dramatic improvement and reached a plateau after moving away from the Min setting.

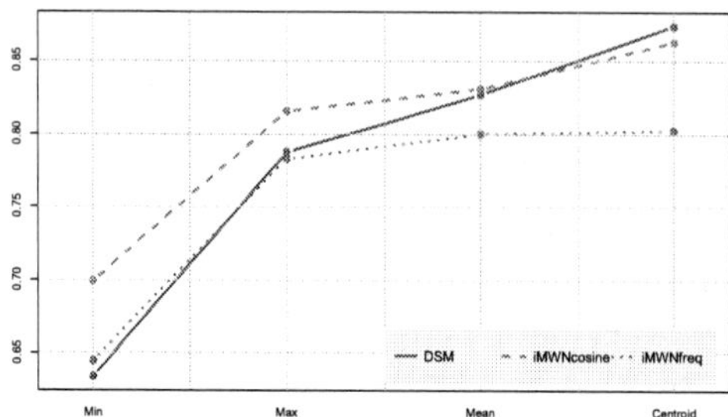

Figure 4: IAP, measure / model.

Figure 5 shows that in the F-measure setting the DSM model had a steeper improvement when moving from Min to the other measures, as compared to the iMWN$_{cos}$ and the iMWN$_{freq}$ models.

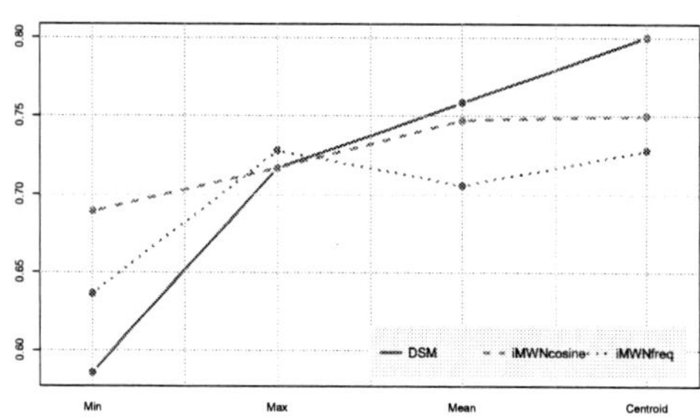

Figure 5: F-measure, measure / model.

Figure 6 shows that in the correlation setting the iMWN$_{cos}$ and the DSM models outperformed the iMWN$_{freq}$ model only when exploiting the Min and the Mean measures. It is worth remarking that the correlational scores with the human ratings are negative and therefore points that are positioned lower on the y-axis indicate better performance.

Figures 7 and 8 plot the interaction between *model* and the way of encoding *non-attested variants* in the IAP and in the ρ models, respectively. In both cases, only the two iMWN models appeared to be sensitive to the way non-attested variants are handled. In the IAP model, zero variants appeared to be the outperforming setting, while the ρ model showed the opposite pattern. In both

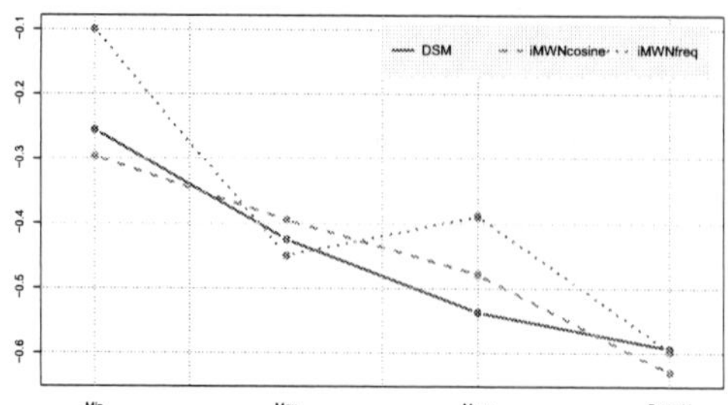

Figure 6: ρ, measure / model.

models, moreover, the best overall setting always involve the iMWN$_{cos}$ model.

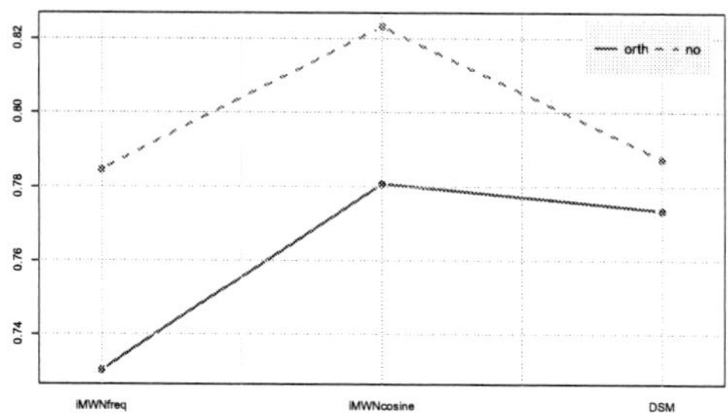

Figure 7: IAP, model / non-attested variants.

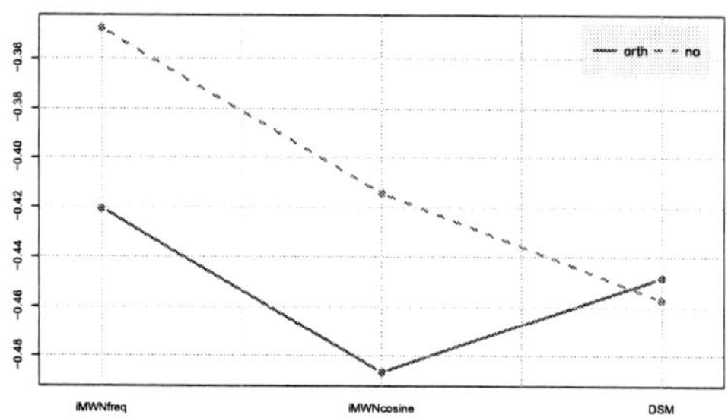

Figure 8: ρ, model / non-attested variants.

Figures 9 and 10 display the interactions between *measure* and the way of encoding *non-attested variants*. In the IAP model, ignoring the non-attested variants resulted in a significantly better performance only when using the Max and Centroid measures. In the ρ model, however, accounting for the effects of non-attested variants outperformed the other setting only when using the Min and Mean measures.

The interaction between the number of *variants per target* and the *model* when modeling IAP is displayed in Figure 11. We observed a strong effect of the variants number on the performance of

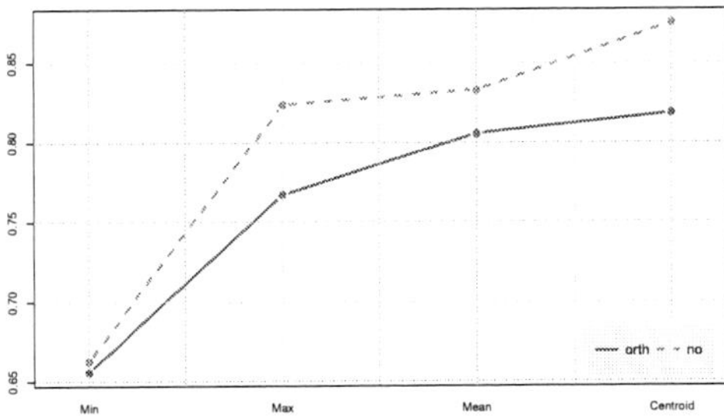

Figure 9: IAP, measure / non-attested variants.

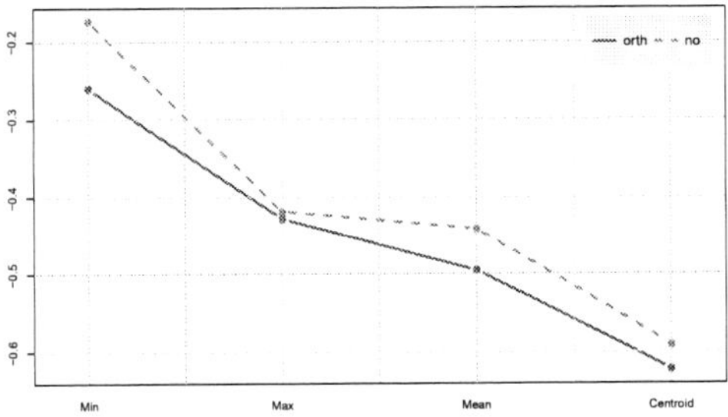

Figure 10: ρ, measure / non-attested variants.

iMWN$_{freq}$, with more variants leading to a better performance. There was a significant advantage of iMWN$_{cos}$ over the other models when using 15 variants, but this advantage was lost as the number of variants increased.

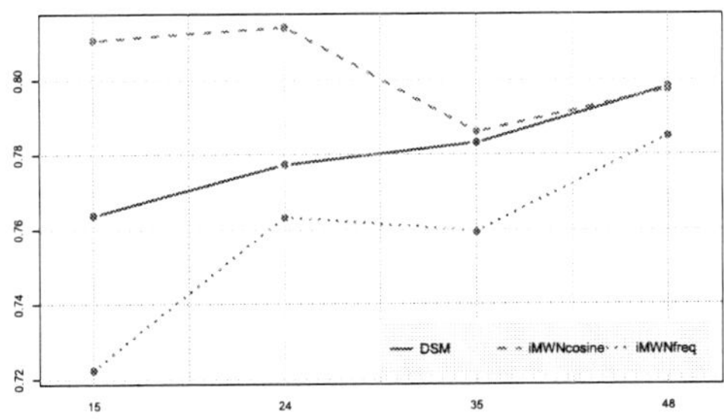

Figure 11: IAP, variants per target / model.

All in all, the Centroid measure appeared to perform better than the other three measures, with Min obtaining the worst results. The DSM and the iMWN$_{cos}$ models performed consistently better than iMWN$_{freq}$, while the advantage of either way of encoding non-attested variants (*no* vs. *orth*) over the other depended on the evaluation setting. Finally, the number of variants per target did not appear to consistently influence the performance of our models.

Error Analysis. A qualitative inspection of the data revealed that the most frequent false positives (i.e. non-idioms classified as idioms) include expressions like *giocare a carte* ('to play cards') or *mostrare interesse* ('to show interest'). Despite being literal and compositional, these word combinations display some form of collocational behavior, being less lexically free than the other literal combinations. Conversely, among the most common false negatives (i.e. idioms that were classified as non-idioms), we find expressions like *cadere dal cielo* ('to fall from the sky, to be heaven-sent') or *aprire gli occhi* ('to open one's eyes') that happen to be highly ambiguous in that they make both an idiomatic and a literal reading possible according to the context. It is possible that the evidence available in our corpus privileged a literal reading for them. Such ambiguous expressions should be analyzed in more detail in following contributions by means of *token detection* algorithms that might tell apart idiomatic and literal usages of these expressions in context.

6   Conclusions

In this paper we carried out an idiom type identification task based on the idea that idiomatic expressions tend to allow for more restricted variability in the lexical choice of their subparts with respect to non-idiomatic ones. Starting from a list of target Italian V-NP and V-PP constructions, comprising both idioms and non-idioms, we generated a set of lexical variants by replacing their components with semantically related words extracted distributionally or from Italian MultiWordNet. We then measured the cosine similarity between the vectors of the original expressions and the vectors of their variants, expecting idioms to be less similar to their variants with respect to non-idioms. All in all, this proved to be the case. More specifically, cosine similarity between the vector of the original expressions and the centroid of their variants stood out as the best performing measure. The best models used DSM variants or iMWN variants filtered by their cosine similarity with the components of the target expressions. In the second place, our methods proved to be successful also when applied to idioms most of which had many scarcely or not at all attested variants. In devising our variant-based distributional idiomaticity measures we also tried to take this negative evidence into consideration, still achieving high and reliable performances.

References

Ron Artstein and Massimo Poesio. 2008. Inter-coder agreement for computational linguistics. *Computational Linguistics*, 34(4):555–596.

Timothy Baldwin, Colin Bannard, Takaaki Tanaka, and Dominic Widdows. 2003. An empirical model of multiword expression decomposability. In *Proceedings of the ACL-SIGLEX Workshop on Multiword Expressions: Analysis, Acquisition and Treatment*, pages 89–96.

Colin Bannard. 2007. A measure of syntactic flexibility for automatically identifying multiword expressions in corpora. In *Proceedings of the Workshop on a Broader Perspective on Multiword Expressions*, pages 1–8.

Marco Baroni, Silvia Bernardini, Federica Comastri, Lorenzo Piccioni, Alessandra Volpi, Guy Aston, and Marco Mazzoleni. 2004. Introducing the La Repubblica Corpus: A Large, Annotated, TEI(XML)-Compliant Corpus of Newspaper Italian. In *Proceedings of the 4th International Conference on Language Resources and Evaluation*, pages 1771–1774.

Marco Baroni, Silvia Bernardini, Adriano Ferraresi, and Eros Zanchetta. 2009. The wacky wide web: a collection of very large linguistically processed web-crawled corpora. *Language Resources and Evaluation*, 43(3):209–226.

Cristina Cacciari and Sam Glucksberg. 1991. Understanding idiomatic expressions: The contribution of word meanings. *Advances in Psychology*, 77:217–240.

Cristina Cacciari. 2014. Processing multiword idiomatic strings: Many words in one? *The Mental Lexicon*, 9(2):267–293.

Noam Chomsky. 1980. Rules and representations. *Behavioral and Brain Sciences*, 3:1–15, 3.

Kenneth W. Church and Patrick Hanks. 1991. Word association norms, mutual information, and lexicography. *Computational Linguistics*, 16(1):22–29.

Scott Deerwester, Susan T. Dumais, George W. Furnas, Thomas K. Landauer, and Richard Harshman. 1990. Indexing by latent semantic analysis. *Journal of the American society for information science*, 41(6):391.

Patrick J. Duffley. 2013. How creativity strains conventionality in the use of idiomatic expressions. In Mike Borkent, Barbara Dancygier, and Jennifer Hinnell, editors, *Language and the creative mind*, pages 49–61. CSLI Publications.

Stefan Evert. 2008. Corpora and collocations. In Anke Lüdeling and Merja Kytö, editors, *Corpus Linguistics. An International Handbook*, volume 2, pages 1212–1248. Mouton de Gruyter.

Afsaneh Fazly and Suzanne Stevenson. 2008. A distributional account of the semantics of multiword expressions. *Italian Journal of Linguistics / Rivista di Linguistica*, 1(20):157–179.

Afsaneh Fazly, Paul Cook, and Suzanne Stevenson. 2009. Unsupervised type and token identification of idiomatic expressions. *Computational Linguistics*, 1(35):61–103.

John R. Firth. 1957. *Papers in Linguistics*. Oxford University Press.

Jerry A. Fodor and Ernest Lepore. 2002. *The compositionality papers*. Oxford University Press.

Raymond W. Gibbs, Nandini P. Nayak, John L. Bolton, and Melissa E. Keppel. 1989. Speakers' assumptions about the lexical flexibility of idioms. *Memory & Cognition*, 17(1):58–68.

Adele E. Goldberg. 1995. *Constructions. A Construction Grammar Approach to Argument Structure*. University of Chicago Press.

Filip Graliński. 2012. Mining the web for idiomatic expressions using metalinguistic markers. In *Proceedings of Text, Speech and Dialogue: 15th International Conference*, pages 112–118.

Zellig S. Harris. 1954. Distributional structure. *Word*, 10(2-3):146–162.

Thomas Hoffmann and Graeme Trousdale, editors. 2013. *The Oxford Handbook of Construction Grammar*. Oxford University Press.

Ray Jackendoff. 1997. *The Architecture of the Language Faculty*. MIT Press.

Klaus Krippendorff. 2012. *Content analysis: An introduction to its methodology*. Sage.

Gabriella Lapesa and Stefan Evert. 2014. A large scale evaluation of distributional semantic models: Parameters, interactions and model selection. *Transactions of the Association for Computational Linguistics*, 2:531–545.

Dekang Lin. 1999. Automatic identification of non-compositional phrases. In *Proceedings of the 37th Annual Meeting of the Association for Computational Linguistics*, pages 317–324.

Diana McCarthy, Bill Keller, and John Carroll. 2003. Detecting a continuum of compositionality in phrasal verbs. In *Proceedings of the ACL-SIGLEX Workshop on Multiword Expressions: Analysis, Acquisition and Treatment*, pages 73–80.

Matthew S. McGlone, Sam Glucksberg, and Cristina Cacciari. 1994. Semantic productivity and idiom comprehension. *Discourse Processes*, 17(2):167–190.

Rosamund Moon. 1998. *Fixed expressions and idioms in English: A corpus-based approach.* Oxford University Press.

Grace Muzny and Luke S. Zettlemoyer. 2013. Automatic Idiom Identification in Wiktionary. In *Proceedings of the 2013 Conference on Empirical Methods in Natural Language Processing*, pages 1417–1421.

Geoffrey Nunberg, Ivan Sag, and Thomas Wasow. 1994. Idioms. *Language*, 70(3):491–538.

Emanuele Pianta, Luisa Bentivogli, and Christian Girardi. 2002. Multiwordnet: Developing and aligned multilingual database. In *Proceedings of the First International Conference on Global WordNet*, pages 293–302.

Monica B. Quartu. 1993. *Dizionario dei modi di dire della lingua italiana.* RCS Libri, Milano.

Ivan A. Sag, Timothy Baldwin, Francis Bond, Ann Copestake, and Dan Flickinger. 2002. Multiword Expressions: A Pain in the Neck for NLP. In *Proceedings of the 3rd International Conference on Intelligent Text Processing and Computational Linguistics*, pages 1–15.

Magnus Sahlgren. 2008. The distributional hypothesis. *Italian Journal of Linguistics*, 20(1):33–54.

John Sinclair. 1991. *Corpus, concordance, collocation.* Oxford University Press.

Anna Siyanova-Chanturia and Ron Martinez. 2014. The idiom principle revisited. *Applied Linguistics*, pages 1–22.

Frank Smadja. 1993. Retrieving collocations from text: Xtract. *Computational Linguistics*, 19(1):143–177.

Peter D. Turney and Patrick Pantel. 2010. From Frequency to Meaning: Vector Space Models of Semantics. *Journal of Artificial Intelligence Research*, 37:141–188.

Sriram Venkatapathy and Aravid Joshi. 2005. Measuring the relative compositionality of verb-noun (V-N) collocations by integrating features. In *Proceedings of Joint Conference on Human Language Technology and Empirical Methods in Natural Language Processing*, pages 899–906.

Dominic Widdows and Beate Dorow. 2005. Automatic extraction of idioms using graph analysis and asymmetric lexicosyntactic patterns. In *Proceedings of the ACL-SIGLEX Workshop on Deep Lexical Acquisition*, pages 48–56.

Filtering and Measuring the Intrinsic Quality of Human Compositionality Judgments

Silvio Cordeiro[1,2], Carlos Ramisch[1], Aline Villavicencio[2]
[1] Aix Marseille Université, CNRS, LIF UMR 7279 (France)
[2] Institute of Informatics, Federal University of Rio Grande do Sul (Brazil)
silvioricardoc@gmail.com   carlos.ramisch@lif.univ-mrs.fr   avillavicencio@inf.ufrgs.br

Abstract

This paper analyzes datasets with numerical scores that quantify the semantic compositionality of MWEs. We present the results of our analysis of crowdsourced compositionality judgments for noun compounds in three languages. Our goals are to look at the characteristics of the annotations in different languages; to examine intrinsic quality measures for such data; and to measure the impact of filters proposed in the literature on these measures. The cross-lingual results suggest that greater agreement is found for the extremes in the compositionality scale, and that outlier annotation removal is more effective than outlier annotator removal.

1   Introduction

Noun compounds (NCs) are a pervasive class of multiword expressions (MWEs) in many languages. They are conventionalized noun phrases whose semantics range from idiomatic to fully compositional interpretations (Nakov, 2013). In idiomatic NCs, the meaning of the whole does not come directly from the meaning of its parts (Baldwin and Kim, 2010). For instance, an *ivory tower* is not a physical place, but a non-realistic perspective. Its semantic interpretation has little or nothing to do with a literal *tower* built out of *ivory*.

The semantic compositionality of MWEs can be represented as a numerical score. Its value indicates how much individual words contribute to the meaning of the whole: e.g. *olive oil* may be seen as 80% *olive* and 100% *oil*, whereas *dead end* is 5% *dead* and 90% *end*.

Low values imply idiomaticity, while high values imply compositionality. This information can be useful, e.g. to decide how an MWE should be translated (Cap et al., 2015).

Many datasets with compositionality judgments have been collected (e.g. Gurrutxaga and Alegria (2013) and McCarthy et al. (2003)). Reddy et al. (2011) asked Mechanical Turkers to annotate 90 English noun-noun compounds on a scale from 0 to 5 with respect to the literality of member words. This resource has been used to evaluate compositionality prediction systems (Salehi et al., 2015). A similar resource has been created for German by Roller et al. (2013), who propose two filtering techniques adopted in our experiments. Farahmand et al. (2015) created a dataset of 1042 compounds in English with binary annotations by 4 experts. The sum of the binary judgments has been used as a numerical score to evaluate compositionality prediction functions (Yazdani et al., 2015).

In this paper we report a cross-lingual examination of quality measures and filtering strategies for compound compositionality annotations. Using the dataset by Reddy et al. (2011) and its extension to English, French and Portuguese by Ramisch et al. (2016), we examine the filters reported by Roller et al. (2013) for German and assess whether they improve overall dataset quality in these three languages. This analysis aims at studying the distributions and characteristics of the human ratings, examining quality measures for the collected data, and measuring the impact of simple filtering techniques on these quality measures. In particular, we look at how the scores obtained are distributed across the compositionality scale, whether the scores of the individual components are correlated with

Proceedings of the 12th Workshop on Multiword Expressions, pages 32–37,
Berlin, Germany, August 7-12, 2016. ©2016 Association for Computational Linguistics

those of the compounds, and if there are cases of compounds that are more difficult to annotate than others. This paper is structured as follows: the three compositionality datasets are presented in §2. The quality measures and filtering strategies are described in §3 and the results of the analysis in §4. The paper concludes with discussion of the results and of future work (§5).

2 Compostionality Datasets

In this task, we built three datasets, in French (`fr`), Portuguese (`pt`) and English (`en`), containing human-annotated compositionality scores for 2-word NCs. Annotators were native speakers using an online non-timed questionnaire. They were shown a NC (e.g. `en` *ivory tower*) and three sentences where the compound occurs in a particular sense as context for disambiguation. They then provide three numerical scores in a scale from 0 (idiomatic) to 5 (compositional): the contribution of the head word to the whole (s_H), the contribution of the modifier word to the whole (s_M) and the contribution of both words to the whole (s_{NC}). Each entry in the raw dataset can be represented as a tuple, containing:

- **annot**: identifier of a human annotator
- **H**: syntactic head of the NC (noun).
- **M**: syntactic modifier of the head, can be a noun (`en`) or an adjective (`en pt fr`).
- s_{NC}: integer rating given by the human annotator **annot** assessing the compositionality of the NC.
- s_H and s_M: Same as s_{NC} for the contribution of **H** and **M** to the meaning of the whole NC.
- **equiv**: A list of at least two paraphrases, synonyms or equivalent formulations. For instance, for *ivory tower*, common paraphrases include *privilege* and *utopia*.

The datasets contain comparable data collected using different methodologies due to the requirement and availability of native speakers. For `en` and `fr`, we used Amazon Mechanical Turk (AMT). Native `en` speakers abound on the platform, unlike for the other languages. For `fr`, the annotation took considerably longer, and the quality was not as good

as `en`. For `pt`, not enough native speakers were found. Therefore, we developed a stand-alone interface for collecting `pt` judgments from volunteer annotators.

The `pt` and `fr` datasets contain 180 manually selected noun–adjective NCs each. The `en` dataset is the combination of 2 parts: REDDY (Reddy et al., 2011) with the original dataset downloaded from the authors' websites, and en_+, with 90 manually selected noun–noun and adjective–noun compounds.

For each NC, the final scores are calculated as the average of all its annotations. For instance, if the 5 annotations for the contribution of *ivory* to *ivory tower* were [0,1,0,2,0], the final μ_M score would be 3/5. In other words, we obtain 3 scores per compound (for the contribution of **H**, **M** and for both) by aggregating individual annotator's scores using the arithmetic mean μ.

3 Quality Measures and Filtering

To calculate the quality of a compositionality dataset, we adopt measures that reflect agreement among the different annotators. We also compare strategies for removing outlier data (which may have introduced noise among the judgments), and the impact of such removal in terms of data retention.

3.1 Quality Measures

Our hypothesis is that, if the task is well defined, native speaker annotators should *agree* with each other even in the absence of common training or expertise. Low agreement could be motivated by several reasons: unclear/vague instructions, ill-formed or highly polysemous NCs, etc.

Inter-Annotator Agreement (α) A classical measure of inter-annotator agreement is the kappa score, which not only considers the proportion of agreeing pairs but also factors out chance agreement. In our case, however, ratings are not categorical but ordinal, so the α score, would be more adequate (Artstein and Poesio, 2008). Nonetheless, it is only possible to calculate α when all annotators rate the same items, which is not our case. We do not report this score in our evaluation.

Standard Deviation (μ_σ and $P_{\sigma>1.5}$) The standard deviation σ of a score s estimates its average distance from the mean. Therefore, if human annotators agree, σ should be low as they tend to provide similar ratings that converge toward the average score μ. On the other hand, high σ values indicate high disagreement. We propose two metrics:

- μ_σ Average standard deviation of a score s over all NCs.
- $P_{\sigma>1.5}$ Proportion of NCs in the dataset whose σ is higher than 1.5, following Reddy et al. (2011).

Rank Correlation (ρ_{oth}) If two annotators agree, the ranking of the NCs annotated by both must be similar. Since in an AMT like setting it is difficult to compare pairs of annotators because they may not annotate the same NCs, we compare the ranking of the NCs rated by an individual annotator a with the ranking of the same NCs according to the average of all other annotators $\mu_{\Omega-a}$. In order to consider only order differences rather than value differences, we use Spearman's rank correlation score, noted ρ_{oth}.

3.2 Filtering

This analysis focuses on the filtering strategies described by Roller et al. (2013).

Z-score Filtering Our first filtering strategy aims at removing outlier *annotations*, who perhaps were distracted or did not fully understand the meaning of a given NC. It is similar to the filter proposed by Roller et al. (2013). We remove individual NC annotations whose score s is more than z standard deviations σ away from the average $\mu_{\Omega-s}$ of other scores for the same compound. In other words, we remove a compound if $\dfrac{|s - \mu_{\Omega-s}|}{\sigma_{\Omega-s}} > z$ for one of the three ratings (NC, **H** or **M**).[1]

Spearman Filtering Our second filtering strategy aims at removing outlier *annotators*, e.g. spammers and non-native speakers. We define a threshold R on the rank-correlation with others ρ_{oth} below which we discard all scores provided by **annot**. This technique was also used by Roller et al. (2013).

---

[1] Differently from Roller et al. (2013), we do not include the score being filtered out in μ and σ estimates. Moreover, we apply the filter to the three scores of an NC simultaneously.

We employed two additional filters, not analyzed here. First, we only accept annotators who confirm they are native speakers by answering general demographic questions in an external form. Second, we manually remove annotators who provided malformed **equiv** answers, not only containing typos but also major errors, suggesting non-native status.

3.3 Filtering Impact

To determine the impact of outlier removal, we calculate two measures. The first one is used by Roller et al. (2013) in the context of data filtering. They consider the data retention rate DRR as the proportion of NCs in the dataset after filtering n_{filtered} with respect to the initial number of compounds n, that is, how much was retained after filtering. The second measure is the average number of annotations μ_n across all NCs.

4 Data Analysis

In this paper we discuss 4 questions in particular, related to the quality of the annotations.

Does filtering improve quality? Table 1 presents the quality results for all datasets, in their original form as well as filtered. The filter threshold configurations adopted in these analyses were, for **en** and **pt**: $z = 2.2$, $\rho = 0.5$, and for **fr**: $z = 2.5$, $\rho = 0.5$.

As can be seen in Table 1, filtering does improve the quality of the annotations. The more restrictive the filtering, the lower the number of annotations available, but also the higher is the agreement among annotators, for all languages. When no filtering is performed, there is an average of 14.92 annotations per compound, but average standard deviation values ranging from 1.08 to 1.21. The proportion of high standard deviation compounds is between 22.78% and 30.56%. With filtering, the number of annotations per compound drops to 13.03, but so does the average standard deviation, which becomes smaller than 1. The proportion of high standard deviation compounds is between 14% and 19%.

Figures 1 and 2 show the variation in the **pt** dataset's quality as a function of z-score and Spearman ρ choices, respectively. The former is quite effective at improving the quality of the annotations for these languages, while the

Dataset	μ_n	$\mu_{\sigma\mathbf{NC}}$	$\mu_{\sigma\mathbf{H}}$	$\mu_{\sigma\mathbf{M}}$	$P_{\sigma\mathbf{NC}>1.5}$	$P_{\sigma\mathbf{H}>1.5}$	$P_{\sigma\mathbf{M}>1.5}$	DRR
Reddy	15	0.99	0.94	0.89	5.56%	11.11%	8.89%	–
en$_+$ raw	18.8	1.17	1.05	1.18	18.89%	16.67%	27.78%	–
en$_+$ filter	15.7	0.87	0.66	0.88	3.33%	10.00%	14.44%	83.61%
fr raw	14.9	1.15	1.08	1.21	22.78%	24.44%	30.56%	–
fr filter	13	0.94	0.83	0.96	13.89%	15.00%	18.89%	87.34%
pt raw	31.8	1.22	1.09	1.20	14.44	17.22%	19.44%	–
pt filter	27.9	1.0	0.83	0.97	6.11%	8.89%	12.22%	87.81%

Table 1: Intrinsic quality measures for the raw and filtered datasets

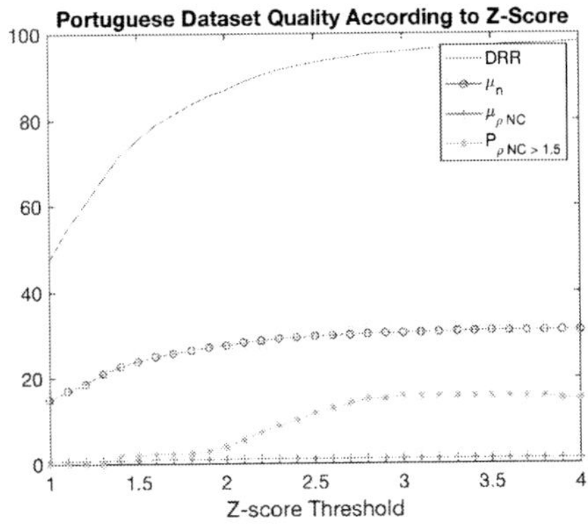

Figure 1: Quality of z-score filtering

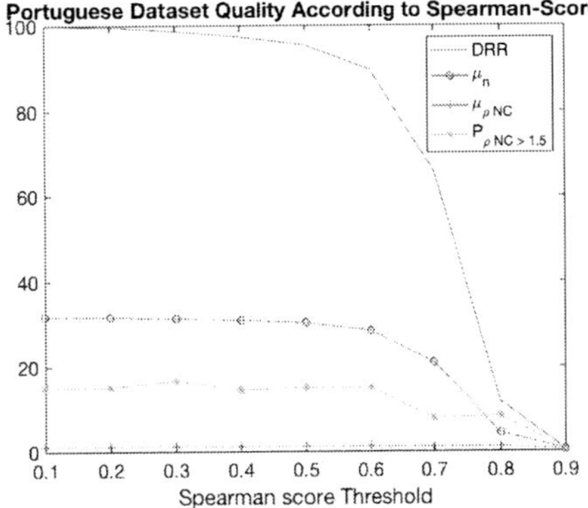

Figure 2: Quality of Spearman filtering

later does not seem to provide any real benefit. This differs from the results obtained by Roller et al. (2013) for German, but we see the same results consistently in our three datasets.

Are scores evenly distributed? Figure 3 shows the widespread distribution of compositionality scores of compounds (x-axis), compared with the combination of heads and modifiers (y-axis). This indicates that they are representative of the various compositionality scores, in a balanced manner.

Are the individual scores correlated? As can be seen in Figure 3, the average score for each compound can be reasonably approximated by the individual scores of head and modifier. Considering the goodness of fit measures R^2_{geom} and R^2_{arith} (for arithmetic and geometric means), we can see that the geometric model better represents the data. Whenever annotators judged an element of the compound as too idiomatic, they have also rated the whole compound as highly idiomatic.

Which NCs are harder to annotate? Figure 4 presents the standard deviation for each compound as a function of its average scores. One can visually attest that the least consensual compound judgments fall in the middle section of the graph. Even if we account for the fact that the extremities cannot follow a two-tailed distribution, those compounds still end up being easier than the ones in the middle.

5 Conclusions and Future Work

In this paper, we discussed the quality of human compositionality judgments, in English, French and Portuguese. We examined measures and filters for ensuring high agreement among annotators across languages. The cross-lingual results suggest that a greater agreement is obtained with outlier annotation removal than with outlier annotator removal, and that more agreement is found for the extremes of the compositionality scale.

Future work includes proposing a cross-lingual compositionality judgment protocol

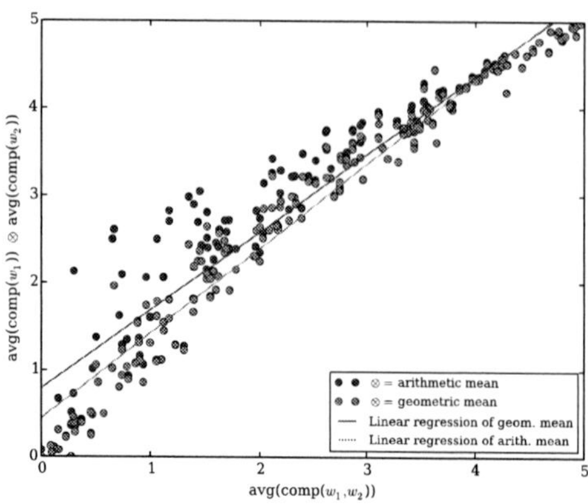

Figure 3: Distribution of $s_H \otimes s_M$ according to s_{NC} in pt.

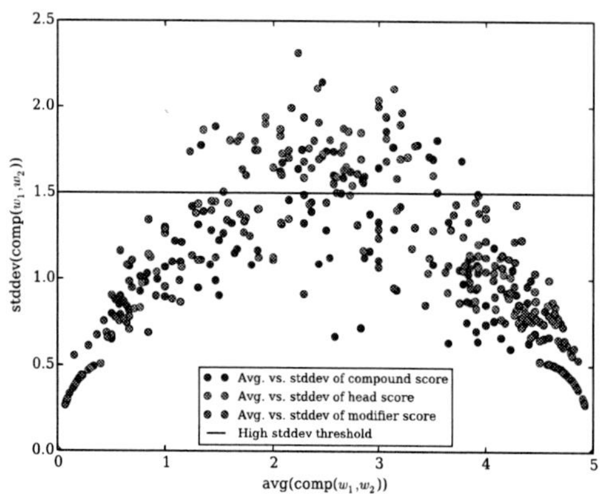

Figure 4: Distribution of σ_{NC} according to μ_{NC} in fr.

that maximizes agreement among annotators. We also intend to examine the impact of factors like polysemy and concreteness of compound elements on annotator agreement. The complete resource, including filtered and raw data, is freely available.[2]

Acknowledgements

This work has been partly funded by projects "Simplificação Textual de Expressões Complexas", sponsored by Samsung Eletrônica da Amazônia Ltda. under the terms of Brazilian federal law No. 8.248/91, PARSEME (Cost Action IC1207), PARSEME-FR (ANR-14-CERA-0001), AIM-WEST (FAPERGS-INRIA 1706-2551/13-7) and CNPq 482520/2012-4, 312114/2015-0.

References

Ron Artstein and Massimo Poesio. 2008. Intercoder agreement for computational linguistics. *Comp. Ling.*, 34(4):555–596.

Timothy Baldwin and Su Nam Kim. 2010. Multiword expressions. In Nitin Indurkhya and Fred J. Damerau, editors, *Handbook of Natural Language Processing*, pages 267–292. CRC Press, Taylor and Francis Group, Boca Raton, FL, USA, 2 edition.

Fabienne Cap, Manju Nirmal, Marion Weller, and Sabine Schulte im Walde. 2015. How to account for idiomatic German support verb constructions in statistical machine translation. In *Proc. of the 11th Workshop on MWEs (MWE 2015)*, pages 19–28, Denver, Colorado, USA. ACL.

Meghdad Farahmand, Aaron Smith, and Joakim Nivre. 2015. A multiword expression data set: Annotating non-compositionality and conventionalization for English noun compounds. In *Proc. of the 11th Workshop on MWEs (MWE 2015)*, pages 29–33, Denver, Colorado, USA. ACL.

Antton Gurrutxaga and Iñaki Alegria. 2013. Combining different features of idiomaticity for the automatic classification of noun+verb expressions in Basque. In Valia Kordoni, Carlos Ramisch, and Aline Villavicencio, editors, *Proc. of the 9th Workshop on MWEs (MWE 2013)*, pages 116–125, Atlanta, GA, USA, Jun. ACL.

Diana McCarthy, Bill Keller, and John Carroll. 2003. Detecting a continuum of compositionality in phrasal verbs. In Francis Bond, Anna Korhonen, Diana McCarthy, and Aline Villavicencio, editors, *Proc. of the ACL Workshop on MWEs: Analysis, Acquisition and Treatment (MWE 2003)*, pages 73–80, Sapporo, Japan, Jul. ACL.

Preslav Nakov. 2013. On the interpretation of noun compounds: Syntax, semantics, and entailment. *Nat. Lang. Eng. Special Issue on Noun Compounds*, 19(3):291–330.

Carlos Ramisch, Silvio Ricardo Cordeiro, Leonardo Zilio, Marco Idiart, Aline Villavicencio, and Rodrigo Wilkens. 2016. How naked is the naked truth? A multilingual lexicon of nominal compound compositionality. In *Proc. of ACL 2016*. ACL. To appear.

---

[2] `http://pageperso.lif.univ-mrs.fr/~carlos.ramisch/?page=downloads/compounds`

Siva Reddy, Diana McCarthy, and Suresh Manandhar. 2011. An empirical study on compositionality in compound nouns. In *Proceedings of The 5th International Joint Conference on Natural Language Processing 2011 (IJCNLP 2011)*, November.

Stephen Roller, Sabine Schulte im Walde, and Silke Scheible. 2013. The (un)expected effects of applying standard cleansing models to human ratings on compositionality. In Valia Kordoni, Carlos Ramisch, and Aline Villavicencio, editors, *Proc. of the 9th Workshop on MWEs (MWE 2013)*, pages 32–41, Atlanta, GA, USA, Jun. ACL.

Bahar Salehi, Nitika Mathur, Paul Cook, and Timothy Baldwin. 2015. The impact of multiword expression compositionality on machine translation evaluation. In *Proc. of the 11th Workshop on MWEs (MWE 2015)*, pages 54–59, Denver, Colorado, USA. ACL.

Majid Yazdani, Meghdad Farahmand, and James Henderson. 2015. Learning semantic composition to detect non-compositionality of multiword expressions. In *Proceedings of the 2015 Conference on Empirical Methods in Natural Language Processing*, pages 1733–1742, Lisbon, Portugal, September. Association for Computational Linguistics.

Graph-based Clustering of Synonym Senses for German Particle Verbs

Moritz Wittmann and **Marion Weller-Di Marco** and **Sabine Schulte im Walde**
Institut für Maschinelle Sprachverarbeitung, Universität Stuttgart
Pfaffenwaldring 5B, 70569 Stuttgart, Germany
{wittmamz,wellermn,schulte}@ims.uni-stuttgart.de

Abstract

In this paper, we address the automatic induction of synonym paraphrases for the empirically challenging class of German particle verbs. Similarly to Cocos and Callison-Burch (2016), we incorporate a graph-based clustering approach for word sense discrimination into an existing paraphrase extraction system, (i) to improve the precision of synonym identification and ranking, and (ii) to enlarge the diversity of synonym senses. Our approach significantly improves over the standard system, but does not outperform an extended baseline integrating a simple distributional similarity measure.

1 Introduction

Alignments in parallel corpora provide a straightforward basis for the extraction of paraphrases by means of re-translating pivots and then ranking the obtained set of candidates. For example, if the German verb *aufsteigen* is aligned with the English pivot verbs *rise* and *climb up*, and the two English verbs are in turn aligned with the German verbs *aufsteigen, ansteigen* and *hochklettern*, then *ansteigen* and *hochklettern* represent two paraphrase candidates for the German verb *aufsteigen*. Bannard and Callison-Burch (2005) were the first to apply this method to gather paraphrases for individual words and multi-word expressions, using translation probabilities as criteria for ranking the obtained paraphrase candidates.

This standard re-translation approach however suffers from a major *re-translation sense problem*, because the paraphrase candidates cannot distinguish between the various senses of the target word or phrase. Consequently, (i) the different senses of the original word or phrase are merged,

paraphrase	valid	sense	gloss
richten	-		*to direct*
abzielen	+	1	*to concentrate*
konzentrieren	+	1	*to concentrate*
orientieren	-		*to orientate*
organisieren	+	2	*to organize*
beruhen	-		*to rely*
anstreben	-		*to strive*
lenken	-		*to steer*
zielen	-		*to aim*
erreichen	+	3	*to achieve*

Table 1: Top-ranked paraphrases for *ausrichten*.

when the back translations of all pivot words are collected within one set of paraphrase candidates; and (ii) the ranking step does not guarantee that all senses of a target are covered by the top-ranked candidates, as more frequent senses amass higher translation probabilities and are favoured.

Recently, Cocos and Callison-Burch (2016) proposed two approaches to distinguish between paraphrase senses (i.e., aiming to solve problem (i) above). In this paper, we address both facets (i) and (ii) of the *re-translation sense problem*, while focusing on an emprically challenging class of multi-word expressions, i.e., German particle verbs (PVs). German PVs can appear morphologically joint or separated (such as *steigt ... auf*), and are often highly ambiguous. For example, the 138 PVs we use in this paper have an average number of 5.3 senses according to the *Duden*[1] dictionary.

Table 1 illustrates the re-translation sense problem for German PVs. It lists the 10 top-ranked paraphrases for the target verb *ausrichten* obtained with the standard method. Four synonyms in the 10 top-ranked candidates were judged valid according to the *Duden*, covering three out of five senses listed in the *Duden*. Synonyms for a fourth sense *"to tell"* (*sagen, übermitteln, weitergeben*) existed in the candidate list, but were ranked low.

---

[1] www.duden.de

Proceedings of the 12th Workshop on Multiword Expressions, pages 38–43,
Berlin, Germany, August 7-12, 2016. ©2016 Association for Computational Linguistics

Our approach to incorporate word senses into the standard paraphrase extraction applies a *graph-based clustering* to the set of paraphrase candidates, based on a method described in (Apidianaki and He, 2010; Apidianaki et al., 2014). It divides the set of candidates into clusters by reducing edges in an originally fully-connected graph to those exceeding a dynamic similarity threshold. The resulting clusters are taken as paraphrase senses, and different parameters from the graphical clustering (such as connectedness in clusters; cluster centroid positions; etc.) are supposed to enhance the paraphrase ranking step. With this setting, we aim to achieve higher precision in the top-ranked candidates, and to cover a wider range of senses as the original re-translation method.

2 Related Work

Bannard and Callison-Burch (2005) introduced the idea of extracting paraphrases with the re-translation method. Their work controls for word senses regarding specific test sentences, but not on the type level. Subsequent approaches improved the basic re-translation method, including Callison-Burch (2008) who restrict paraphrases by syntactic type; and Wittmann et al. (2014) who add distributional similarity between paraphrase candidate and target word as a ranking feature. Approaches that applied extracted paraphrases relying on the re-translation method include the evaluation of SMT (Zhou et al., 2006) and query expansion in Q-A systems (Riezler et al., 2007).

Most recently, Cocos and Callison-Burch (2016) proposed two clustering algorithms to address one of the sense problems: They discriminate between target word senses, exploiting hierarchical graph factorization clustering and spectral clustering. The approaches cluster all words in the Paraphrase Database (Ganitkevitch et al., 2013) and focus on English nouns in their evaluation.

A different line of research on synonym extraction has exploited distributional models, by relying on the contextual similarity of two words or phrases, e.g. Sahlgren (2006), van der Plas and Tiedemann (2006), Padó and Lapata (2007), Erk and Padó (2008). Typically, these methods do not incorporate word sense discrimination.

3 Synonym Extraction Pipeline

This section lays out the process of extracting, clustering and ranking synonym candidates.

3.1 Synonym Candidate Extraction

Following the basic approach for synonym extraction outlined by Bannard and Callison-Burch (2005), we gather all translations (i.e., pivots) of an input particle verb, and then re-translate the pivots. The back translations constitute the set of synonym candidates for the target particle verb.

In order to rank the candidates according to how likely they represent synonyms, each candidate is assigned a probability. The *synonym probability* $p(e_2|e_1)_{e2 \neq e1}$ for a synonym candidate verb e_2 given a target particle verb e_1 is calculated as the product of two translation probabilities: the *pivot probability* $p(f_i|e_1)$, i.e. the probability of the English pivot f_i being a translation of the particle verb e_1, and the *return probability* $p(e_2|f_i)$, i.e. the probability that the synonym candidate e_2 is a translation of the English pivot f_i. The final synonym score for e_2 is the sum over all pivots $f_{1..n}$ that re-translate into the candidate:

$$p(e_2|e_1)_{e2 \neq e1} = \sum_{i=1}^{n} p(f_i|e_1)p(e_2|f_i) \quad (1)$$

The translation probabilities are based on relative frequencies of the counts in a parallel corpus, cf. section 4.1.

Filtering We apply filtering heuristics at the *pivot probability step* and the *return probability step*: obviously useless pivots containing only stop-words (e.g. articles) or punctuation are discarded. In the back-translation step, synonym candidates that did not include a verb are removed. Furthermore, we removed pivots (*pivot probability step*) and synonym candidates (*return probability step*) consisting only of light verbs, due to their lack of semantic content and tendency to be part of multi-word expressions. If left unfiltered, light verbs often become super-nodes in the graphs later on (see section 3.2) due to their high distributional similarity with a large number of other synonym candidates. This makes it difficult to partition the graphs into meaningful clusters with the algorithm used here.

Distributional Similarity We add distributional information as an additional feature for the ranking of synonym candidates, because weighting the score from equation (1) by simple multiplication with the distributional similarity between the candidate and the target (as obtained from large corpus data, cf. section 4.1), has been found to improve the ranking (Wittmann et al., 2014).

Properties of the clusters:	
C(#(cand))	number of synonym candidates in a cluster
C(av-sim(cand,c))	average distributional similarity between synonym candidates in a cluster and the cluster centroid
C(av(#(e)))	average number of edges in the clusters of the cluster analyses
C(#(e))	total number of edges in a cluster
C(av-sim(cand,v))	average distributional similariy between synonym candidates in a cluster and the target PV
C(av-sim(cand,gc))	average distributional similariy between all synonym candidates and the global centroid
C(sim(c,v))	distributional similarity between a cluster centroid and the target PV
C(con)	connectedness of a cluster
Properties of the synonym candidates:	
S(tr)	translation probability of a synonym candidate
S(#(e))	number of edges of a synonym candidate
S(cl%(#(e)))	proportion of cluster edges for a synonym candidate
S(sim(cand,v))	distributional similarity between a synonym candidate and the target PV
S(sim(cand,c))	distributional similarity between a synonym candidate and the cluster centroid
S(sim(cand,gc))	distributional similarity between a synonym candidate and the global centroid

Table 2: Properties of synonym candidates and clusters.

3.2 Graph-Based Clustering of Candidates

The clustering algorithm suggested by Apidianaki et al. (2014) is adopted for clustering all extracted synonym candidates for a specific particle verb target. In a first step, a fully connected undirected graph of all synonym candidates is created as a starting point, with nodes corresponding to synonym candidates and edges connecting two candidates; edge weights are set according to their distributional similarity. In a second step, a similarity threshold is calculated, in order to delete edges with weights below the threshold. The threshold is initialized with the mean value between all edge weights in the fully connected graph. Subsequently, the threshold is updated iteratively:

1. The synonym candidate pairs are partitioned into two groups: P_1 contains pairs with similarities below the current threshold, and P_2 contains pairs with similarities above the current threshold **and** sharing at least one pivot.

2. A new threshold is set: $T = \frac{A_{P_1} + A_{P_2}}{2}$, where A_{P_i} is the mean over all similarities in P_i.

After convergence, the resulting graph consists of disconnected clusters of synonym candidates. Singleton clusters are ignored. The sub-graphs represent the cluster analysis to be used in the ranking of synonyms for the target particle verb.

Iterative Application of Clustering Algorithm
Because the resulting clusterings of the synonym candidates typically contain one very large (and many small) clusters, we extend the original algorithm and iteratively re-apply the clustering: After one pass of the clustering algorithm as described

above (T_1), the resulting set of connected synonym candidates becomes the input to another iteration of the algorithm ($T_{2...n}$). Each iteration of the algorithm results in a smaller and more strongly partitioned sub-graph of the initially fully connected graph because the similarity threshold for edges becomes successively higher.

3.3 Synonym Candidate Ranking

Assuming that clusters represent senses, we hypothesize that combining properties of individual synonym candidates with properties of the graph-based clusters of synonym candidates results in a ranking of the synonym candidates that overcomes both facets of the *re-translation sense problem*: Including synonym candidates from various clusters should ensure more senses of the target particle verbs in the top-ranked list; and identifying salient clusters should improve the ranking. Table 2 lists the properties of the individual synonym candidates S and the properties of the graph-based cluster analyses C that we consider potentially useful. For the experiments in section 4, we use all combinations of S and C properties.

4 Experiments, Results and Discussion

4.1 Data and Evaluation

For the extraction of synonym candidates, we use the German–English version of Europarl (1.5M parallel sentences) with GIZA++ word alignments for the extraction of synonym candidates. In the alignments, the German data is lemmatized and re-ordered in order to treat split occurrences of particle and verb as a single word (Schmid et al., 2004; Schmid, 2004; Fraser, 2009).

	system	ranking	prec. top 10	prec. top 20	no. of senses	prop. of senses
1	basic	S(tr)	34.57	25.76	1.99	45.59
2	basic + distr. sim.	S(tr) · sim(cand,v)	38.19	27.79	**2.04**	**46.89**
3	clustering + ranking (1)	S(tr) · S(sim(cand,v)) · C(#(e))	**38.41**	**27.90**	2.04	46.89
4	clustering + ranking (2)	S(tr) · S(sim(cand,v)) · C(av-sim(cand,gc))	38.26	**27.90**	2.04	46.89
5	clustering + ranking (3)	S(tr) · S(sim(cand,v))	38.19	**27.90**	2.04	46.89
6	clustering + ranking (4)	S(tr) · S(sim(cand,v)) · C(sim(cand,v))	38.12	**27.90**	2.04	46.89
7	clustering + ranking (5)	S(tr) · S(sim(cand,v)) · C(con)	37.97	27.83	2.03	46.65

Table 3: Evaluation of basic approaches and best five rankings: precision & no./proportion of senses.

The distributional similarity *sim* is determined by cosine similarities between vectors relying on co-occurrences in a window of 20 words. We use the German web corpus *DECOW14AX* (Schäfer and Bildhauer, 2012; Schäfer, 2015) containing 12 billion tokens, with the 10,000 most common nouns as vector dimensions. The feature values are calculated as *Local Mutual Information (LMI)*, cf. (Evert, 2005).

Our dataset contains the same 138 German particle verbs from Europarl as in previous work (Wittmann et al., 2014), all PVs with a frequency $f \geq 15$ and at least 30 synonyms listed in the *Duden* dictionary. For the evaluation, we also rely on the *Duden*, which provides synonyms for the target particle verbs and groups the synonyms by word sense. We consider four evaluation measures, and compare the ranking formulas by macro-averaging each of the evaluation measures over all 138 particle verbs:

- *Precision* among the *10/20 top-ranked* synonym candidates.

- *Number and proportion of senses* represented among the 10 top-ranked synonyms.

4.2 Results

The basic system (line 1 in table 3) only relies on the translation probabilities ($S(tr)$). It is extended by incorporating the distributional similarity between the target particle verb and the synonym candidates (line 2).

Our five best rankings with one iteration of graphical clustering (T_1) are shown in lines 3-7. All of these include the translation probability and the distributional similarity between candidate and particle verb; only one makes use of cluster information. Thus, the simple distributional extension is so powerful that additional cluster information cannot improve the system any further. The most relevant cluster measure is the number of edges

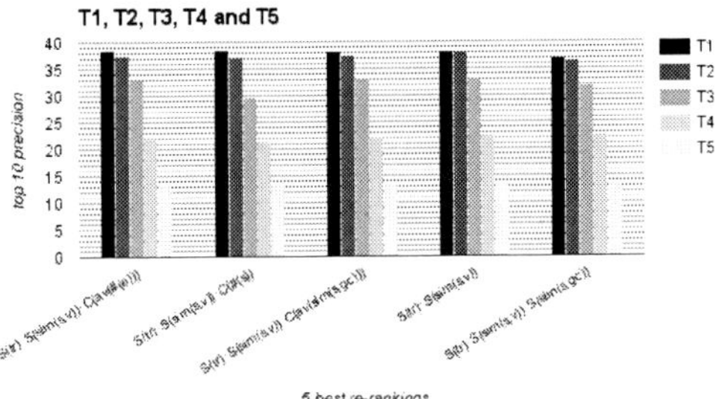

Figure 1: Evaluating an iterative application of the clustering algorithm ($T_{1...5}$).

of the cluster $C(\#(e))$, an indication of cluster size and connectedness.

While the best three clustering systems[2] outperform the extended basic system (line 2) in terms of top-10/top-20 precision, none of the improvements is significant.[3]

Also, the number and proportion of senses remain the same as in the basic approach with distributional extension. Further iterations of the clustering step ($T_{2...n}$) up to $n = 8$ lead to increasingly worse precision scores and sense detection, cf. figure 1 for $T_{1...5}$.

4.3 Discussion

Overall, the distributional similarity between the target word and the synonym candidates represents the strongest extension of the basic re-translation approach, and the cluster graphs do not provide further useful information. A breakdown of the cluster analyses revealed that the cluster sizes are very unevenly distributed. Typically, there is one very large cluster and several considerably smaller clusters, as shown by the first part of table 4, which depicts the proportion of *synonym candidates* in the largest cluster vs. the average

---

[2]The systems in lines 2 and 5 use the same ranking information but have different results, due to the removal of singletons from the graphs in the clustering, see section 3.2.

[3]χ^2 without Yates' correction

candidates		T_1	T_2	T_3	T_4	T_5
prop. largest	[%]	99.95	97.09	59.69	8.19	7.15
avg. prop rest	[%]	0.13	0.16	0.34	0.80	1.60

...

synonyms		T_1	T_2	T_3	T_4	T_5
prop. largest	[%]	99.90	96.18	60.24	9.70	8.55
avg. prop. rest	[%]	0.25	0.21	0.33	0.79	1.58

...

senses		T_1	T_2	T_3	T_4	T_5
prop. largest	[%]	100.00	96.85	74.30	15.25	9.83
avg. prop. rest	[%]	1.23	0.92	1.08	1.58	2.34

Table 4: Distribution of *candidates*, *synonyms* and *senses* in the largest cluster vs. all other clusters in the iterations T_1-T_5.

proportion of candidates in the remaining clusters. In addition, we found that most *correct synonyms* are also in the largest cluster (middle part of table 4). Accordingly, the cluster analyses do not represent partitions of the target verb senses, but most *senses* are in the largest cluster (bottom part of table 4).

Consequently, while the synonym features are useful for ranking the set of candidates, cluster-level features are ineffective as they are derived from effectively meaningless cluster analyses.[4] While re-applying the clustering step gradually overcomes the uneven cluster distribution (iterations T_2-T_5 in table 4), the sizes of the graphs decrease dramatically. For example (not depicted in table 4), on average there are only 169 candidates left in T_5 compared to 1,792 in T_1, with an average of 2.8 correct synonyms instead of 22.5, and an average of 1.7 senses instead of 4.5.

We assume that partitioning the candidate set according to senses in combination with the cluster-level measures is a valid approach to deal with the word sense problem, but based on our analysis we conclude that either (i) the context vectors are not suitable to differentiate between senses, or that (ii) the clustering algorithm is inapt for this scenario. A possible solution might be to apply the algorithms suggested in Cocos and Callison-Burch (2016). Finally, no weighting was applied to any of the properties listed in table 2. This could be improved by using a held-out data development set, and a greater number of particle verbs (we only use 138) would probably be needed as well.

---

[4]Intuitively, many of the smaller clusters are actually semantically coherent, but often not semantically related to the target verb and thus not helpful.

5 Summary

We hypothesized that graph-based clustering properties in addition to synonym candidate properties should improve the precision of synonym identification and ranking, and extend the diversity of synonym senses. Unfortunately, our extensions failed, and analyses of cluster properties revealed that future work should improve the vector representations and compare other clustering algorithms. One should keep in mind, however, that we focused on a specifically challenging class of multi-word expressions: highly ambiguous German particle verbs.

Acknowledgments

This work was funded by the DFG Research Project "Distributional Approaches to Semantic Relatedness" (Moritz Wittmann, Marion Weller-Di Marco) and the DFG Heisenberg Fellowship SCHU-2580/1-1 (Sabine Schulte im Walde).

References

Marianna Apidianaki and Yifan He. 2010. An Algorithm for Cross-Lingual Sense-Clustering tested in a MT Evaluation Setting. In *Proceedings of the International Workshop on Spoken Language Translation*, pages 219–226, Paris, France.

Marianna Apidianaki, Emilia Verzeni, and Diana McCarthy. 2014. Semantic Clustering of Pivot Paraphrases. In *Proceedings of the 9th International Conference on Language Resources and Evaluation*, pages 4270–4275, Reykjavik, Iceland.

Colin Bannard and Chris Callison-Burch. 2005. Paraphrasing with Bilingual Parallel Corpora. In *Proceedings of the 43rd Annual Meeting of the Association for Computational Linguistics*, pages 597–604, Ann Arbor, MI, USA.

Chris Callison-Burch. 2008. Syntactic Constraints on Paraphrases Extracted from Parallel Corpora. In *Proceedings of the Conference on Empirical Methods in Natural Language Processing*, pages 196–205, Honolulu, Hawaii, USA.

Anne Cocos and Chris Callison-Burch. 2016. Clustering Paraphrases by Word Sense. In *Proceedings of the 15th Annual Conference of the North American Chapter of the Association for Computational Linguistics: Human Language Technologies*, pages 1463–1472, San Diego, CA, USA.

Katrin Erk and Sebastian Padó. 2008. A Structured Vector Space Model for Word Meaning in Context. In *Proceedings of the joint Conference on Empirical*

Methods in Natural Language Processing and Computational Natural Language Learning, pages 897–906, Waikiki, Hawaii, USA.

Stefan Evert. 2005. *The Statistics of Word Co-Occurrences: Word Pairs and Collocations.* Ph.D. thesis, Institut für Maschinelle Sprachverarbeitung, Universität Stuttgart.

Alexander Fraser. 2009. Experiments in Morphosyntactic Processing for Translating to and from German. In *Proceedings of the 4th Workshop on Statistical Machine Translation*, pages 115–119, Athens, Greece.

Juri Ganitkevitch, Benjamin van Durme, and Chris Callison-Burch. 2013. PPDB: The Paraphrase Database. In *Proceedings of the 14th Conference of the North American Chapter of the Association for Computational Linguistics: Human Language Technologies*, pages 758–764, Atlanta, GA, USA.

Sebastian Padó and Mirella Lapata. 2007. Dependency-based Construction of Semantic Space Models. *Computational Linguistics*, 33(2):161–199.

Stefan Riezler, Alexander Vasserman, Ioannis Tsochantaridid, Vibhu Mittal, and Yi Liu. 2007. Statistical Machine Translation for Query Expansion in Answer Retrieval. In *Proceedings of the 45th Annual Meeting of the Association for Computational Linguistics*, pages 464–471, Prague, Czech Republic.

Magnus Sahlgren. 2006. *The Word-Space Model: Using Distributional Analysis to Represent Syntagmatic and Paradigmatic Relations between Words in High-Dimensional Vector Spaces.* Ph.D. thesis, Stockholm University.

Roland Schäfer and Felix Bildhauer. 2012. Building Large Corpora from the Web Using a New Efficient Tool Chain. In *Proceedings of the 8th International Conference on Language Resources and Evaluation*, pages 486–493, Istanbul, Turkey.

Roland Schäfer. 2015. Processing and Querying Large Web Corpora with the COW14 Architecture. In *Proceedings of the 3rd Workshop on Challenges in the Management of Large Corpora*, pages 28–34, Mannheim, Germany.

Helmut Schmid, Arne Fitschen, and Ulrich Heid. 2004. SMOR: A German Computational Morphology Covering Derivation, Composition and Inflection. In *Proceedings of the 4th International Conference on Language Resources and Evaluation*, pages 1263–1266, Lisbon, Portugal.

Helmut Schmid. 2004. Efficient Parsing of Highly Ambiguous Context-Free Grammars with Bit Vectors. In *Proceedings of the 20th International Conference on Computational Linguistics*, pages 162–168, Geneva, Switzerland.

Lonneke van der Plas and Jörg Tiedemann. 2006. Finding Synonyms using Automatic Word Alignment and Measures of Distributional Similarity. In *Proceedings of the 21st International Conference on Computational Linguistics and the 44th Annual Meeting of the Association for Computational Linguistics*, pages 866–873, Sydney, Australia.

Moritz Wittmann, Marion Weller, and Sabine Schulte im Walde. 2014. Automatic Extraction of Synonyms for German Particle Verbs from Parallel Data with Distributional Similarity as a Re-Ranking Feature. In *Proceedings of the 9th International Conference on Language Resources and Evaluation*, pages 1430–1437, Reykjavik, Iceland.

Liang Zhou, Chin-Yew Lin, and Eduard Hovy. 2006. Re-evaluating Machine Translation Results with Paraphrase Support. In *Proceedings of the Conference on Empirical Methods in Natural Language Processing*, pages 77–84, Sydney, Australia.

Accounting ngrams and multi-word terms can improve topic models

Michael Nokel
Yandex,
Moscow, Russian Federation
mnokel@yandex-team.ru

Natalia Loukachevitch
Lomonosov Moscow State University,
Moscow, Russian Federation
louk_nat@mail.ru

Abstract

The paper presents an empirical study of integrating ngrams and multi-word terms into topic models, while maintaining similarities between them and words based on their component structure. First, we adapt the PLSA-SIM algorithm to the more widespread LDA model and ngrams. Then we propose a novel algorithm LDA-ITER that allows the incorporation of the most suitable ngrams into topic models. The experiments of integrating ngrams and multi-word terms conducted on five text collections in different languages and domains demonstrate a significant improvement in all the metrics under consideration.

1 Introduction

Topic models, such as PLSA (Hofmann, 1999) and LDA (Blei et al., 2003), have shown great success in discovering latent topics in text collections. They have considerable applications in the information retrieval, text clustering and categorization (Zhou et al., 2009), word sense disambiguation (Boyd-Graber et al., 2007), etc.

However, these unsupervised models may not produce topics that conform to the user's existing knowledge (Mimno et al., 2011). One key reason is that the objective functions of topic models do not correlate well with human judgements (Chang et al., 2009). Therefore, it is often necessary to incorporate semantic knowledge into topic models to improve the model's performance. Recent work has shown that interactive human feedback (Hu et al., 2011) and information about words (Boyd-Graber et al., 2007) can improve the inferred topic quality.

Another key limitation of the original algorithms is that they rely on a "bag-of-words" as-

sumption, which means that words are assumed to be uncorrelated and generated independently. While this assumption facilitates computational efficiency, it loses the rich correlations between words. There are several studies, in which the integration of collocations, ngrams and multi-word terms is investigated. However, they are often limited to bigrams (Wallach, 2006; Griffiths et al., 2007) and often result in a worsening of the model quality due to increasing the size of a vocabulary or to a complication of the model, which requires time-intensive computation (Wang et al., 2007).

The paper presents two novel methods that take into account ngrams and maintain relationships between them and the words in topic models (e.g, *weapon – nuclear weapon – weapon of mass destruction; discrimination – discrimination on basis of nationality – racial discrimination*). The proposed algorithms do not rely on any additional resources, human help or topic-independent rules. Moreover, they lead to a huge improvement of the quality of topic models.

All experiments were carried out using the LDA algorithm and its modifications on five corpora in different domains and languages.

2 Related work

The idea of using ngrams in topic models is not a novel one. Two kinds of methods are proposed to deal with this problem: the creation of a unified topic model and preliminary extraction of collocations for further integration into topic models.

Most studies belong to the first kind of methods and are limited to bigrams: i.e, the Bigram Topic Model (Wallach, 2006) and LDA Collocation Model (Griffiths et al., 2007). Besides, Wang et al. (2007) proposed the Topical N-Gram Model that allows the generation of ngrams based on the context. However, all these models are mostly

44

Proceedings of the 12th Workshop on Multiword Expressions, pages 44–49,
Berlin, Germany, August 7-12, 2016. ©2016 Association for Computational Linguistics

of theoretical interest since they are very complex and hard to compute on real datasets.

The second type of methods includes those proposed in (Lau et al., 2013; Nokel and Loukachevitch, 2015). These works are also limited to bigrams. Nokel and Loukachevitch (2015) extend the first work and propose the PLSA-SIM algorithm, which integrates top-ranked bigrams and maintains the relationships between bigrams sharing the same words. The authors achieve an improvement in topic model quality.

Our first method in the paper extends the PLSA-SIM algorithm (Nokel and Loukachevitch, 2015) by switching to ngrams and the more widespread LDA model. Also we propose a novel iterative LDA-ITER algorithm that allows the automatic choice of the most appropriate ngrams for further integration into topic models.

The idea of utilizing prior knowledge in topic models is not a novel one, but the current studies are limited to words. So, Andrzejewski et al. (2011) incorporated knowledge by Must-Link and Cannot-Link primitives represented by a Dirichlet Forest prior. These primitives were then used in (Petterson et al., 2010; Newman et al., 2011), where similar words are encouraged to have similar topic distributions. However, all such methods incorporate knowledge in a hard and topic-independent way, which is a simplification since two words that are similar in one topic are not necessarily of equal importance for another topic.

Also several works seek to utilize the domain-independent knowledge available in online dictionaries or thesauri (such as WordNet) (Xie et al., 2015). We argue that this knowledge may be insufficient in the particular text corpus.

Our current work proposes an approach to maintain the relationships between ngrams, sharing the same words. Our method does not require any complication of the original LDA model and just gives advice on whether ngrams and words can be in the same topics or not.

3 Proposed algorithms

First, we adapt the PLSA-SIM algorithm proposed in (Nokel and Loukachevitch, 2015). We argue that the more widespread model is LDA (Blei et al., 2003). So we transfer the idea of the PLSA-SIM algorithm to LDA and adapt it to multi-word expressions and terms of any length.

The main idea of the approach of including multi-word expressions into topic models is that similar ngrams sharing the same words (e.g, *hidden – hidden layer – hidden Markov model – number of hidden units*) often belong to the same topics, under one important condition that they often co-occur within the same texts.

To implement the approach, we introduce the sets of similar ngrams and words: $S = \{S_w\}$, where S_w is the set of ngrams similar to w, that is $S_w = \{w \bigcup (\bigcup\limits_{n \; w_1 \ldots w_n : \exists i : w_i = w} w_1 \ldots w_n)\}$, where w is the lemmatized word, and $w_1 \ldots w_n$ is the lemmatized ngram. While adding ngrams to the vocabulary as single tokens, we decrease the frequencies of unigram components by the frequencies of encompassing ngrams in each document d. The resulted frequencies are denoted as n_{dw}.

The pseudocode of the resulting LDA-SIM algorithm is presented in Algorithm 1.

Algorithm 1: LDA-SIM algorithm

Input: collection D, vocabulary W, number of topics $|T|$, initial $\{p(w|t)\}$ and $\{p(t|d)\}$, sets of similar ngrams S, hyperparameters $\{\alpha_t\}$ and $\{\beta_w\}$
Output: distributions $\{p(w|t)\}$ and $\{p(t|d)\}$

1   **while** *not meet the stop criterion* **do**

2   **for** $d \in D, w \in W, t \in T$ **do**

3       $p(t|d, w) = \dfrac{p(w|t)p(t|d)}{\sum\limits_{u \in T} p(w|u)p(u|d)}$

4   **for** $d \in D, w \in W, t \in T$ **do**

5       $n'_{dw} = n_{dw} + \sum\limits_{s \in S_w} n_{ds}$

6       $p(w|t) = \dfrac{\sum\limits_{d \in D} n'_{dw} p(t|d,w) + \beta_w}{\sum\limits_{d \in D} \sum\limits_{w \in d} n'_{dw} p(t|d,w) + \sum\limits_{w \in W} \beta_w}$

7       $p(t|d) = \dfrac{\sum\limits_{w \in d} n'_{dw} p(t|d,w) + \alpha_t}{\sum\limits_{w \in W} \sum\limits_{t \in T} n'_{dw} p(t|d,w) + \sum\limits_{t \in T} \alpha_t}$

So, if similar ngrams co-occur within the same document, we sum up their frequencies during calculation of probabilities, trying to carry similar ngrams and words to the same topics. Otherwise we make no modification to the original algorithm.

Then we hypothesized that it is possible to automatically choose the most suitable ngrams to incorporate into topic models. For this purpose we can compose all possible ngrams from the top elements from each previously inferred topic and further incorporate them into a topic model (e.g., we can compose *"support vector machine"* from the top words *"machine"*, *"vector"*, *"support"*). To be precise, we can choose the most frequent ngram that can be composed from the given set of words.

To verify this hypothesis, we propose the novel **LDA-ITER** algorithm that utilizes the LDA and LDA-SIM algorithms (Algorithm 2). In fact, there is some similarity in extracting ngrams with the approach presented in (Blei and Lafferty, 2009), where the authors visualize topics with ngrams consisting of words mentioned in these topics. But in that approach the authors do not create a new topic model taking into account extracted ngrams.

Algorithm 2: LDA-ITER algorithm

---

1 Infer topics via the LDA algorithm using vocabulary W containing only words
2 **while** *not meet the stop criterion* **do**
3   Form sets C_t from the top-10 elements from each topic t
4   Form sets B_t containing all possible ngrams from the elements in each set C_t
5   Create sets of similar ngrams and words
$$S = \bigcup_t (B_t \cup C_t)$$
6   Run LDA-SIM using set of similar ngrams and words S and vocabulary
$$W = W \cup \left(\bigcup_t B \right)$$

In the proposed LDA-ITER algorithm we select top-10 elements from each topic at each iteration. We established experimentally that topic coherence does not depend highly on this parameter, while the best value for perplexity is achieved when selecting top-5 or top-7 elements. Nevertheless in all experiments we set this parameter to 10.

We should note that the number of parameters in the proposed algorithms equals to $|W||T|$ as in the original LDA, where $|W|$ is the size of vocabulary, and $|T|$ is the number of topics (cf. $|W|^N|T|$ parameters in the topical n-gram model (Wang et al., 2007), where N is the length of n-grams).

4 Datasets and evaluation

In our experiments we used English and Russian text collections in different domains (Table 1).

---
[1]http://www.stamt.org/europarl
[2]http://ipsc.jrc.ec.europa.eu/index.php?id=198
[3]http://acl-arc.comp.nus.edu.sg/
[4]http://www.cs.nyu.edu/~rowels/data.html

Text collection	Number of texts	Number of words
Russian banking texts	10422	$\approx$ 32 mln
English part of Europarl corpus[1]	9672	$\approx$ 56 mln
English part of JRC-Acquiz corpus[2]	23545	$\approx$ 53 mln
ACL Anthology Reference corpus[3]	10921	$\approx$ 48 mln
NIPS Conference Papers (2000–2012)[4]	17400	$\approx$ 5 mln

Table 1: Text collections for experiments

As the sources of multi-word terms, we took two real information-retrieval thesauri in the following domains: socio-political (EuroVoc thesaurus comprising 15161 terms) and banking (Russian Banking Thesaurus comprising 15628 terms). We used the Eurovoc thesaurus in the processing of the Europarl and JRC-Acquiz corpora. The Russian Banking Thesaurus was employed for the processing of Russian banking texts.

At the preprocessing step, documents were processed by morphological analyzers. We do not consider function and low frequency words as elements of vocabulary since they do not play a significant role in forming topics. Also we extracted all collocations in the form of the regular expression $((Adj|Noun)^+|(Adj|Noun)^*(Noun\ Prep)^?(Adj|Noun)^*)^*Noun$ (similar to the one proposed in (Frantzi and Ananiadou, 1999)). We take into account only such ngrams since topics are mainly identified by noun groups. Also we emphasize that the proposed sets of similar ngrams cannot be formed by prepositions.

As for the quality of the topic models, we consider three intrinsic measures. The first one is **Perplexity**, which is the standard criterion of topic quality (Daud et al., 2010):

$$Perplexity(D) = e^{-\frac{1}{n} \sum_{d \in D} \sum_{w \in d} n_{dw} \ln p(w|d)}, \quad (1)$$

where n is the number of all considered words in the corpus, D is the set of documents in the corpus, n_{dw} is the number of occurrences of the word w in the document d, $p(w|d)$ is the probability of appearing the word w in the document d.

Another method of evaluating topic models is topic coherence (**TC-PMI**) proposed by Newman et al. (2010), which measures the interpretability of topics based on human judgment:

$$TC\text{-}PMI = \frac{1}{|T|} \sum_{j=2}^{10} \sum_{i=1}^{j-1} \log \frac{P(w_j, w_i)}{P(w_j)P(w_i)}, \quad (2)$$

where $(w_1, w_2, \ldots, w_{10})$ are the top-10 elements in a topic, $P(w_i)$, $P(w_j)$ and $P(w_j, w_i)$ are probabilities of w_i, w_j and ngram (w_j, w_i) respectively.

Following the idea of Nokel and Loukachevitch (2015), we also used the variation of this measure – **TC-PMI-nSIM**, which considers top-10 terms, no two of which are from the same set of similar ngrams. To avoid the effect of considering very long ngrams, we took the most frequent item in each found set of similar ngrams.

5 Experiments

To compare the proposed algorithms with the original one, we extracted all the ngrams in each text corpus. For ranking ngrams we used *Term Frequency* (*TF*) and one of the eight context measures: *C-Value* (Frantzi and Ananiadou, 1999), two versions of *NC-Value* (Frantzi and Ananiadou, 1997; Frantzi and Ananiadou, 1999), *Token-FLR, Token-LR, Type-FLR, Type-LR* (Nakagawa and Mori, 2003), and *Modified Gravity Count* (Nokel and Loukachevitch, 2013). We should note that context measures are the most well-known method for extracting ngrams and multi-word terms.

According to the results of (Lau et al., 2013) we decided to integrate the top-1000 ngrams and multi-word terms into all the topic models under consideration. We should note that in all experiments we fixed the number of topics $|T| = 100$ and the hyperparameters $\alpha_t = \frac{50}{|T|}$ and $\beta_w = 0.01$.

We conducted experiments with all **nine** aforementioned measures on all the text collections to compare the quality of the LDA, the LDA with top-1000 ngrams or multi-word terms added as "black boxes" (similar to (Lau et al., 2013)), and the LDA-SIM with the same top-1000 elements.

In Table 2 we present the results of integrating the top-1000 ngrams and multi-word terms ranked by *NC-Value* (Frantzi and Ananiadou, 1999) for all five text collections. Other measures under consideration demonstrate similar results.

As we can see, there is a huge improvement in topic coherence using the proposed algorithm in all five text collections. This means that the inferred topics become more interpretable. As for

Corpus	Model	Perplexity	TC-PMI	TC-PMI-nSIM
Banking	*LDA*	1654	81.3	81.3
	LDA + ngrams	2497.1	90.1	90.1
	LDA-SIM + ngrams	**1472.8**	120.6	114.9
	LDA-SIM + terms	**1621.4**	**133**	**118**
Europarl	*LDA*	1466.1	54	54
	LDA + ngrams	2084.9	53.6	53.6
	LDA-SIM + ngrams	**1343.4**	**122.1**	**121.2**
	LDA-SIM + terms	1594.7	**105.4**	**98.3**
JRC	*LDA*	807.7	64.1	64.1
	LDA + ngrams	1140.6	65.6	65.6
	LDA-SIM + ngrams	**795.8**	**85.4**	**80.4**
	LDA-SIM + terms	885.4	**76.6**	**73.9**
ACL	*LDA*	1779.8	73.4	73.4
	LDA + ngrams	2277.5	69.6	69.6
	LDA-SIM + ngrams	2059.3	**95.2**	**90.1**
NIPS	*LDA*	1284.4	72.2	72.2
	LDA + ngrams	1968.5	69.3	69.3
	LDA-SIM + ngrams	1526.7	**127.9**	**116.3**

Table 2: Results of integrating top-1000 ngrams and terms ranked by *NC-Value* into topic models

perplexity, there is also a significant improvement compared to LDA with ngrams as "black boxes". Moreover, sometimes the perplexity is even better than in the original LDA, although the proposed algorithm works on the larger vocabularies, which usually leads to the increase of perplexity.

We should note that the results of the ACL and NIPS corpora are a little different. This is because the ACL corpus contains a lot of word segments hyphenated at ends of lines, while the NIPS corpus is relatively small.

At the last stage of the experiments, we compare the iterative and original algorithms. In Table 3 we present the results of the first iteration of the LDA-ITER algorithm (with the numbers of the added ngrams and terms) alongside the LDA.

As we can see, there is also an improvement in the topics, despite the fact that the LDA-ITER algorithm selects much more ngrams than in the experiments with the LDA-SIM. As for the multi-word terms, selecting just a few hundreds of them results in the similar or even better topic quality

Corpus	Model	Perplexity	TC-PMI	TC-PMI-nSIM
Banking	LDA	1654	81.3	81.3
	LDA-ITER + 2514 ngrams	**1448.8**	**106**	**108.7**
	LDA-ITER + 371 terms	**1384**	101.6	99.7
Europarl	LDA	1466.1	54	54
	LDA-ITER + 1848 ngrams	**1455.5**	**56.4**	**66.1**
	LDA-ITER + 210 terms	**1278.9**	**88.3**	**79.4**
JRC	LDA	807.7	64.1	64.1
	LDA-ITER + 2497 ngrams	**806.5**	**68.4**	**65.7**
	LDA-ITER + 225 terms	**741.5**	**73.8**	**70.2**
ACL	LDA	1779.8	73.4	73.4
	LDA-ITER + 2311 ngrams	1972.5	**95.9**	**79.7**
NIPS	LDA	1284.4	72.2	72.2
	LDA-ITER + 1161 ngrams	1434.2	**108**	**94.3**

Table 3: Results of integrating ngrams and multi-word terms into the LDA-ITER algorithm

than selecting regular ngrams. Thus, it seems very important that in the case of the LDA-ITER algorithm there is no need to select the desired number of integrating ngrams (cf. the LDA-SIM algorithm). We should also note that on the next iterations the results start to hover around the same values of the measures.

In Table 4 we present working time of the LDA-SIM and the first iteration of the LDA-ITER alongside the original LDA. All the algorithms conducted on a notebook with 2.1 GHz Intel Core i7-4600U and 8 GB RAM, running Lubuntu 16.04.

Corpus	LDA	LDA-SIM	LDA-ITER
Banking	11 min	13 min	11 min
ACL	13 min	15 min	16 min
Europarl	10 min	14 min	14 min
JRC	10 min	14 min	15 min
NIPS	1.75 min	2 min	1.75 min

Table 4: Working time of the algorithms

At the end, as an example of the inferred topics, we present in Table 5 the top-10 elements from the two random topics inferred by the LDA-SIM with 1000 most frequent ngrams and the first iteration of the LDA-ITER on the ACL corpus.

6 Conclusion

The paper presents experiments on integrating ngrams and multi-word terms along with similar-

LDA-SIM	
translation model	speech
statistical machine translation	speech recognition
machine translation	speech communication
statistical translation	spontaneous speech
translation	speech processing
language model	speech recognizer
translation probability	spoken language processing
reference translation	speech synthesis
translation quality	automatic speech
translation system	automatic speech recognition

LDA-ITER	
translation model	speech recognition system
statistical translation model	speech recognition
source word	speech
machine translation	recognition system
translation	speech system
language model	recognition
statistical translation	system
target word	speaker
translation system	speech recognizer
model	speak

Table 5: Topics inferred by the LDA-SIM and LDA-ITER on the ACL corpus

ities between them and words into topic models. First, we adapted the existing PLSA-SIM algorithm to the LDA model and ngrams. Then we propose the LDA-ITER algorithm, which allows us to incorporate the most suitable ngrams and multi-word terms. The experiments conducted on five text collections in different domains and languages demonstrate a huge improvement in all the metrics of quality using the proposed algorithms.

Acknowledgments

This work is partially supported by RFBR grant N14-07-00383.

References

David Andrzejewski, Xiaojin Zhu, and Mark Craven. 2011. Incorporating domain knowledge into topic modeling via dirichlet forest priors. In *Proceedings of the 26th Annual International Conference on Machine Learning*, pages 25–32.

David M. Blei and John D. Lafferty. 2009. Visualizing topics with multi-word expressions. `https://arxiv.org/pdf/0907.1013.pdf`.

David M. Blei, Andrew Y. Ng, and Michael Jordan. 2003. Latent dirichlet allocation. *Journal of Machine Learning Research*, 3(3):993–1002.

Jordan Boyd-Graber, David M. Blei, and Xiaojin Zhu. 2007. A topic model for word sense disambiguation. In *Proceedings of Empirical Methods in Natural Language Processing*, pages 1024–1033.

Jonathan Chang, Jordan Boyd-Graber, Chong Wang, Sean Gerrich, and David M. Blei. 2009. Reading tea leaves: How humans interpret topic models. In *Proceedings of the 24th Annual Conference on Neural Information Processing Systems*, pages 288–296.

Ali Daud, Juanzi Li, Lizhu Zhou, and Faqir Muhammad. 2010. Knowledge discovery through directed probabilistic topic models: a survey. *Frontiers of Computer Science in China*, 2(2):280–301.

Katerina Frantzi and Sophia Ananiadou. 1997. Automatic term recognition using contextual cues. In *Proceedings of the IJCAI Workshop on Multilinguality in Software Industry: the AI Contribution*, pages 73–80.

Katerina Frantzi and Sophia Ananiadou. 1999. The c-value/nc-value domain-independent method for multi-word term extraction. *Journal of Natural Language Processing*, 6(3):145–179.

Thomas L. Griffiths, Mark Steyvers, and Joshua B. Tenenbaum. 2007. Topics in semantic representation. *Psychological Review*, 114(2):211–244.

Thomas Hofmann. 1999. Probabilistic latent semantic indexing. In *Proceedings of the 22nd Annual International SIGIR Conference on Research and Development in Information Retrieval*, pages 50–57.

Yuening Hu, Jordan Boyd-Graber, and Brianna Satinoff. 2011. Interactive topic modeling. In *Proceedings of the Association for Computational Linguistics*, pages 248–257.

Jey Han Lau, Timothy Baldwin, and David Newman. 2013. On collocations and topic models. *ACM Transactions on Speech and Language Processing*, 10(3):1–14.

David Mimno, Hanna M. Wallach, Edmund Talley, Miriam Leenders, and Andrew McCallum. 2011. Optimizing semantic coherence in topic models. In *Proceedings of EMNLP'11*, pages 262–272.

Hiroshi Nakagawa and Tatsunori Mori. 2003. Automatic term recognition based on statistics of compound nouns and their components. *Terminology*, 9(2):201–219.

David Newman, Jey Han Lau, Kari Grieser, and Timothy Baldwin. 2010. Automatic evaluation of topic coherence. In *Proceedings of Human Language Technologies: The 11th Annual Conference of the North American Chapter of the Association for Computational Linguistics,* pages 100–108.

David Newman, Edwin V Bonilla, and Wray Buntine. 2011. Improving topic coherence with regularized topic models. In *Advances in Neural Information Processing Systems*, pages 496–504.

Michael Nokel and Natalia Loukachevitch. 2013. An experimental study of term extraction for real information-retrieval thesauri. In *Proceedings of the 10th International Conference on Terminology and Artificial Intelligence*, pages 69–76.

Michael Nokel and Natalia Loukachevitch. 2015. A method of accounting bigrams in topic models. In *Proceedings of North American Chapter of the Association for Computational Linguistics – Human Language Technologies*, pages 1–9.

James Petterson, Wray Buntine, Shravan M Narayanamurthy, Tiberio S Caetano, and Alex J Smola. 2010. Word features for latent dirichlet allocation. In *Advances in Neural Information Processing Systems*, pages 1921–1929.

Hanna M. Wallach. 2006. Topic modeling: Beyond bag-of-words. In *Proceedings of the 23rd International Conference on Machine Learning*, pages 977–984.

Xuerui Wang, Andrew McCallum, and Xing Wei. 2007. Topical n-grams: Phrase and topic discovery, with an application to information retrieval. In *Proceedings of the 2007 Seventh IEEE International Conference on Data Mining*, pages 697–702.

Pengtao Xie, Diyi Yang, and Eric P. Xing. 2015. Incorporating word correlation knowledge into topic modeling. In *Proceedings of North American Chapter of the Association for Computational Linguistics – Human Language Technologies*, pages 725–734.

Shibin Zhou, Kan Li, and Yushu Liu. 2009. Text categorization based on topic model. *International Journal of Computational Intelligence Systems*, 2(4):398–409.

Top a Splitter:
Using Distributional Semantics for Improving Compound Splitting

Patrick Ziering   **Stefan Müller**
Institute for Natural Language Processing
University of Stuttgart, Germany
`{zierinpk,muellesn}`
`@ims.uni-stuttgart.de`

Lonneke van der Plas
Institute of Linguistics
University of Malta, Malta
`Lonneke.vanderPlas@um.edu.mt`

Abstract

We present a flexible method that re-arranges the ranked output of compound splitters (i.e., decomposers of one-word compounds such as the German *Kinderlied* 'children's song') using a distributional semantics model. In an experiment, we show that our re-ranker improves the quality of various compound splitters.

1 Introduction

Closed nominal compounds (i.e., one-word compounds such as the German *Eidotter* 'egg yolk') are one of the most productive word formation types in Germanic languages such as German, Dutch or Swedish, and constitute a major class of multi-word expressions (MWEs). Baroni (2002) presents a German corpus study showing that almost half of the corpus types are compounds, while the token frequency of individual compounds is low. This makes it hard to process closed compounds with general-purpose statistical methods and necessitates automatic compound analysis as a principal part of many natural language processing tasks such as statistical machine translation (SMT).

Therefore, previous work has tried to tackle the task of compound splitting (e.g., decomposing *Eidotter* to *Ei* 'egg' and *Dotter* 'yolk'). Most compound splitters follow a generate-and-rank procedure. Firstly, all possible candidate splits are generated, e.g., *Ei|dotter, Eid|otter, ..., Eidott|er* (Koehn and Knight, 2003) or a knowledge-rich morphological analyzer provides a set of plausible candidate splits (Fritzinger and Fraser, 2010). In a second step, the list of candidate splits is ranked according to statistical features such as constituent frequency (Stymne, 2008; Macherey et al., 2011; Weller and Heid, 2012) or frequency

of morphological operations (Ziering and Van der Plas, 2016). By considering each constituent in isolation, approaches limited to frequency neglect the semantic compatibility between a compound and its constituents. For example, while *Eidotter* is usually understood as the yolk of an egg (i.e., *Ei|dotter*), the low frequency of *Dotter* often makes frequency-based splitters rank a less plausible interpretation higher: *Eid|otter* 'oath otter'.

We try to tackle this pitfall by enriching the ranked output of various splitters with a semantic compatibility score. Our method is inspired by recent work on the prediction of compound compositionality using distributional semantics (Reddy et al., 2011; Schulte im Walde et al., 2013). The distributional measures that are used to predict the compositionality of compounds are in fact measuring the semantic similarity between the compound and its constituents. Our assumption is that they can therefore be used readily to rank the candidate constituents a splitter proposes and help to promote more plausible candidate splits (e.g., *Eidotter* is distributionally more similar to *Dotter* than to *Otter*). Previously, Weller et al., (2014) applied compositionality measures to compound splitting as a pre-processing step in SMT. Their intuition is that non-compositional compounds benefit less from splitting prior to SMT. However, they found no improvements in the extrinsic evaluation. Neither did they find improvements from applying distributional semantics directly to the unordered list of candidate splits. We will show in an intrinsic evaluation that distributional semantics, when combined with the initial ranked output of various splitters does lead to a statistically significant improvement in compound splitting.

Other works that used semantic information for compound splitting include Bretschneider and Zillner (2015), who developed a splitting approach relying on a semantic ontology of the medical do-

Proceedings of the 12th Workshop on Multiword Expressions, pages 50–55,
Berlin, Germany, August 7-12, 2016. ©2016 Association for Computational Linguistics

main. They disambiguated candidate splits using semantic relations from the ontology (e.g., *Beckenbodenmuskel* 'pelvic floor muscle' is binary split to *Beckenboden | muskel* using the `part_of` relation). As back-off strategy, if the ontology lookup fails, they used constituent frequency. We do not restrict to a certain domain and related ontology but use distributional semantics in combination with frequency-based split features for the disambiguation.

Daiber et al., (2015) developed a compound splitter based on semantic analogy (e.g., *bookshop* is to *shop* as *bookshelf* is to *shelf*). From word embeddings of compound and head word, they learned prototypical vectors representing the modification. During splitting, they determined the most suitable modifier by comparing the analogy to the prototypes. While Daiber et al., (2015) developed an autonomous splitter and focused on semantic analogy, we present a re-ranker that combines distributional similarity with additional splitting features.

Very recently, Riedl and Biemann (2016) developed a semantic compound splitter that uses a pre-compiled distributional thesaurus for searching semantically similar substrings of a compound subject to decomposition. While their stand-alone method focuses on knowledge-lean split point determination, our approach improves splitters including the task of constituent normalization.

Our contributions are as follows. We are the first to show that distributional semantics information as an additional feature helps in determining the best split among the candidate splits proposed by various compound splitters in an intrinsic evaluation. Moreover, we present an architecture that allows for the addition of distributional similarity scores to any compound splitter by re-ranking a system's output.

2 Re-ranking based on distributional semantics

2.1 Initial split ranking

Our method is applicable to any compound splitter that produces a ranked output of split options[1] with their corresponding ranking score.

For example, the target compound *Fischerzeugnis* 'fish product' is processed by a compound splitter yielding the output as given in Table 1.

---

[1]Following Weller et al., (2014), we focus on true compounds and ignore non-split options.

The top-ranked candidate split is the result from a falsely triggered normalization rule (i.e., *+er* is not a valid linking element for *Fisch*).

Ranking score	Candidate split	Correct?
14264	*Fisch + Zeugnis* 'fish certificate'	✗
9390	*Fisch + Erzeugnis* 'fish product'	✓
5387	*Fischer + Zeugnis* 'fisherman certificate'	✗

Table 1: Initial split ranking

2.2 Determination of distributional similarity

For each candidate split of a target compound (e.g., *Fisch | erzeugnis* given *Fischerzeugnis*), the cosine similarity between the target compound and each candidate constituent is determined as a standard measure that is used for computing the distributional similarity (DS). In a following step, these cosine values are used to predict the degree of semantic relatedness between the target compound and the candidate modifier (MOD) or head (HEAD), respectively. As proposed by Weller et al., (2014), a possible combination of the candidate constituents' cosine values is the geometric mean (GEO). For example, let $\cos(\overrightarrow{Fischerzeugnis}, \overrightarrow{Fisch})$ be 0.455 and $\cos(\overrightarrow{Fischerzeugnis}, \overrightarrow{Erzeugnis})$ be 0.10. The GEO DS score for the lexemes derived from *Fisch|erzeugnis* is $\sqrt{0.455 \cdot 0.10} \approx 0.22$.

2.3 Combination and re-ranking

In the next step, we multiply the DS scores with the initial split ranking scores and finally re-rank the splits according to the resulting product. Table 2 shows the result from re-ranking the output presented in Table 1 with GEO DS scores.

Re-ranking score	Candidate split	Correct?
9390 · 0.22 ≈ **2034**	*Fisch + Erzeugnis* 'fish product'	✓
14264 · 0.05 ≈ **709**	*Fisch + Zeugnis* 'fish certificate'	✗
5387 · 0.01 ≈ **70**	*Fischer + Zeugnis* 'fisherman certificate'	✗

Table 2: Split re-ranking with GEO DS scores

3 Experiments

3.1 Data

We use the German Wikipedia[2] corpus comprising 665M words. We tokenize, lemmatize and PoS-tag using TreeTagger (Schmid, 1995). While we are aware of the fact that there are German corpora larger than Wikipedia which can boost the perfomance of distributional semantics methods, we decided to use the same corpora as used in previous work for the inspected compound splitters (Ziering and Van der Plas, 2016). By controlling for corpus size, we can contrast the differences in splitting performance with respect to information type (i.e., distributional similarity vs. frequency information) irrespective of corpus size.

3.2 Distributional model

In analogy to the distributional model of Weller et al., (2014), we adopt a setting whose parameters are tuned on a development set and prove best for compositionality (Schulte im Walde et al., 2013). It employs corpus-based co-occurrence information extracted from a window of 20 words to the left and 20 to the right of a target word. We restrict to the 20K most frequent nominal co-occurrents.

3.3 Distributional similarity modes

Inspired by Weller et al., (2014), the distributional similarity mode (DS MODE) refers to the selected cosine values, determined with our distributional model. We compare the distributional similarity of both individual constituents (i.e., modifier (MOD) and head (HEAD)) with the geometric mean of them (GEO). Moreover, we used standard arithmetic operations (Widdows, 2008; Mitchell and Lapata, 2010) and combine the vectors of modifier and head by vector addition (ADD), and multiplication (MULT) as shown to be beneficial in Schulte im Walde et al., (2013).

3.4 Rankings in comparison

We compare the performance of the initial ranking (INITIAL) of a compound splitter, based on all individual features, with the splitting performance after re-ranking by multiplying the selected DS value with the initial ranking score (RR_{ALL}). Our baseline (RR_{DS}) is inspired by the aggressive splitting mode (DIST) of Weller et al., (2014): we re-rank the unordered list of candidate splits proposed by a splitter according to the DS scores only.

3.5 Inspected compound splitters

We inspect three different types of German compound splitters, ranging from knowledge-lean to knowledge-rich. **Ziering and Van der Plas (2016)** developed a corpus-based approach, where morphological operations are learned automatically from word inflection. **Weller and Heid (2012)** used a frequency-based approach with a list of PoS-tagged lemmas and an extensive hand-crafted set of normalization rules. **Fritzinger and Fraser (2010)** combined the splitting output of the morphological analyzer SMOR (Schmid et al., 2004) with corpus frequencies.

3.6 Evaluation setup

While Weller at al., (2014) did not observe a difference in SMT performance between ranking candidate splits according to frequency and compositionality, we use an intrinsic evaluation measure actually revealing significant differences. We follow the evaluation approach of Ziering and Van der Plas (2016), who defined splitting accuracy[3] in terms of determining the correct split point (SPAcc) and correctly normalizing the resulting constituents (NormAcc), and use the GermaNet[4] gold standard developed by Henrich and Hinrichs (2011). We remove hyphenated compounds, which should be trivial splitting cases that do not need improvement by re-ranking. The final set comprises 51,230 compounds.

System	Test set size	Coverage
ZvdP_2016	51,194	99.9%
WH_2012	49.999	97.6%
FF_2010	47,940	93.6%

Table 3: Coverage of compound splitters

Some of the compound splitters described in Section 3.5 can only process a subset of the gold standard. For example, the approach of Fritzinger and Fraser (2010) is limited to a hand-crafted lexicon (i.e., it misses compounds with unknown constituents such as *Barbiepuppe* 'Barbie doll'). Moreover, it uses the analyzer SMOR, which considers some gold standard compounds as cases of derivation which are not subject to decomposition (e.g., *Unterbesetzung* 'understaffing' is primarily derived from the verb *unterbesetzen* 'to understaff'). Besides, for some compounds, there are

[2]de.wikipedia.org

[3]Accuracy refers to the top-ranked candidate split.
[4]sfs.uni-tuebingen.de/GermaNet

Accuracy	SPAcc					NormAcc				
DS MODE	MOD	HEAD	GEO	MULT	ADD	MOD	HEAD	GEO	MULT	ADD
ZIERING AND VAN DER PLAS (2016)										
INITIAL	97.5%					87.4%				
RR_{DS}	93.6%	94.6%	95.4%	92.7%	92.0%	75.9%	84.7%	77.8%	69.6%	61.2%
RR_{ALL}	97.5%	97.9%†	**98.0%**†	97.8%†	**98.0%**†	88.6%†	87.7%†	**89.0%**†	88.5%†	88.7%†
WELLER AND HEID (2012)										
INITIAL	98.1%					90.4%				
RR_{DS}	96.9%	97.0%	97.7%	96.9%	95.8%	86.5%	89.3%	87.1%	81.8%	75.3%
RR_{ALL}	98.2%†	98.2%†	**98.3%**†	98.2%†	**98.3%**†	**91.3%**†	90.5%†	91.1%†	90.9%†	90.9%†
FRITZINGER AND FRASER (2010)										
INITIAL	98.4%					94.9%				
RR_{DS}	97.9%	97.9%	98.4%	98.3%	98.2%	94.3%	94.3%	94.7%	94.5%	94.3%
RR_{ALL}	98.4%	98.3%	**98.5%**	98.4%	98.4%	94.8%	94.7%	**95.0%**	94.8%	94.7%

Table 4: Results of split re-ranking; † indicates significantly better than INITIAL

no binary splits in a system's ranking. These compounds are excluded from the respective splitter's test set. Table 3 shows the test set sizes and coverage of the inspected compound splitters.

4 Results and discussion

In the following section, we show results on splitting performance of various compound splitters before and after adding our re-ranking method. As shown in Table 3, the systems are evaluated on different test sets. It is not our goal to compare different splitting methods against each other, but to show the universal applicability of our re-ranker for different types of splitters.

4.1 General trends

Table 4 shows the performance numbers for all inspected compound splitters and all DS modes. A **first result** is that the INITIAL accuracy (both SPAcc and NormAcc) is always outperformed by re-ranking with DS scores as additional feature (RR_{ALL}) for at least one DS MODE.

The **baseline** of using pure DS scores (RR_{DS}) worsens the INITIAL performance. This is in line with previous work (Weller et al., 2014) and shows that isolated semantic information does not suffice but needs to be introduced as an additional feature. In an error analysis, we observed that the corpus frequency, which is missing for RR_{DS}, is a crucial feature for compound splitting and helps to demote analyses based on typographical errors or unlikely modifier normalization. For example, while RR_{ALL} analyzes the compound *Haarwasser*

'hair tonic' with the correct and highly frequent modifier *Haar* 'hair', RR_{DS} selects the morphologically plausible but yet unlikely and infrequent verbal modifier *haaren* 'to molt', which happens to have the higher cosine similarity to *Haarwasser*.

Another type of compound analysis that benefits from corpus frequency is binary splitting of left-branched tripartite compounds (i.e., bracketing). For example, the compound *Blinddarmoperation* 'appendix operation' (lit.: 'blind intestine operation') is frequency-based correctly split into *Blinddarm | operation* '[appendix] operation', whereas RR_{DS} prefers the right-branched splitting into *Blind | darmoperation* 'blind [intestine operation]'. Since the rightmost constituent *Operation* 'surgery/operation' is more ambiguous, it has a smaller cosine similarity to the entire compound than the right-branched compound *Darmoperation* 'intestinal operation'. In contrast, the high corpus frequency of the non-compositional *Blinddarm* 'appendix' and the head *Operation*, make a frequency-based splitter choose the correct structure. However, bracketing also benefits from cosine similarity. For example, using re-ranking by RR_{ALL}, the wrong compound split *Arbeits|platzmangel* 'labor [lack of space]' is corrected to *Arbeitsplatz|mangel* 'job scarcity'. As conclusion, we argue that the combination of corpus frequency and semantic plausibility (in terms of cosine similarity) is working best for splitting.

Comparing the accuracy types, we see that the determination of the correct split point is the easier task and achieves a SPAcc of 98.5%

(GEO@RR_{ALL} for Fritzinger and Fraser's (2010) splitter). However, there is only a small benefit for SPAcc when adding semantic support. In contrast, constituent normalization (measured as NormAcc) can be improved by +1.6% (GEO@RR_{ALL} for Ziering and Van der Plas' (2016) splitter).

Comparing the DS modes, we see that for NormAcc, the more demanding task that leads to the largest differences in performance between the different modes, the MOD mode outperforms the HEAD mode (for RR_{ALL}). However, the modes that combine head and modifier scores mostly outperform those based on heads or modifiers in isolation. This is in line with tendencies found in previous work on compositionality of compounds (Schulte im Walde et al., 2013). In addition, we find that for NormAcc, the GEO mode outperforms the modes based on vector arithmetic, whereas for SPAcc, the performance of GEO and the vector addition (ADD) is comparable.

4.2 Individual splitter improvement

Ziering and Van der Plas (2016) automatically learned constituent transformations taking place during compounding (e.g., *s*-suffixation) from word inflection. Based on corpus frequency and transformation plausibility, they produced a ranked list of candidate splits. However, misleading inflections can rank false splits high. For example, +*ge*, as in the participle *aufgewachsen* 'grown up' (*aufwachsen* 'grow up'), leads to the falsely top-ranked candidate split *Fu(ge)nk | elle* 'radio ulna' instead of *Fugen | kelle* 'filling trowel'. Re-ranking with RR_{ALL} promotes the correct candidate split. We achieve significant[5] improvements for almost all DS MODEs.

Weller and Heid (2012) extended a frequency-based approach (Koehn and Knight, 2003) with a hand-crafted set of morphological rules. Even restricted to only valid constituent transformations, some rules are falsely triggered and lead to wrong splits. For example, the *er*-suffix (as in *Kinder | buch* 'children's book') is used for the compound *Text | erkennung* 'text recognition' and results in the false split *Text(er) | kennung* 'text ID'. Our re-ranking method (RR_{ALL}) again helps to promote the correct candidate split. In all DS MODES, the performance is improved significantly.

For the system of **Fritzinger and Fraser (2010)**, the GEO mode improves the INITIAL split-

---

⁵Approximate randomization test (Yeh, 2000), $p < 0.05$

ting accuracy (+0.1%), but we do not achieve statistically significant results. The main reason for this is due to the lexicon-based morphological analyzer SMOR. While having the smallest coverage on the gold standard, utilizing a hand-crafted lexicon results in only correctly triggered transformation rules. This leads to a smaller list of candidate splits. In fact, the average number of analyses provided by Fritzinger and Fraser (2010) is much smaller than for Ziering and Van der Plas (2016) as shown in Table 5.

System	Avg # candidate splits
ZvdP_2016	4.31
WH_2012	2.25
FF_2010	1.11

Table 5: Average number of candidate splits

As a consequence, re-ranking has only a limited impact on the splitting performance. We can conclude that a knowledge-rich morphological resource can mitigate the need for semantic support, however, at the expense of coverage.

5 Conclusion

We presented a flexible method for re-arranging the ranked output of a compound splitter, by adding a feature for the semantic compatibility between compound and potential constituents derived from a distributional semantics model. We showed that the addition of distributional similarity significantly improves different types of compound splitters.

Acknowledgments

We thank the anonymous reviewers for their helpful feedback. We also thank Marion Di Marco and Fabienne Cap for providing their splitting methods. This research was funded by the German Research Foundation (Collaborative Research Centre 732, Project D11).

References

Marco Baroni, Johannes Matiasek, and Harald Trost. 2002. Predicting the Components of German Nominal Compounds. In *ECAI*, pages 470–474. IOS Press.

Claudia Bretschneider and Sonja Zillner. 2015. Semantic Splitting of German Medical Compounds. In *Text, Speech, and Dialogue*. Springer International Publishing.

Joachim Daiber, Lautaro Quiroz, Roger Wechsler, and Stella Frank. 2015. Splitting Compounds by Semantic Analogy. *CoRR*.

Fabienne Fritzinger and Alexander Fraser. 2010. How to Avoid Burning Ducks: Combining Linguistic Analysis and Corpus Statistics for German Compound Processing. In *Proceedings of the ACL 2010 Joint 5th Workshop on Statistical Machine Translation and Metrics MATR*, pages 224–234.

Verena Henrich and Erhard W. Hinrichs. 2011. Determining Immediate Constituents of Compounds in GermaNet. In *RANLP 2011*, pages 420–426.

Philipp Koehn and Kevin Knight. 2003. Empirical methods for compound splitting. In *EACL*.

Klaus Macherey, Andrew M. Dai, David Talbot, Ashok C. Popat, and Franz Och. 2011. Language-independent Compound Splitting with Morphological Operations. In *ACL HLT 2011*.

Jeff Mitchell and Mirella Lapata. 2010. Composition in distributional models of semantics. *Cognitive Science*, 34:1388–1429.

Siva Reddy, Diana McCarthy, and Suresh Manandhar. 2011. An Empirical Study on Compositionality in Compound Nouns. In *IJCNLP 2011*.

Martin Riedl and Chris Biemann. 2016. Unsupervised Compound Splitting With Distributional Semantics Rivals Supervised Methods. In *NAACL-HTL 2016*.

Helmut Schmid, Arne Fitschen, and Ulrich Heid. 2004. SMOR: A German Computational Morphology Covering Derivation, Composition, and Inflection. In *LREC 2004*, pages 1263–1266.

Helmut Schmid. 1995. Improvements in Part-of-Speech Tagging with an Application to German. In *ACL SIGDAT-Workshop*.

Sabine Schulte im Walde, Stefan Müller, and Stephen Roller. 2013. Exploring Vector Space Models to Predict the Compositionality of German Noun-Noun Compounds. In *Second Joint Conference on Lexical and Computational Semantics (*SEM), Volume 1: Proceedings of the Main Conference and the Shared Task: Semantic Textual Similarity*.

Sara Stymne. 2008. German Compounds in Factored Statistical Machine Translation. In *GoTAL*.

Marion Weller and Ulrich Heid. 2012. Analyzing and Aligning German compound nouns. In *LREC 2012*.

Marion Weller, Fabienne Cap, Stefan Müller, Sabine Schulte im Walde, and Alexander Fraser. 2014. Distinguishing Degrees of Compositionality in Compound Splitting for Statistical Machine Translation. In *ComAComA 2014*.

Dominic Widdows. 2008. Semantic Vector Products: Some Initial Investigations. In *Proceedings of the Second AAAI Symposium on Quantum Interaction*.

Alexander Yeh. 2000. More Accurate Tests for the Statistical Significance of Result Differences. In *COLING 2000*.

Patrick Ziering and Lonneke van der Plas. 2016. Towards Unsupervised and Language-independent Compound Splitting using Inflectional Morphological Transformations. In *NAACL-HLT 2016*.

Using Word Embeddings for Improving Statistical Machine Translation of Phrasal Verbs

Kostadin Cholakov and Valia Kordoni
Humboldt-Universität zu Berlin, Germany
`{kostadin.cholakov,kordonieva}@anglistik.hu-berlin.de`

Abstract

We examine the employment of word embeddings for machine translation (MT) of phrasal verbs (PVs), a linguistic phenomenon with challenging semantics. Using word embeddings, we augment the translation model with two features: one modelling distributional semantic properties of the source and target phrase and another modelling the degree of compositionality of PVs. We also obtain paraphrases to increase the amount of relevant training data. Our method leads to improved translation quality for PVs in a case study with English to Bulgarian MT system.

1 Introduction

Phrasal verbs (PVs) are a type of multiword expressions (MWEs) and as such, their semantics is not predictable, or is only partially predictable, from the semantics of their components. In statistical machine translation (SMT) the word-to-word translation of MWEs often results in wrong translations (Piao et al., 2005). Previous work (Ren et al. (2009), Carpuat and Diab (2010), Cholakov and Kordoni (2014)) has shown that dedicated techniques for identification of MWEs and their integration into the translation algorithms improve the quality of SMT. Generally, those techniques are based on categorical representations. MWEs are either treated as a single unit or binary features encoding properties of MWEs are added to the translation table. On the other hand, recent works have successfully applied distributional representations of words and phrases in SMT (Mikolov et al. (2013a), Zhang et al. (2014), Alkhouli et al. (2014)). The idea behind is that similar words and phrases in different languages tend to have similar distributional representations (Mikolov et al., 2013a).

In this paper, we explore the usage of such representations for improving SMT of PVs. We propose three strategies based on word embeddings. First, we employ continuous vectors of phrases learnt using neural networks to provide semantic scoring of aligned phrase pairs containing PVs. The addition of this score to the SMT model is a step toward integration of semantic information about the PVs into the translation process. Second, we use the vectors learnt to find paraphrases of the original phrase pairs and add those to the translation table. This increases the amount of relevant parallel data. Third, we make use of word embeddings to map a PV onto a continuous-valued compositionality score and add this score as a feature in the SMT model. The score indicates the semantic similarity between a PV and the verb forming that PV, i.e. the degree of compositionality of the PV. The meaning of (semi-)compositional PVs can be (partially) derived from the meaning of their lexemes, e.g. *carry in*. Previous work (Cholakov and Kordoni, 2014) treats PVs as either compositional or idiomatic while we handle compositionality as a continuous phenomenon.

We perform a case study with an English to Bulgarian SMT system. An English PV is generally translated to a single Bulgarian verb. This many-to-one mapping poses difficulties for SMT. The combined integration of all three strategies presented above outperforms the results reported in previous work both in automated and manual evaluation. Thus we show that word embeddings help SMT to handle better such a challenging linguistic phenomenon as PVs.

Proceedings of the 12th Workshop on Multiword Expressions, pages 56–60,
Berlin, Germany, August 7-12, 2016. ©2016 Association for Computational Linguistics

2   Related Work

Previous work on SMT of MWEs (Lambert and Banchs (2005), Carpuat and Diab (2010), Simova and Kordoni (2013)) suggests training the SMT system on corpora in which each MWE is treated as a single unit, e.g. *call_off*. Ren et al. (2009) treat bilingual MWEs pairs as parallel sentences which are then added to the training data. Other methods (Simova and Kordoni (2013), Cholakov and Kordoni (2014)) perform feature mining and modify directly the translation table. In addition to the standard translational probabilities, those methods add binary features which indicate whether a source phrase contains MWEs and whether an MWE is compositional or idiomatic. Our work modifies both the training data (via the addition of paraphrases) and the translation table. However, the modifications come from the usage of word embeddings assuming that those allow for a better incorporation of semantic information into SMT.

Following the work of Mikolov et al. (2013a), Mikolov et al. (2013b), and Alkhouli et al. (2014), we exploit the idea that vector representations of similar words in different languages are related by a linear transformation. However, we focus on exploring this idea on a specific phenomenon with challenging semantics, namely PVs. Finally, there has been significant research on predicting the compositionality of MWEs (e.g., Schulte im Walde et al. (2013), Salehi et al. (2015)) under the assumption that this could be helpful in applications. Here, we go a step further and prove this assumption correct by integrating compositionality into a real-life application such as SMT.

3   English–Bulgarian SMT System

Translation of PVs. In (1) the PV *called off* has to be mapped to the single Bulgarian verb *otmeni*. For more convenience, the Bulgarian sentence is transcribed with Latin letters.

(1)   Toj *otmeni*   sreshtata.
      he cancelled meeting-the
      'He *called off* the meeting.'

Another challenge is the mapping of an English PV to a 'da'-construction. Such constructions are very frequent in Bulgarian since they denote complex verb tenses, modal verb constructions, and subordinating conjunctions. Guessing whether to add a 'da' particle or not is problematic for the SMT system.

Language Resources. We employ the SeTimes news corpus[1] which contains parallel articles in English and 9 Balkan languages. The training data consist of approximately 151,000 sentences. Another 2,000 sentences are used for tuning. The test set consists of 800 sentences, 400 of which contain one or more instances of PVs. We manually identified 138 unique PVs with a total of 403 instances. A language model for the target language is created based on a 50 million words subset of the Bulgarian National Reference Corpus (BNRC).[2] Finally, Moses is employed to build a factored phrase-based translation model which operates on lemmas and POS tags due to the rich Bulgarian morphology.

4   Integration of Word Embeddings

In our work, we construct word embeddings of English phrases which contain PVs and of their aligned counterparts in Bulgarian. Then we use those representations to augment the translation table with new features and phrase alignments. The word embeddings are obtained using the *word2vec* toolkit.[3] We used the continuous bag-of-words (CBOW) model. Experiments with the skip-gram model showed very close results and are not reported here.

4.1   Phrase Corpus

When training phrase vectors using neural networks, the network is presented with a *phrase corpus*. The phrase corpus is similar to a word corpus except that some words are joined to make up phrases. For example, Mikolov et al. (2013b) identify phrases using a monolingual point-wise mutual information criterion with discounting. However, since our goal is to generate phrase vectors that are helpful for translation of PVs, we limit the construction of phrases in the training data for *word2vec* only to those English and Bulgarian phrases which: i) are aligned in the phrase table and ii) the English phrase contains PVs. To determine the latter, we use an automatically created lexicon of English PVs (Simova and Kordoni, 2013) and the jMWE library (Kulkarni and Finlayson, 2011) to mark potential PVs in the data.

---

[1] http://www.setimes.com
[2] http://webclark.org/
[3] https://code.google.com/p/word2vec

We ran this method on the MT test set of 800 sentences in order to examine its performance. It achieved 91% precision and 93% recall.

As training data for *word2vec*, we use the English part of the SeTimes corpus and the English Wikipedia dump from November 2014. Since the phrase table contains lemmas, the Wikipedia corpus was lemmatised using the TreeTagger (Schmid, 1994). For Bulgarian, the SeTimes corpus and the BNRC were employed. *Word2vec* generates a vector of fixed dimensionality d for each phrase in the training corpus. In our experiments, d is set to 300 and the size of the context window is set to 5.

4.2 Semantic Scoring Feature

Following the work in Mikolov et al. (2013b) and Alkhouli et al. (2014), we introduce an additional feature in the translation model:

$$(2) \quad sim(Wx_{\widetilde{f}}, z_{\widetilde{e}})$$

where sim is a similarity function, $x_{\widetilde{f}}$ and $z_{\widetilde{e}}$ are the S-dimensional source and T-dimensional target vectors corresponding to the source (English) phrase $\widetilde{f}$ and target (Bulgarian) phrase $\widetilde{e}$, respectively. W is an $S \times T$ linear projection matrix that maps the source space to the target space. The matrix is estimated by optimizing the following criterion with stochastic gradient descent:

$$(3) \quad \min_{W} \sum_{i=1}^{N} \|Wx_i - z_i\|^2$$

where the training data consists of the pairs $(x_1, z_1), \ldots, (x_N, z_N)$ corresponding to the source and target vectors. For any given phrase or word and its continuous vector representation x, we can map it to the other language space by computing $z = Wx$. Then we find the word or phrase whose representation is closest to z in the target language space, using cosine similarity as the distance metric.

Since the source and target phrase vectors are learned separately, we do not have an immediate mapping between them. That is why we resort to the phrase table to obtain it. A source and a target vectors are paired if there is a corresponding phrase pair entry in the phrase table.

4.3 Paraphrases

We use the vectors produced for Bulgarian to augment the phrase table with additional entries. Us-ing cosine similarity, we find the top 5 similar phrases and consider them paraphrases of the original Bulgarian phrase. This is done only for entries mapped to a source English phrase containing a PV. The newly generated phrase pair is assigned the same feature values as the pair used to induce it. In order to differentiate the original phrase pair from the induced paraphrases, we introduce an additional feature which indicates the similarity between the Bulgarian phrase and its paraphrase. The value of this feature for the original phrase pair is set to 1. Finally, note that since we are interested in the proper translation of English PVs, we do not paraphrase the source English phrase.

4.4 Compositionality Score

In Cholakov and Kordoni (2014) a binary feature indicates whether a PV is compositional (1) or idiomatic (0). This solution does not reflect the different degrees of compositionality PVs exhibit. We follow the research in Schulte im Walde et al. (2013) and Salehi et al. (2015) and map each PV to a continuously-valued compositionality score which is then added as a feature to the translation model. This score is calculated as:

$$(4) \quad comp(PV) = sim(PV, V)$$

where PV is the vector associated with the phrase verb in question, V is the vector associated with the verb forming the PV, and sim is a vector similarity function. We use *word2vec* to calculate the similarity sim between the two vectors. The idea behind the score is that the more similar the meaning of the PV is to the meaning of the verb, the more compositional this PV is. Note that in light of the findings reported in Salehi et al. (2014) and Salehi et al. (2015), we do not take into account the vector of the particle.

5 Results

Our work is directly comparable to that in Cholakov and Kordoni (2014) since we used the same datasets and MT system setup. Furthermore, we have successfully reproduced the results reported there.

Automatic Evaluation. Table 1 presents the results from the automatic evaluation, in terms of BLEU (Papineni et al., 2002) and NIST (Doddington, 2002) scores. All results are averages of 3 MERT optimizer runs. Statistical significance is computed using the Approximate Randomization

	with PVs		all	
	bleu	nist	bleu	nist
baseline	0.244	5.97	0.237	6.14
4 binary features	0.267	6.01	0.256	6.16
semantic scoring feature	0.268	6.00	0.258	6.15
paraphrases	0.270	**6.02**	0.261	**6.18**
compositionality feature	0.269	6.01	0.260	6.17
our 3 strategies combined	**0.272**	**6.02**	**0.262**	**6.18**

Table 1: Automatic evaluation of MT quality.

(AR) test. We used the *multeval* toolkit (Clark et al., 2011) for evaluation.

In the baseline case Moses is run in a standard configuration, i.e. without any explicit MWE knowledge. Table 1 also shows the best results from Cholakov and Kordoni (2014) where 4 binary features indicate: 1) whether a phrase contains a PV; 2) whether a detected PV is transitive or not; 3) whether the particle in a PV is separable or not; and 4) whether a PV is compositional or not. We evaluated the contribution of each of our 3 strategies based on word embeddings as well as various combinations thereof. Note that, for reasons of space, we do not report on the 400 test sentences without a PV. The results for those are very close for all setups which shows that our modifications do not harm the MT quality for sentences without PVs.

The combination of our three strategies based on word embeddings achieves the best performance in terms of BLEU, with the results being statistically significant compared to all other settings at $p < 0.01$. The semantic scoring feature alone outperforms the baseline but achieves the same performance as the setting with 4 the binary features. On the other hand, the usage of paraphrases or the incorporation of compositionality feature achieve very close results and both are significantly better than the binary features setting. In fact, those settings are almost as good as the best configuration. This shows that: i) paraphrases found using *word2vec* are of good quality and help MT and ii) treating compositionality of PVs as a continuous phenomenon has positive effects on MT and outperforms the binary compositional/idiomatic setting. Last, apart from the baseline, the differences in NIST scores are not significant. We attribute this to the fact that our method improves translation of more frequent and thus less informative for NIST PVs.

Manual Evaluation. A native speaker of Bul-

	good	acceptable	incorrect
baseline	0.21	0.41	0.38
4 binary features	0.3	0.5	0.2
semantic scoring feature	0.3	0.54	0.16
paraphrases	**0.31**	0.53	0.16
compositionality feature	0.3	**0.57**	0.13
our 3 strategies combined	**0.31**	**0.57**	**0.12**

Table 2: Manual evaluation of MT quality.

garian was asked to judge the translations of PVs produced by the MT system. A translation was judged as:

- *good* - correct translation of the PV, correct verb inflection

- *acceptable* - correct translation of the PV but wrong inflection, or wrongly built *da-* or reflexive construction

- *incorrect* - wrong translation which changes the meaning of the sentence

Table 2 shows the results. Compared to previous work, all our strategies achieve a significantly higher number of acceptable translations and reduce the number of wrong translations. The improvement in translation comes mostly from better translations of semi-compositional verbs which underlines the importance of better treatment of this phenomenon. Note the good performance of the setting involving the compositionality feature which directly tackles this issue.

6 Conclusion

In this paper we used word embeddings to augment the phrase table of an SMT system with new features and aligned phrase pairs which led to improved SMT of PVs. The new features aim at capturing distributional semantic properties and the degree of compositionality of PVs. In a case study with an English-Bulgarian SMT system, our work clearly outperformed previous research. In future work, we will extend our approach to other types of MWEs.

References

Tamer Alkhouli, Andreas Guta, and Hermann Ney. 2014. Vector space models for phrase-based machine translation. In *Proceedings of SSST-8, Eighth Workshop on Syntax, Semantics and Structure in Statistical Translation*, pages 1–10, Doha, Qatar.

Marine Carpuat and Mona Diab. 2010. Task-based evaluation of multiword expressions: a pilot study in statistical machine translation. In *Human Language Technologies: The 2010 Annual Conference of the North American Chapter of the Association for Computational Linguistics.*, HLT '10., pages 242–245, Stroudsburg, PA, USA. Association for Computational Linguistics.

Kostadin Cholakov and Valia Kordoni. 2014. Better statistical machine translation through linguistic treatment of phrasal verbs. In *Proceedings of the 2014 Conference on Empirical Methods in Natural Language Processing (EMNLP)*, pages 196–201, Doha, Qatar, October. Association for Computational Linguistics.

Jonathan H. Clark, Chris Dyer, Alon Lavie, and Noah A. Smith. 2011. Better hypothesis testing for statistical machine translation: Controlling for optimizer instability. In *49th Annual Meeting of the Association for Computational Linguistics:shortpapers*, pages 176–181, Portland, Oregon.

George Doddington. 2002. Automatic evaluation of machine translation quality using n-gram co-occurrence statistics. In *Proceedings of the second international conference on Human Language Technology Research*, pages 138–145, San Francisco, CA, USA.

Nidhi Kulkarni and Mark Alan Finlayson. 2011. JMWE – a Java toolkit for detecting multiword expressions. In *Proceedings of the 2011 Workshop on Multiword Expressions*, pages 122–124.

Patrik Lambert and Rafael Banchs. 2005. Data inferred multi-word expressions for statistical machine translation. In *Proceedings of the X Machine Translation Summit*, pages 396–403.

Tomas Mikolov, Quoc V Le, and Ilya Sutskever. 2013a. Exploiting similarities among languages for machine translation. *arXiv preprint arXiv:1309.4168*.

Tomas Mikolov, Ilya Sutskever, Kai Chen, Greg S Corrado, and Jeff Dean. 2013b. Distributed representations of words and phrases and their compositionality. In *Advances in Neural Information Processing Systems*, pages 3111–3119.

Kishore Papineni, Salim Roukos, Todd Ward, and Wei-Jing Zhu. 2002. BLEU: A method for automatic evaluation of machine translation. In *Proceedings of the 40th Annual Meeting on Association for Computational Linguistics*, pages 311–318, Stroudsburg, PA, USA.

Scott Songlin Piao, Paul Rayson, and and Tony McEnery Dawn Archer. 2005. Comparing and combining a semantic tagger and a statistical tool for MWE extraction. *Comuter Speech and Language*, 19(4):378–397.

Zhixiang Ren, Yajuan Lu, Jie Cao, Qun Liu, and Yun Huang. 2009. Improving statistical machine translation using domain bilingual multiword expressions. In *Proceedings of the ACL Workshop on Multiword Expressions: Identification, Interpretation, Disambiguation and Applications*, pages 47–54, Singapore.

Bahar Salehi, Paul Cook, and Timothy Baldwin. 2014. Using distributional similarity of multi-way translations to predict multiword expression compositionality. In *Proceedings of the 14th Conference of the European Chapter of the Association for Computational Linguistics (EACL 2014)*, pages 472–481, Gothenburg, Sweden.

Bahar Salehi, Paul Cook, and Timothy Baldwin. 2015. A word embedding approach to predicting the compositionality of multiword expressions. In *Proceedings of the 2015 Annual Meeting of the North American Chapter of ACL – Human Language Technologies (NAACL HLT)*, Denver, Colorado. Association for Computational Linguistics.

Helmut Schmid. 1994. Probabilistic part-of-speech tagging using decision trees. In *Proceedings of the International Conference on New Methods in Language Processing*, Manchester, UK.

Sabine Schulte im Walde, Stefan Muller, and Stephen Roller. 2013. Exploring vector space models to predict the compositionality of German noun-noun compounds. In *Second Joint Conference on Lexical and Computational Semantics (*SEM), Volume 1: Proceedings of the Main Conference and the Shared Task*, pages 255–265, Atlanta, Georgia.

Iliana Simova and Valia Kordoni. 2013. Improving English-Bulgarian statistical machine translation by phrasal verb treatment. In *Proceedings of MT Summit XIV Workshop on Multi-word Units in Machine Translation and Translation Technology*, Nice, France.

Jiajun Zhang, Shujie Liu, Mu Li, Ming Zhou, and Chengqing Zong. 2014. Bilingually-constrained phrase embeddings for machine translation. In *Proceedings of the 52th Annual Meeting on Association for Computational Linguistics. Association for Computational Linguistics*.

Modeling the Non-Substitutability of Multiword Expressions
with Distributional Semantics and a Log-Linear Model

Meghdad Farahmand
Department of Computer Science
University of Geneva
meghdad.farahmand@unige.ch

James Henderson
Xerox Research Centre Europe
james.henderson@xrce.xerox.com

Abstract

Non-substitutability is a property of Multiword Expressions (MWEs) that often causes lexical rigidity and is relevant for most types of MWEs. Efficient identification of this property can result in the efficient identification of MWEs. In this work we propose using distributional semantics, in the form of word embeddings, to identify candidate substitutions for a candidate MWE and model its substitutability. We use our models to rank MWEs based on their lexical rigidity and study their performance in comparison with association measures. We also study the interaction between our models and association measures. We show that one of our models can significantly improve over the association measure baselines, identifying collocations.

1 Introduction

Multiword expressions (MWEs), commonly referred to as collocations,[1] are idiosyncratic sequences of words whose idiosyncrasy can be broadly classified into semantic, statistical, and syntactic classes. Semantic idiosyncrasy (also referred to as non-compositionality) means that the meaning of an MWE cannot be inferred from the meaning of its components, as in *loan shark*. Syntactic idiosyncrasy refers to the situation where the syntax of an MWE does not follow syntactic rules, as in *in short*. Statistical idiosyncrasy means that components of a statistically idiosyncratic MWE

co-occur more than expected by chance, as in *swimming pool*. The range of types of idiosyncrasy included in MWEs has been characterized in several other ways (Baldwin and Kim, 2010; Sag et al., 2002). To avoid getting mired down in this uncertainty, which mainly emerges while dealing with borderline MWEs, between completely idiosyncratic and fully compositional, we subscribe to the viewpoint of McCarthy et al. (2007) and treat idiosyncrasy as a spectrum and focus only on the (very) idiosyncratic end of this spectrum. MWEs have application in different areas in NLP and linguistics, for instance statistical machine translation (Ren et al., 2009; Carpuat and Diab, 2010); shallow parsing (Korkontzelos and Manandhar, 2010); language generation (Hogan et al., 2007); opinion mining (Berend, 2011); corpus linguistics and language acquisition (Ellis, 2008). In general, as Green et al. (2011) point out, "MWE knowledge is useful, but MWEs are hard to identify."

In this work, we propose a method of identifying MWEs based on their non-substitutability. Non-substitutability means that the components of an MWE cannot be replaced with their synonyms (Manning and Schütze, 1999; Pearce, 2001). It implies statistical idiosyncrasy, which is relevant for all kinds of MWEs, and identifying non-substitutability in text results in the identification of a wide range of MWEs. In MWE research, non-substitutability has been widely considered but never thoroughly studied, except for a few work that present low coverage and limited models of this concept.

We develop a model that takes into account the semantics of words for identifying statistical idiosyncrasy, but is highly generalizable and does not require supervision or labor-intensive resources. The proposed model uses distributional semantics, in the form of word embeddings, and

---

[1] In older work, the term collocation refers to all kinds of MWEs. In more recent work, however, it mainly refers to statistically idiosyncratic MWEs. In any case, statistical idiosyncrasy can be considered as a general property of all kinds of MWEs, regardless of other forms of idiosyncrasy they may have.

Proceedings of the 12th Workshop on Multiword Expressions, pages 61–66,
Berlin, Germany, August 7-12, 2016. ©2016 Association for Computational Linguistics

uses them to identify semantically similar words for the components of a candidate MWE. Non-substitutability is then measured for the candidate MWE using log-linear model(s), also computed using word embeddings. Our proposed models result in an improvement over the state-of-the-art.

1.1 Syntactic Categories of MWEs

From a syntactic point of view, MWEs are very heterogeneous, including light verb constructions, phrasal verbs, noun compounds, verb-object combinations and others. In this work, however, we focus only on noun compounds for the following reasons: (i) They are the most productive and frequent category of MWEs.() (ii) There are more datasets of compounds available for evaluation. (iii) Focusing on one controlled category allows us to focus on modeling and detecting idiosyncrasy in isolation, avoiding complexities such as gappy MWEs. We also focus only on two-word noun compounds, because higher order ones are relatively rare.

2 Related Work

Identification of statistical idiosyncrasy of MWEs seems to have been first formally discussed in Choueka et al. (1983) by proposing a statistical index to identify collocates and further developed into more efficient measures of collocation extraction such as Pointwise Mutual Information (Church and Hanks, 1990), t-score (Church et al., 1991; Manning and Schütze, 1999), and Likelihood Ratio (Dunning, 1993). Smadja (1993) proposes a set of statistical scores that can be used to extract collocations. Evert (2005) and Pecina (2010) study a wide range of association measures that can be employed to rank and classify collocations, respectively.

Farahmand and Nivre (2015) assume that a word pair is a true MWE if the conditional probability of one word given the other is greater than the conditional probability of that word given synonyms of the other word, and Riedl and Biemann (2015), and Farahmand and Martins (2014) use contextual features to identify MWEs.

The above-mentioned methods target statistical idiosyncrasy of MWEs. There are however many other approaches to extraction of MWEs which do not explicitly focus on statistical idiosyncrasy. For instance, some identify MWEs based on their semantic idiosyncrasy (Yazdani et al., 2015; Im Walde et al., 2013; Hermann et al., 2012; Reddy et al., 2011; Baldwin et al., 2003; McCarthy et al., 2003), some approaches are rule-based (Seretan, 2011; Baldwin, 2005), and some are both rule-based and statistical (Ramisch, 2012; Seretan and Wehrli, 2006).

3 Modeling Non-Substitutability

As discussed earlier, we model statistical idiosyncrasy based on an assumption inspired by *non-substitutability*, which means that the components of an MWE cannot be replaced with their near synonyms. Let $w_1 w_2$ represent a word pair. We make the same assumption as Farahmand and Nivre (2015) that $w_1 w_2$ is statistically idiosyncratic if:

$$P(w_2|w_1) > P(w_2|sim(w_1)) \qquad (1)$$

where $sim(w_i)$ (defined below in Section 3.1) represents the words that are similar to w_i. With respect to noun noun compounds, this inequality roughly means that for an idiosyncratic compound, the probability of the headword (w_2) co-occurring with the modifier (w_1) is greater than the probability of the headword co-occurring with "synonyms" of the modifier (e.g. *climate change* is more probable than *weather change*). This, however, is not the case for non or less idiosyncratic compounds (e.g. *film director* which is substitutable with *movie director*).

Farahmand and Nivre (2015) estimate a similar probability, in both directions, with the help of WordNet *synsets*. They show that the model that considers the probabilities in both directions outperforms the model that considers only one direction (head conditioned on modifier).

To study and model the effects of *direction* we also consider the following inequality:

$$P(w_1|w_2) > P(w_1|sim(w_2)) \qquad (2)$$

Intuitively, inequality 1 plays a more important role in lexical rigidity than inequality 2, but this is something we study in section 4.

In related work, (Pearce, 2001) extracts the synonyms of the constituents of a compound, creates new phrases called *anti-collocations*, and based on the number of *anti-collocations* of the candidate MWE decides whether it is a true MWE.

3.1 Modeling Semantically Similar Words

In previous work, WordNet synsets were employed to model the $sim()$ function. The obvious limitation of such an approach is coverage. Other limitations include costliness and labor intensiveness of updating and expanding such a knowledge base. In this work, we use cosine similarity between word embeddings to represent semantically similar words (that include but are not limited to synonyms). This may result in a drop in precision, but the coverage will be immensely improved. Moreover, similarity in the word embedding space is shown to provide a relatively good approximation of synonymy (Chen et al., 2013).

3.2 Ranking with Log-Linear Models

We estimate the probabilities presented in (1) and (2) using a log linear model. Let $\phi(w_i)$ represent the word embedding of w_i where $\phi \in \mathbb{R}^{50}$.

$$P(w_2|w_1) = \frac{exp(v_{w_2} \cdot \phi(w_1))}{\sum_{w_2'} exp(v_{w_2'} \cdot \phi(w_1))} \quad (3)$$

where v_{w_i} is a parameter vector and v is the model's parameter matrix. The analogous equation is used to define $P(w_1|w_2)$.

Let S_{w_i} represent the set of top-n $\phi(w_j)$ that are most similar to $\phi(w_i)$, $S_{w_i} = \{w_j|w_j \in nGreatest(w_i.w_j)\}$. $P(w_2|sim(w_1))$ can then be estimated as:

$$P(w_2|sim(w_1)) = \frac{1}{|S_{w_1}|} \sum_{w_j \in S_{w_1}} P(w_2|w_j)$$

where $P(w_2|w_j)$ is defined in (3).

And again, the analogous equation defines $P(w_1|sim(w_2))$.

Combining these gives us the following version of (1), and an analogous version of (2).

$$\frac{exp(v_{w_2} \cdot \phi(w_1))}{\sum_{w_2'} exp(v_{w_2'} \cdot \phi(w_1))}$$
$$> \frac{1}{|S_{w_1}|} \sum_{w_j \in S_{w_1}} \frac{exp(v_{w_2} \cdot \phi(w_j))}{\sum_{w_2'} exp(v_{w_2'} \cdot \phi(w_j))} \quad (4)$$

Given that MWEs lie on a continuum of idiosyncrasy, it is natural to treat identification of MWEs as a ranking problem. We therefore define an unsupervised ranking function as follows:

$$\delta_{21} = \frac{exp(v_{w_2} \cdot \phi(w_1))}{\sum_{w_2'} exp(v_{w_2'} \cdot \phi(w_1))}$$
$$- \frac{1}{|S_{w_1}|} \sum_{w_j \in S_{w_1}} \frac{exp(v_{w_2} \cdot \phi(w_j))}{\sum_{w_2'} exp(v_{w_2'} \cdot \phi(w_j))} \quad (5)$$

And an analogous function δ_{12}.

4 Evaluation

As our evaluation set we used the dataset of Farahmand et al. (2015) who annotate 1042 English noun compounds for statistical and semantic idiosyncrasy. Each compound is annotated by four judges with two binary votes, one for their semantic and one for their statistical idiosyncrasy.

As our baselines we use three measures that have been widely used as a means of identifying collocations: Pointwise Mutual Information (PMI) (Church and Hanks, 1990; Evert, 2005; Bouma, 2009; Pecina, 2010), t-score (Manning and Schütze, 1999; Church et al., 1991; Evert, 2005; Pecina, 2010), and Log-likelihood Ratio (LL_r) (Dunning, 1993; Evert, 2005).

Since we are concerned with the idiosyncratic end of the spectrum of MWEs, we look at the identification of MWEs as a ranking problem. To evaluate this ranking, we use precision at k ($p@k$) as the evaluation metric, considering different values of k.

4.1 Individual Models

To train the log-linear model, we first extracted all noun-noun compounds from a POS-tagged Wikipedia dump (only articles) with a frequency of at least 5. This resulted in a list of $\approx 560,000$ compounds. We created word embeddings of size 50 for words of Wikipedia that had the frequency of at least 5 using *word2vec*[2]. These word embeddings were used both to determine the set of similar words for each word of a compound and to train the log-linear model by stochastic minimization of the cross entropy. We discarded 30 instances of the evaluation set because (having type frequency of below 5) word embeddings were not available for at least one of their components.

To measure precision, we assume those evaluation set instances that were annotated as statistically or semantically idiosyncratic by three or more judges (out of four) are MWE and other instances are not. This results in the total of 369 positive instances. Figure 1 shows the performance of the different models.

At the top of the ranked list, δ_{21} outperforms one of the baselines (t-score) but performs similarly to the other two baselines, PMI and LL_r. It, however, shows a more steady performance up

---

[2] https://code.google.com/archive/p/word2vec/

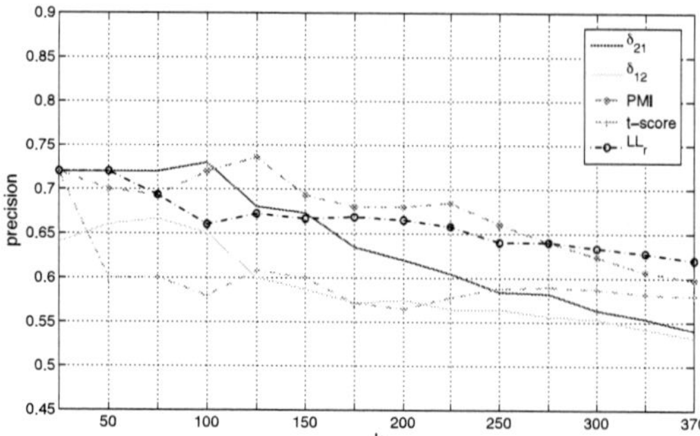

Figure 1: $p@k$ for our models and the baselines.

---

until $p@100$. As it moves further from the idiosyncratic end of the spectrum its precision drops further. δ_{12}, on the other hand, shows a weaker performance. It, however, outperforms t-score for the most part. The best baseline is PMI, the worst is t-score. Again, considering lexicalization, the main process that MWEs should undergo to become useful for other NLP applications, a high precision at a small (proportional) k is what we should be really concerned about: lexicons cannot grow too large so every multi-word entry should be sufficiently idiosyncratic and lexically rigid. On the other hand, we do not want to limit a model's ability to generalize by lexicalizing every word sequence that appears slightly idiosyncratic. Looking back at the models, we know that δ_{21}, PMI, and LL_r independently perform well at the top of their ranked list. On the other hand, we know that in theory δ_{21} bases its ranking on relatively different criteria from PMI and LL_r. The question we seek to answer in the next section is whether merging these criteria (semantic non-substitutability and statistical association) can improve on the best performance.

4.2 Combining Non-Substitutability and Association

Our first combined model of non-substitutability integrates both directions (head to modifier and modifier to head). To emphasize precision, we propose a combination function H_1 that requires both δ_{21} and δ_{12} to be high.

$$H_1 = min(\delta_{21}, \delta_{12})$$

By ranking according to the minimum of the scores δ_{21} and δ_{12}, each highly-ranked data point

must be highly ranked by both individual models.[3]

To combine an association measure with our non-substitutability models we chose PMI because its performance at the top of the ranked list is better than other baselines. The values of PMI and the δs have different scales. We measured the linear correlation in terms of Pearson r between PMI and δs in order to see whether we can scale up the δs' by a linear factor. The correlation was very small and almost negligible, so instead of using $min()$ we combined the two rankings as:

$$H_2 = H_1 \circ \text{PMI}$$

where $\circ$ denotes the element-wise product.

We perform the same experiments as in Section 4.1 with the combined models[4] and compare their performance with the best models from the previous experiments. The results can be seen in Figure 2.

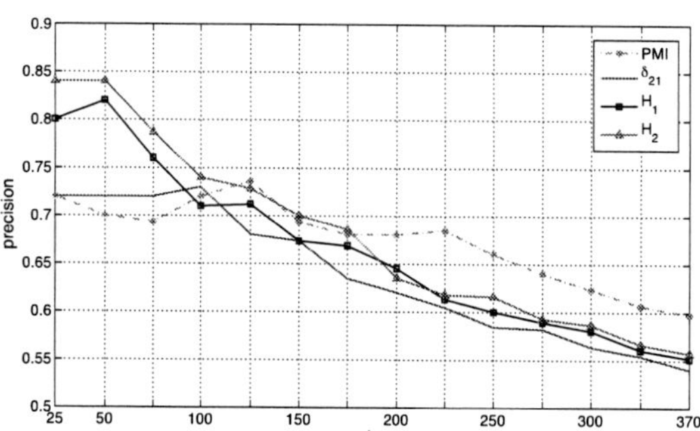

Figure 2: $p@k$ for H_1, H_2 and previous best models.

H_2 clearly outperforms other models at the top of the ranked list. It reaches a significantly higher precision than other models. This confirms our assumption that in practice association measures and substitutability based models that are semantically motivated[5] base their decisions on different pieces of information that are complementary. Also, the results for H_1 show that combining both δ_{21} and δ_{12} gives us an improvement for high precision and performs similarly to the best one (δ_{21}) at lower k.

---

[3] We also tried element-wise multiplication in order to combine these models. The performance of $min()$, however, was slightly better.

[4] We also combined different association measures which resulted in models with performances that were mainly similar to the performance of their sub-models.

[5] Assuming that word embeddings represent semantics in a slightly more meaningful way than first order statistical association.

5 Conclusions

We presented a method for identifying MWEs based on their semantic non-substitutability. We assumed that non-substitutability implies statistical idiosyncrasy and modeled this property with word embedding representations and a log-linear model. We looked at MWE identification as a ranking problem due the nature of idiosyncrasy, which is better defined as a continuum than as a binary phenomenon. We showed our best model can reach the same performance as the best baseline. We showed that joining our models lead to a better performance compared to that of the baselines and individual models. We also showed that joining our models -that are aware of semantic non-substitutability, and association measures (baselines) can result in a model with a performance that is significantly higher than the performance of the baselines.

References

[Baldwin and Kim2010] Timothy Baldwin and Su Nam Kim. 2010. Multiword expressions. *Handbook of Natural Language Processing, second edition. Morgan and Claypool.*

[Baldwin et al.2003] Timothy Baldwin, Colin Bannard, Takaaki Tanaka, and Dominic Widdows. 2003. An empirical model of multiword expression decomposability. In *Proceedings of the ACL 2003 workshop on Multiword expressions: analysis, acquisition and treatment-Volume 18*, pages 89–96. Association for Computational Linguistics.

[Baldwin2005] Timothy Baldwin. 2005. Deep lexical acquisition of verb–particle constructions. *Computer Speech & Language*, 19(4):398–414.

[Berend2011] Gábor Berend. 2011. Opinion expression mining by exploiting keyphrase extraction. In *IJCNLP*, pages 1162–1170. Citeseer.

[Bouma2009] G. Bouma. 2009. Normalized (pointwise) mutual information in collocation extraction. In *From Form to Meaning: Processing Texts Automatically, Proceedings of the Biennial GSCL Conference 2009*, volume Normalized, pages 31–40, Tübingen.

[Carpuat and Diab2010] Marine Carpuat and Mona Diab. 2010. Task-based evaluation of multiword expressions: a pilot study in statistical machine translation. In *Human Language Technologies: The 2010 Annual Conference of the North American Chapter of the Association for Computational Linguistics*, pages 242–245. Association for Computational Linguistics.

[Chen et al.2013] Yanqing Chen, Bryan Perozzi, Rami Al-Rfou, and Steven Skiena. 2013. The expressive power of word embeddings. *arXiv preprint arXiv:1301.3226.*

[Choueka et al.1983] Yaacov Choueka, Shmuel T Klein, and E Neuwitz. 1983. Automatic retrieval of frequent idiomatic and collocational expressions in a large corpus. *Association for Literary and Linguistic Computing Journal*, 4(1):34–38.

[Church and Hanks1990] Kenneth Ward Church and Patrick Hanks. 1990. Word association norms, mutual information, and lexicography. *Computational linguistics*, 16(1):22–29.

[Church et al.1991] Kenneth Church, William Gale, Patrick Hanks, and Donald Hindle. 1991. Using statistics in lexical analysis. In *Lexical Acquisition: Exploiting On-Line Resources to Build a Lexicon*, pages 115–164. Erlbaum.

[Dunning1993] Ted Dunning. 1993. Accurate methods for the statistics of surprise and coincidence. *Computational linguistics*, 19(1):61–74.

[Ellis2008] Nick C Ellis. 2008. The periphery and the heart of language. *Phraseology: An interdisciplinary perspective*, pages 1–13.

[Evert2005] Stefan Evert. 2005. *The statistics of word cooccurrences*. Ph.D. thesis, Dissertation, Stuttgart University.

[Farahmand and Martins2014] Meghdad Farahmand and Ronaldo Martins. 2014. A supervised model for extraction of multiword expressions based on statistical context features. In *Proceedings of the 10th Workshop on Multiword Expressions (MWE)*, pages 10–16. Association for Computational Linguistics.

[Farahmand and Nivre2015] Meghdad Farahmand and Joakim Nivre. 2015. Modeling the statistical idiosyncrasy of multiword expressions. In *Proceedings of NAACL-HLT*, pages 34–38.

[Farahmand et al.2015] Meghdad Farahmand, Aaron Smith, and Joakim Nivre. 2015. A multiword expression data set: Annotating non-compositionality and conventionalization for english noun compounds. In *Proceedings of the 11th Workshop on Multiword Expressions (MWE-NAACL 2015)*. Association for Computational Linguistics.

[Green et al.2011] Spence Green, Marie-Catherine De Marneffe, John Bauer, and Christopher D Manning. 2011. Multiword expression identification with tree substitution grammars: A parsing tour de force with french. In *Proceedings of the Conference on Empirical Methods in Natural Language Processing*, pages 725–735. Association for Computational Linguistics.

[Hermann et al.2012] Karl Moritz Hermann, Phil Blunsom, and Stephen Pulman. 2012. An unsupervised ranking model for noun-noun compositionality. In *Proceedings of the First Joint Conference on Lexical and Computational Semantics*, pages 132–141. Association for Computational Linguistics.

[Hogan et al.2007] Deirdre Hogan, Conor Cafferkey, Aoife Cahill, and Josef Van Genabith. 2007. Exploiting multi-word units in history-based probabilistic generation. Association for Computational Linguistics.

[Im Walde et al.2013] Sabine Schulte Im Walde, Stefan Müller, and Stephen Roller. 2013. Exploring vector space models to predict the compositionality of german noun-noun compounds. In *Proceedings of the 2nd Joint Conference on Lexical and Computational Semantics*, pages 255–265.

[Korkontzelos and Manandhar2010] Ioannis Korkontzelos and Suresh Manandhar. 2010. Can recognising multiword expressions improve shallow parsing? In *Human Language Technologies: The 2010 Annual Conference of the North American Chapter of the Association for Computational Linguistics*, pages 636–644. Association for Computational Linguistics.

[Manning and Schütze1999] Christopher D Manning and Hinrich Schütze. 1999. *Foundations of statistical natural language processing*. MIT press.

[McCarthy et al.2003] Diana McCarthy, Bill Keller, and John Carroll. 2003. Detecting a continuum of compositionality in phrasal verbs. In *Proceedings of the ACL-SIGLEX Workshop on Multiword Expressions: Analysis, Acqusation and Treatment*, pages 73–80.

[McCarthy et al.2007] Diana McCarthy, Sriram Venkatapathy, and Aravind K Joshi. 2007. Detecting compositionality of verb-object combinations using selectional preferences. In *EMNLP-CoNLL*, pages 369–379.

[Pearce2001] Darren Pearce. 2001. Synonymy in collocation extraction. In *Proceedings of the Workshop on WordNet and Other Lexical Resources, Second meeting of the North American Chapter of the Association for Computational Linguistics*, pages 41–46. Citeseer.

[Pecina2010] Pavel Pecina. 2010. Lexical association measures and collocation extraction. *Language resources and evaluation*, 44(1-2):137–158.

[Ramisch2012] Carlos Ramisch. 2012. A generic framework for multiword expressions treatment: from acquisition to applications. In *Proceedings of ACL 2012 Student Research Workshop*, pages 61–66. Association for Computational Linguistics.

[Reddy et al.2011] Siva Reddy, Diana McCarthy, and Suresh Manandhar. 2011. An empirical study on compositionality in compound nouns. In *IJCNLP*, pages 210–218.

[Ren et al.2009] Zhixiang Ren, Yajuan Lü, Jie Cao, Qun Liu, and Yun Huang. 2009. Improving statistical machine translation using domain bilingual multiword expressions. In *Proceedings of the Workshop on Multiword Expressions: Identification, Interpretation, Disambiguation and Applications*, pages 47–54. Association for Computational Linguistics.

[Riedl and Biemann2015] Martin Riedl and Chris Biemann. 2015. A single word is not enough: Ranking multiword expressions using distributional semantics. In *Proceedings of the 2015 Conference on Empirical Methods in Natural Language Processing (EMNLP 2015)*, Lisboa, Portugal.

[Sag et al.2002] Ivan A Sag, Timothy Baldwin, Francis Bond, Ann Copestake, and Dan Flickinger. 2002. Multiword expressions: A pain in the neck for nlp. In *Computational Linguistics and Intelligent Text Processing*, pages 1–15. Springer.

[Seretan and Wehrli2006] Violeta Seretan and Eric Wehrli. 2006. Accurate collocation extraction using a multilingual parser. In *Proceedings of the 21st International Conference on Computational Linguistics and the 44th annual meeting of the Association for Computational Linguistics*, pages 953–960. Association for Computational Linguistics.

[Seretan2011] Violeta Seretan. 2011. *Syntax-based collocation extraction*, volume 44. Springer.

[Smadja1993] Frank Smadja. 1993. Retrieving collocations from text: Xtract. *Computational Linguistics*, 19:143–177.

[Yazdani et al.2015] Majid Yazdani, Meghdad Farahmand, and James Henderson. 2015. Learning semantic composition to detect non-compositionality of multiword expressions. In *Proceedings of the 2015 Conference on Empirical Methods in Natural Language Processing*, pages 1733–1742, Lisbon, Portugal, September. Association for Computational Linguistics.

Phrase Representations for Multiword Expressions

Joël Legrand[1,2] and Ronan Collobert[*3,1]

[1] Idiap Research Institute, Martigny, Switzerland
[2] Ecole Polytechnique Fédérale de Lausanne (EPFL), Lausanne, Switzerland
[3] Facebook AI Research, Menlo Park (CA), USA

Abstract

Recent works in Natural Language Processing (NLP) using neural networks have focused on learning dense word representations to perform classification tasks. When dealing with phrase prediction problems, is is common practice to use special tagging schemes to identify segments boundaries. This allows these tasks to be expressed as common word tagging problems. In this paper, we propose to learn fixed-size representations for arbitrarily sized chunks. We introduce a model that takes advantage of such representations to perform phrase tagging by directly identifying and classifying phrases. We evaluate our approach on the task of multiword expression (MWE) tagging and show that our model outperforms the state-of-the-art model for this task.

1 Introduction

Traditional NLP tasks such as part-of-speech (POS) tagging or semantic role labeling (SRL) consists in tagging each word in a sentence with a tag. Another class of problems such as Named Entity Recognition (NER) or shallow parsing (chunking) consists in identifying and labeling phrases (*i.e.* groups of words) with predefined tags. Such tasks can be expressed as word classification problems by identifying the phrase boundaries instead of directly identifying the whole phrases. In practice, this consists in prefixing every tag with an extra-label indicating the position of the word inside a phrase (at the beginning (B), inside (I), at the end (E), single word (S) or not in a phrase (O)). Different schemes have been used in the literature, such as the IOB2, IOE1 and IOE2 schemes (Sang and Veenstra, 1999) or IOBES scheme (Uchimoto et al., 2000) with no clear predominance.

These tasks have been tackled using various machine learning methods such as Support Vector Machines (SVM) for POS tagging (Giménez and Màrquez, 2004) or chunking (Kudoh and Matsumoto, 2000), second order random fields for chunking (Sun et al., 2008) or a combination of different classifiers for NER (Radu et al., 2003). All these approaches use carefully selected hand-crafted features.

Recent studies in NLP introduced neural network based systems that can be trained in an end-to-end manner, using minimal prior knowledge. These models take advantage of continuous representations of words. In Collobert et al. (2011) the authors proposed a deep neural network, which learns the word representations (the features) and produces IOBES-prefixed tags discriminatively trained in an end-to-end manner. This system is trained using a conditional random field (Lafferty et al., 2001) that accounts for the structure of the sentence. This architecture has been applied to various NLP tasks, such as POS tagging, NER or semantic role labeling and achieves state-of-the-art performance in all of them.

In this paper, we propose to learn fixed-size continuous representations of arbitrarily sized chunks by composing word embeddings. These representations are used to directly classify phrases without using the classical IOB(ES) prefixing step. The proposed approach is evaluated on the task of multiword expression (MWE) tagging. Using the SPRML 2014 data for French MWE tagging (Seddah et al., 2013), we show that our phrase representations are able to capture enough knowledge to perform on par with the IOBES-based model of Collobert et al. (2011) applied to MWE

---
[*]All research was conducted at the Idiap Research Institute, before Ronan Collobert joined Facebook AI Research

67

Proceedings of the 12th Workshop on Multiword Expressions, pages 67–71,
Berlin, Germany, August 7-12, 2016. ©2016 Association for Computational Linguistics

tagging. Furthermore, we show that our system outperforms the winner of the SPMRL (Syntactic Parsing of Morphologicaly Rich Language) 2013 shared task for MWE tagging (Constant et al., 2013) which is currently the best published system.

2   The model

The proposed model computes fixed-size continuous vectors of arbitrarily sized chunks which are then used as inputs to a classifier. Every possible window of sizes from 1 to K (K being the maximum size) is projected onto a common vector space (the same for all k), using a different neural network for each size k. The resulting representations are passed on to a classifier which outputs a score for every possible tag. To ensure that a word belongs to one chunk at most, decoding is performed using structured graph decoding using the Viterbi algorithm.

2.1   Word representation

Given an input sentence $S = w_1, \ldots, w_N$, each word is embedded into a D-dimensional vector space by applying a lookup-table operation (Bengio et al., 2000):

$$LT_W(w_n) = W_{w_n}$$

where the matrix $W \in \mathbb{R}^{D \times |\mathcal{W}|}$ represents the parameters of the lookup layer. Each column $W_n \in \mathbb{R}^D$ corresponds to the vector embedding of the nth word in the dictionary $\mathcal{W}$.

Additional features, such as part-of-speech tags, can be used by using a different lookup table for each discrete feature. The input becomes the concatenation of the outputs of all these lookup-tables. For simplicity, we consider only one lookup-table in the rest of the architecture description.

2.2   Phrase representation

We denote k-window a window of size $k \in [1, K]$ where K is the maximum window size. Phrase representations for all k-windows within a given sentence are produced by looking, for all sizes from 1 to K, at all successive windows of text, sliding over the sentence, from position 1 to $N - K + 1$. Formally, if we denote

$$x_{n,k} = [LT_W(w_{n-c}), \ldots, LT_W(w_n)$$
$$, \ldots,$$
$$, LT_W(w_{n+k-1}), \ldots, LT_W(w_{n+k-1+c})]$$

the concatenated word representations corresponding to the nth k-window (c being the context from each side of the the k-window), its representation is given by

$$r_{n,k} = M_k^1 x_{n,k},$$

where $M_k^1 \in \mathbb{R}^{(k+2c)D \times nhu}$ is a matrix of parameters and nhu the dimension of the phrase representations (which is the same for all k). Words outside the sentence boundaries are assigned a special "PADDING" embedding.

2.3   Phrase scoring

We denote $\mathcal{T}$ the set of tags and $\mathcal{T}_k$ the set of tags for a k-window. We denote $t_k \in \mathcal{T}_k$ the tag $t \in \mathcal{T}$ for a k-window. The scores for all k-windows are computed by a linear layer, using their corresponding representations as input. Formally, the score for the nth k-window are given by

$$s_{n,k} = tanh(M^2 r_{n,k}),$$

where $M^2 \in \mathbb{R}^{nhu \times |\mathcal{T}|}$ is a matrix of parameters. We define s_{n,t_k} the score for the tag $t_k \in \mathcal{T}_k$ starting at the position $n < N - k + 1$.

2.4   Structure tag inference

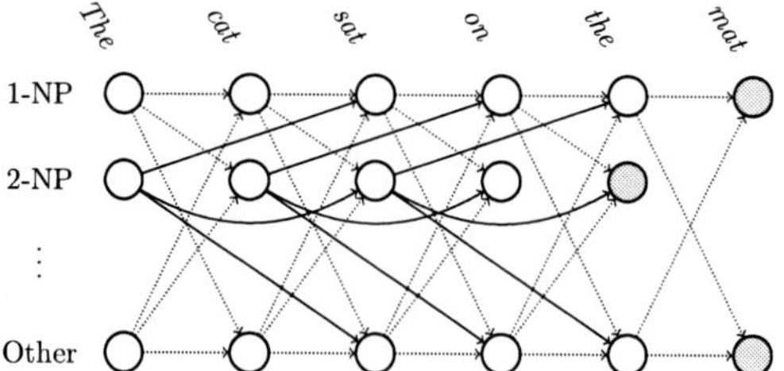

Figure 1: Constrained graph for structured inference. Each node is assigned a score from the scoring layer. For instance, the first node of the line 2-NP correspond to the score for the tag NP for the phrase "the cat". Nodes in gray represent final nodes.

The scoring layer outputs a matrix of $|\mathcal{T}_k| \times (N - k + 1)$ scores for each window size $k \in K$.

The next module (see Figure 1) of our system is a structured graph G constrained in order to ensure that a word is tagged only once. Each node G_{n,t_k} is assigned the score s_{n,t_k} (the score of the tag $t_k \in \mathcal{T}_k$ starting at the position $n < N - k + 1$) from the scoring layer. Only transitions from node G_{n,t_k} to node $G_{n+k,t'_{k'}}$ (with $n + k <= N$) are possible since a word cannot be tagged twice along the same path. The Viterbi algorithm is an efficient choice to find the best path in the lattice. The score for a sentence S of size N along a path of tags $[t]_1^{N_t}$ is then given by the sum of the tag scores:

$$s(S, [t]_1^{N_t}, \theta) = \sum_{n=1}^{N_t} s_{n,t_k}$$

where θ represents all the trainable parameter.

2.5 Training

The proposed neural network is trained by maximizing the likelihood over the training data, using stochastic gradient ascent. Following Collobert et al. (2011), the score $s(S, [t]_1^{N_t}, \theta)$ can be interpreted as a conditional probability by exponentiating this score and normalizing it with respect to all possible path scores. Taking the log, the conditional probability of the true path $[t]_1^{N_t}$ is given by

$$\log p(s(S, [t]_1^{N_t}, \theta)) = s(S, [t]_1^{N_t}, \theta)$$
$$- \log \left(\sum_u s(S, [u]_1^{N_u}), \theta \right)$$

Following Rabiner (1990), the normalization term (second term of this equation) can be computed in linear time thanks to a recursion similar to the Viterbi algorithm. The whole architecture (including the input feature, phrase representations and scoring layer) is trained through the graph in order to encourage valid paths of tags during training, while discouraging all other paths.

3 Experiments

3.1 Multiword expression

Multiword expressions are groups of tokens which act as single units at some level of linguistic analysis. They cover a wide range of linguistic constructions such as idioms ("kick the bucket"), noun compound ("traffic light") or fixed phrases ("ad hoc"). As they can carry meaning that can not

be inferred directly from the meaning of individual constituents (as for idioms), they are difficult to handle by automatic systems and represent a key issue for many NLP systems addressing, for instance, machine translation and text generation tasks.

3.2 Corpus

Experiments were conducted on the SPMRL french corpus provided for the Shared Task 2013 (Seddah et al., 2013). This dataset provides 14.7k sentences (443k tokens) with 22.6k identified MWE. A given MWE is defined as a continuous sequence of terminals, plus a POS tag among the 10 possible POS tags. As presented in Table 1, a wide majority of the chunks are 2-chunks or 3-chunks (91.2%).

Chunk size	2	3	4	5	5+
#chunk	11108	10188	1702	309	250
percentage	47.2	43.2	7.2	1.3	1.1

Table 1: Number of k-sized chunks in the training corpus

3.3 Evaluation

We evaluate the performance of the proposed network on MWE tagging using the three metrics described in Seddah et al. (2013), reporting for each of them the recall, precision and F-score. MWE correspond to the full MWEs, in which a predicted MWE counts as correct if it has the correct span (same group as in the gold data). MWE+POS is defined in the same fashion, except that the predicted MWE counts as correct if it has both correct span and correct POS tag. COMP correspond to the non-head components of MWEs: a non-head component of MWE counts as correct if it is attached to the head of the MWE, with the specific label indicating that it is part of an MWE.

3.4 Baseline models

We compare the proposed model to our implementation of the IOBES-based model described in Collobert et al. (2011), applied to MWE tagging. We also report the results of the LIGM-Alpage architecture which obtained the best results for French SPMRL 2013 MWE recognition shared task (Constant et al., 2013). Their system is based on Conditional Random Fields (CRF) (Lafferty et al., 2001) and on external lexicons which are known to greatly improve MWE segmentation (Constant and Tellier, 2012).

3.5 Setup

The network is trained using stochastic gradient descent over the training data, until convergence on the validation set. Hyper-parameters are tuned on the validation set. The look-up table size for the words is 64. Word embeddings are pre-trained by performing PCA on the matrix of word co-occurrences (Lebret and Collobert, 2014) using Wikipedia data. These embeddings are fine-tuned during the training process. As additional features, we only use the part-of-speech tags obtained using the freely available tool MarMoT (Mueller et al., 2013)[1]. The POS-tag embedding size is 32. The context size is $c = 2$ The maximum size for a window is $K = 7$. The common embedding size for the k-window is $nhu = 300$. We fix the learning rate to 0.01. Following Legrand and Collobert (2015), to prevent units from co-adapting, we adopt a dropout regularization strategy (Srivastava et al., 2014) after every lookup-table, as the capacity of our network mainly lies on the input embeddings.

For the IOBES-based model, we use the following parameters: the context size is set to 2, word and tags feature sizes are 64 and 32 respectively, the hidden layer size is 300 and the learning rate is 0.001. We use the same dropout regularization strategy and the same word initialization as for the proposed model.

4 Results

We first compare our approach with the IOBES-model from Collobert et al. (2011). Table 2 presents the results obtained for the two models. We see that, our model performs on par with the IOBES-based model. Interestingly, adding the POS features has little effect on the performance for MWE identification but helps to determine the MWE POS-tags.

In Table 3, we compare our model with the winner of the SPMRL 2013 shared task for MWE recognition (Constant et al., 2013). Both the IOBES and chunk based models are obtained using an ensemble of 5 model and averaging the obtained scores. We see that both our model and the

	COMP	MWE	MWE+POS
IOBES-model	79.4	78.5	75.4
+ WI	80.8	80.1	76.7
+ WI + POS	80.8	80.1	77.6
Chunk-model	79.1	78.3	75.2
+ WI	80.7	79.6	76.4
+ WI + POS	80.9	79.8	77.5

Table 2: Results on the test corpus (4043 MWEs) in terms of F-measure. WI stands for word initialization.

IOBES-based model outperform this state-of-the-art model.

	COMP	MWE	MWE+POS
LIGM-Alpage	81.3	80.7	77.5
IOBES-model	81.4	80.7	78.2
Chunk-model	81.3	80.7	78.1

Table 3: Results on the test corpus (4043 MWEs) in terms of F-measure.

5 Representation analysis

As the proposed chunk-based model produces continuous phrase representations, it allows for phrase comparison. Table 4 presents some of the closest neighbors (in terms of Euclidean distance) for some chosen phrases. We see that close representations correspond to semantically close phrases.

président de la république
chef de l'état
présidence de la république
ministre de l'intérieur

évasion fiscale
fraude fiscale
détournements financiers
libéralisme sauvage

impôt sur le revenu
impôt sur la fortune
impôt sur le patrimoine
impôts sur la fortune

Table 4: Closest neighbors for three input phrases in terms of euclidean distance.

---

[1] The tags used are available here: `http://cistern.cis.lmu.de/marmot/models/CURRENT/`

6 Conclusion

In this paper, we proposed a neural network model that learns fixed-size continuous representations of arbitrarily-sized chunks by composing word embeddings. These representations are used to directly identify and classify phrases. Evaluating our model on the task of multiword expression tagging, we showed that the proposed representations perform on par with a baseline IOBES-based system. We also showed that it outperforms the model obtaining the best published performance for this task while not using any external lexicon and relying on few input features. As the proposed model computes phrase representations, it allows for comparison between phrases. In the future, the potential of this approach for higher-level tasks such as bilingual word alignment are to be explored.

References

Y. Bengio, R. Ducharme, and P. Vincent. A Neural Probabilistic Language Model. In *NIPS*, 2000.

R. Collobert, J. Weston, L. Bottou, M. Karlen, K. Kavukcuoglu, and P. Kuksa. Natural language processing (almost) from scratch. *Journal of Machine Learning Research*, 2011.

M. Constant, M. Candito, and D. Seddah. The LIGM-Alpage Architecture for the SPMRL 2013 Shared Task: Multiword Expression Analysis and Dependency Parsing. In *Fourth Workshop on Statistical Parsing of Morphologically Rich Languages*, 2013.

J. Giménez and L. Màrquez. Svmtool: A general pos tagger generator based on support vector machines. In *LREC*, 2004.

T. Kudoh and Y. Matsumoto. Use of support vector learning for chunk identification. In *Proceedings of the 2Nd Workshop on Learning Language in Logic and the 4th Conference on Computational Natural Language Learning - Volume 7*, 2000.

J. Lafferty, A. McCallum, and F. Pereira. Conditional random fields: Probabilistic models for segmenting and labeling sequence data. In *Int. Conf. on Machine Learning (ICML 2001)*, 2001.

R. Lebret and R. Collobert. Word Embeddings through Hellinger PCA. In *Proc. of EACL*, 2014.

J. Legrand and R. Collobert. Joint RNN-Based Greedy Parsing and Word Composition. In *Proceedings of ICLR*, 2015.

T. Mueller, H. Schmid, and H. Schütze. Efficient higher-order CRFs for morphological tagging. In *Proceedings of the 2013 Conference on Empirical Methods in Natural Language Processing*, 2013.

L. R. Rabiner. Readings in speech recognition. chapter A Tutorial on Hidden Markov Models and Selected Applications in Speech Recognition. 1990.

F. Radu, I. Abe, J. Hongyan, and Z. Tong. Named entity recognition through classifier combination. In *Proceedings of the Seventh Conference on Natural Language Learning at HLT-NAACL 2003 - Volume 4*, 2003.

E. F. T. K. Sang and J. Veenstra. Representing text chunks. In *Proceedings of the Ninth Conference on European Chapter of the Association for Computational Linguistics*, 1999.

D. Seddah, R. Tsarfaty, S. Kübler, M. Candito, J. D. Choi, R. Farkas, J. Foster, I. Goenaga, K. Gojenola, Y. Goldberg, S. Green, N. Habash, M. Kuhlmann, W. Maier, J. Nivre, A. Przepiórkowski, R. Roth, W. Seeker, Y. Versley, V. Vincze, M. Woliński, A. Wróblewska, and E. Villemonte De La Clergerie. Overview of the SPMRL 2013 shared task: A cross-framework evaluation of parsing morphologically rich languages. In *Proceedings of the 4th Workshop on Statistical Parsing of Morphologically Rich Languages: Shared Task*, 2013.

N. Srivastava, G. Hinton, A. Krizhevsky, I. Sutskever, and R. Salakhutdinov. Dropout: A simple way to prevent neural networks from overfitting. *J. Mach. Learn. Res.*, 2014.

X. Sun, L. Morency, D. Okanohara, and J. Tsujii. Modeling latent-dynamic in shallow parsing: A latent conditional model with improved inference. In *Proceedings of the 22Nd International Conference on Computational Linguistics - Volume 1*, 2008.

K. Uchimoto, Q. Ma, M. Murata, H. Ozaku, and H. Isahara. Named entity extraction based on a maximum entropy model and transformation rules. In *Proceedings of the 38th Annual Meeting on Association for Computational Linguistics*, 2000.

Representing Support Verbs in FrameNet

Miriam R. L. Petruck
1249 Center St, Suite #600
Berkeley, CA 94704
miriamp@icsi.berkeley.edu

Michael Ellsworth
1249 Center St, Suite #600
Berkeley, CA 94704
infinity@icsi.berkeley.edu

Abstract

This paper presents FrameNet's approach to the representation of Support Verbs, as but one type of multiword expression (MWE) included in the database. In addition to motivating and illustrating FrameNet's newly consistent annotation practice for Support Verb constructions, the present work advocates adopting a broad view of what constitutes a multiword expression.

1 Introduction

Natural Language Processing (NLP) research has been interested in the automatic processing of multiword expressions, with reports on and tasks relating to such efforts presented at workshops and conferences for over ten years (e.g. ACL 2003, LREC 2008, COLING 2010, EACL 2014, NAACL 2015). Overcoming the challenge of automatically processing MWEs remains quite elusive because of the difficulty in recognizing and interpreting such forms. Primarily concerned with the mapping of meaning to form via the theory of Frame Semantics (Fillmore 1985, 2012), FrameNet represents MWEs from the perspective of their semantic heads.

Existing statistical approaches to acquiring MWEs (e.g. Villavicencio et al. 2007, Bannard 2005, Nakov 2013) only offer partial solutions to the problem of MWEs. Many, if not most, such approaches focus on identifying MWEs, and do not address the meaning of the MWEs. In the specific case of noun compounds, Nakov (2013) addressed meaning with a fixed set of relationships between members of the compound or by specifying a more explicit paraphrase (Nakov and Hearst 2013). Other efforts have focused on the meaning of verb particle constructions, by distinguishing between meaning classes of parti-

cles (Cook and Stephenson 2006). Salehi et al. (2015) tested newer methods using word embeddings in English and German for compound nouns and verb particle combinations. These studies focused on predicting MWEs, and have not been assessed for the method's utility on vector meaning representations for MWEs. In contrast, the FrameNet analysis of MWEs treats all known kinds of multi-word expressions in English and offers a description of their meaning with the same powerful Frame Semantics system that FN uses for single words.

The rest of this paper is structured as follows. Section 2 describes FrameNet briefly; Section 3 provides background to MWEs, also discussing MWEs in FrameNet and specifically support verb constructions. Section 4 presents the terminology that FN uses in its representation of support verbs, and includes an example. Finally, Section 5 offers concluding remarks.

2 Background to FrameNet

FrameNet (FN) is a knowledge base with unique information about the mapping of meaning to form in the vocabulary of contemporary English through the theory of Frame Semantics (Fillmore 1985, 2012, Fillmore and Baker 2010).

At the heart of Frame Semantics is the **semantic frame**, i.e. an experience-based schematization of the language user's world that allows inferences about participants and objects in and across events, situations, and states of affairs. To date, FN has characterized more than 1,200 frames, nearly 13,500 lexical units (LUs), defined as a pairing of a lemma and a frame, and over 202,000 manually annotated sentences that illustrate the use of each.

A FN frame definition includes a description of a prototypical situation, along with a specification of the frame elements (FEs), or semantic roles, that uniquely characterize that situation. FN distinguishes three types of FEs, core, pe-

Proceedings of the 12th Workshop on Multiword Expressions, pages 72–77,
Berlin, Germany, August 7-12, 2016. ©2016 Association for Computational Linguistics

ripheral, and extrathematic, where core FEs uniquely define a frame. Thus, FrameNet defines the `Revenge`[1] frame as an AVENGER performing a PUNISHMENT on an OFFENDER as a response to an INJURY, inflicted on an IN- JURED_PARTY. These five are core FEs in the `Revenge` frame. Peripheral FEs, such as TIME and PLACE, capture aspects of events more generally. Extrathematic FEs situate an event against the backdrop of another state of affairs; conceptually these FEs do not belong to the frame in which they occur. Example (1) shows a FN analysis of verb *avenge*.v; beyond FEs, FN annotates phrase type and grammatical information.[2]

1. [Sam AVENGER/NP/External] **avenged** [his brother INJURED_PARTY/NP/Object] [after the incident TIME/PP/Dependent].

In (1), *Sam*, the AVENGER, is a NP and functions as the external; *his brother*, the INJURED_PARTY, is a NP and serves the grammatical function object; *after the incident*, the TIME, is a PP dependent. FN lexical entry reports include a table of valence patterns that displays the automatically summarized results of FE, grammatical function and phrase type annotation, as given in Figure 1.

Avenger	Injured_party	Time	
NP Ext	NP Obj	AVP Dep	
Avenger	**Injury**	**Offender**	**Punishment**
CNI --	NP Ext	DNI --	INI --
CNI --	NP Ext	INI --	PP[by] Dep

Figure 1: Partial Valence Table for *revenge*.v

Note that the red arrow in Figure 1 indicates the valence pattern of Example (1).

The FN hierarchy of frames links frames to each other via a number of frame-to-frame relations. For example, **inheritance** is a relation where for each FE, frame relation, and semantic characteristic in the parent, the same or a more specific analogous entity exists in the child. Thus, to illustrate, `Revenge` inherits `Re-`

---

[1] The names of FN frames appear in `Courier New` typeface. An underscore appears between each word of a frame name of more than one word; FN only capitalizes the first word of the name.

[2] FN uses *external* for subjects, including of raising Vs, and a limited set of grammatical functions.

`wards_and_punishments`, which in turn inherits `Response`, as well as `Intention- ally_affect` as Figure 2 depicts.[3]

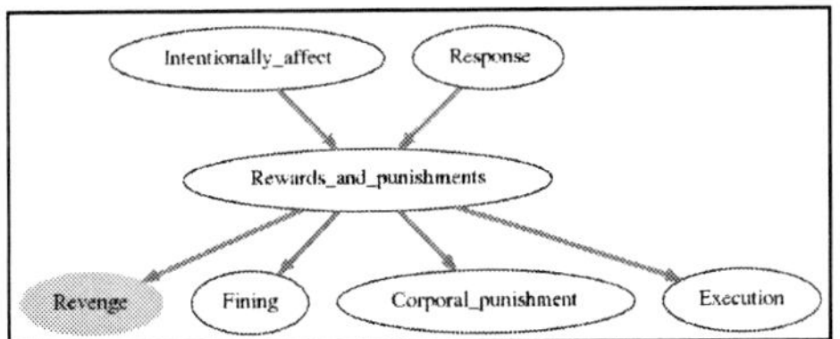

Figure 2: Inheritance Relations in FN

While FN provides frame-specific semantic annotation, its powerful nature becomes most evident when leveraging the larger frame hierarchy, linked through its frame-to-frame relations, of which the local frame is a part.

Not surprisingly, the `Revenge` frame provides the background knowledge structure for defining and understanding a number of MWEs. The following support verb constructions are instances of MWEs defined in terms of `Re- venge`: *get even*.v, *get back*.v, *take revenge*.v, and *exact revenge*.v; details appear in Section 3.

3 Multiword Expressions

3.1 Background

Multiword expressions manifest in a range of linguistic forms (as Sag et al. (2002), among many others, have documented), including: noun + noun compounds (e.g. *fish knife, health hazard* etc.); adjective + noun compounds (e.g. *political agenda, national interest*, etc.); particle verbs (*shut up, take out*, etc.); prepositional verbs (e.g. *look into, talk into*, etc.); VP idioms, such as *kick the bucket*, and *pull someone's leg*, along with less obviously idiomatic forms like *answer the door, mention someone's name*, etc.; expressions that have their own mini-grammars, such as names with honorifics and terms of address (e.g. *Rabbi Lord Jonathan Sacks*), kinship terms (e.g. *second cousin once removed*), and time expressions (e.g. *August 9, 1929*); support verb constructions (e.g. verbs: *take a bath, make a promise*, etc; and prepositions: *in doubt, under review*, etc.). Linguists address issues of polysemy, compositionality, idiomaticity, and continuity for each type of MWE mentioned here.

While native speakers use MWEs with ease, their treatment and interpretation in computa-

---

[3] See, for instance, Petruck and de Melo (2012) for an overview of all of FN's frame-to-frame relations.

tional systems requires considerable effort due to the very issues that concern linguists.

3.2   Multiword Expressions in FrameNet

Although not stated explicitly, Fillmore (2006) suggests that linguists and NLP researchers must consider a very broad view of MWEs instead of limiting the scope of their study to those that fit some analytic or classificatory definition.

While FrameNet includes MWEs in its lexicon, it does not analyze any of them internally. For example, given the (noun + noun) MWE *fish bowl*, FN does not offer an analysis of the relationship between *fish* and *bowl*, the two nouns in the compound when that compound is the focus of the analysis. However, FN does provide semantico-syntactic information about the use of MWEs. Consider the sentence *Smedlap bought a large **fish bowl***, where the (bold-faced) target, i.e. the compound noun, evokes the `Containers` frame, with the core FE CONTAINER and several peripheral FEs, including TYPE. A FN analysis of the sentence indicates that the adjective phrase *a large* is a grammatical dependent of the LU ***fish bowl***, and is annotated with the FE TYPE.

> 2. Smedlap bought [a large TYPE]
>
> [**fish bowl** CONTAINER].

In contrast, if the target LU is the head noun of a noun + noun compound, as in *fish **bowl***, FN annotates the modifier of that compound with the FE that the modifier instantiates, here USE, thus yielding the analysis in (3). Note that both *bowl* and *fish bowl* evoke `Containers`, with analysis of each employing the same set of FEs.

> 3. Smedlap bought a [*fish* USE]
>
> [***bowl*** CONTAINER].

The different analyses in (2) and (3) are a result of the different target LUs in each example.

Table 1, below, lists the types of MWEs found in FrameNet, and provides examples of each.[4]

---

[4] FrameNet also includes support nouns and support adjectives, which the authors believe to be of limited interest to the larger computational linguistics audience.

		Examples
MWE Type		
Compound Noun		fish bowl
Verb + Particle		take off bring out put on
Support Constructions		
Support Verb		make a decision say a prayer find solace
Support Preposition		in possession under attack at large

Table 1: MWE Types in FrameNet

3.3   Support Verbs in FrameNet

This section briefly describes support verbs, very broadly defined (e.g. *give advice, find solace, make a decision*), including plain support verbs, as well as Melcuk's (1996) lexical functions (e.g., causatives), and the discrepancy between the syntactic heads and semantic heads of such forms. Since FN has included

Both Meaning Text Theory (MTT) and Frame Semantics (FS) are interested in characterizing the lexical structure of support verb constructions (as in Table 1), despite the different approaches of each theory. In MTT, lexical functions describe collocations that serve a range of purposes, including, for instance, MAGN, for collocations that emphasize the extremeness of another word (e.g. *red* hot) and CAUS for collocations that express the causation of a word (e.g. *give* a heart attack). Both theories want to describe (a) the verb and the nominal syntactic head of the verb's dependent; (b) the way that the situation or frame that the noun evokes receives expression in the support construction; and (c) how the syntactic dependents of the verb match the semantic roles in the frame that the noun evokes. Some of the shared goals for analyzing support verb constructions motivated exploring the possibility of aligning them (Bouveret and Fillmore 2008), but numerous practical matters, such as different sets of terminology and methodology, precluded any such alignment.

Still, a brief overview of the key differences in the two approaches will illuminate the flexibility of the FrameNet approach. MTT models a limited set of syntactic and semantic relationships between parts of a MWE. Though MTT allows for some multiword expressions involving syntactic and semantic relations beyond these relationships, they do not form part of the larger system. In contrast FrameNet handles all types of meaning relations through its use of frames. The two approaches are complementary in that FN does not model the syntactic relation between the parts of MWEs in a general way, other than the annotation of the syntactic head of the MWE and its part-of-speech.

The support verb construction considered here is but one linguistic form that shows the discrepancy between a syntactic and a semantic head. For example, consider *bottle of champagne*, where *bottle* may refer to a measure (e.g. *They drank a bottle of champagne to celebrate*), or it may indicate a container (e.g. *He broke the bottle of champagne over the newly painted boat*). Regardless of linguistic form, such discrepancies present a challenge to NLP, specifically natural language understanding (NLU). NLU systems must know that *breaking a bottle* is possible, but *breaking champagne* is not. Thus, success in NLP depends, in part, on systems that include the means to resolve the discrepancy between syntactic and semantic heads.

4 Representing Support Vs in FrameNet

This section motivates FrameNet's approach to the representation of support verbs, introduces the terminology that FN uses in their representation, illustrating each, and providing an example that shows the advantage of exploiting FN information for these constructions.

4.1 Motivating FrameNet's Approach

FrameNet began as a lexicography project, and to a large extent remains such, with more attention to the needs of NLP recently than in early phases of the project. As such, FN considered lexicographic factors to determine its approach to representing support verb construction. Nevertheless, FN views the features that it uses in its annotation as showing promise for NLP.

4.2 Terminology

Table 2 displays all possible combinations of the three features that characterize different types of lexically relevant governors, be they supports (as defined in FN), or not. What follows first is a list of features that characterize the relationship between governing and governed words in general: specifically, we define *Bleached, FE-supplying*, and *Idiosyncratic*. Then, this section provides a description of the labels that FrameNet uses for

particular combinations of these features, i.e. *Support, Copula, Controller*, and *Governor*. In the examples that follow, underlining identifies the dependent word with annotation to discuss.

	Bleached		Non-Bleached	
	+FE	-FE	+FE	-FE
+ Idio.	Supp		Supp	
- Idio.	Cop		Ctrlr	Gov

Table 2: Terminology for Lexically Relevant Governors

- **Bleached**: Bleached indicates that the governor does not contribute significant content semantics to the combination of governor and governed word (e.g. *she took revenge, there was rain*). In Non-Bleached cases, added frame annotation models the added meaning from the governor.
- **FE**: FE-supplying (or not) indicates that syntactic dependents of the governing word fill semantic roles of the governed word (e.g. *they gave me a shock*).
- **Idio**: Idiosyncratic covers lexical material whose combination is not predictable from the general meaning of the individual words (e.g. *the US lifted the sanctions*).

These three features underlie the annotation labels that FN employs:

- **Cop**: Copula is for annotating BE, and copula-like verbs (e.g. *seem happy, appear smart*).
- **Ctrlr**: Controller identifies the verb whose subject or object is also the subject or object in the dependent clause (e.g. *attempt a rescue*).
- **Gov**: Governor identifies a word that is used in a prototypical way with a dependent, but without any unusual meaning or any supplying of an FE to its dependent (e.g. *wear boots*)
- **Supp**: Support identifies words that would not mean the same thing without their syntactic dependent (e.g. *take a bath*).

In Table 2, above, the highlighted cell indicates the situation where FrameNet annotates the support item (here, a verb or a preposition) as a separate target, and the combination of Supp + Target is not quite equivalent semantically to the Target alone. (See the example (5).) Regular supports (*exact* in *exact revenge*) need no further analysis and FN does not annotate them further.

4.3 Example

Consider example (4), where the analysis focuses on the support verb expression *took a dirt nap*.[5]

    4. Horatio PROTAGONIST [*took* Supp a **dirt nap**].

FN characterizes *dirt nap*, the target of analysis, in terms of the `Dead_or_alive` frame, defined as a situation in which a PROTAGONIST is in the dynamic, maintained state of being alive or has exited that state. FN records *Horatio*, the syntactic subject of the verb *took* as the PROTAGONIST, and marks *took* with the label Supp. By characterizing *took a dirt nap* in terms of its semantic head, *dirt nap*, FN provides needed information about the participants in the event that the support verb expression describes. Independent of the task, e.g. translation, summarization, search, etc., any NLP system must know that *Horatio* is the participant who is dead. FrameNet provides that information.

Characterizing MWEs for identification and representation in NLP requires systematizing the kinds of combinations that exist. FN provides an elaborate classification system that informs downstream tasks whether the syntactic head or a syntactic dependent is the most important part of a MWE semantically. Importantly, FN provides a unified way to represent the meaning of all types of combinations. This approach includes partially compositional cases, as in (5), where the curly brackets identify the support verb construction.

    5. Officials {lifted Supp [Oslo's EVALUEE] **penalty**}.

In example (5), *Oslo's* fills the EVALUEE role of `Rewards_and_Punishments`, which the noun *penalty* evokes. Additionally, the support verb *lift* evokes another frame, i.e. the `Cause_to_end` frame,with two core FEs, AGENT and PROCESS. In this second frame, the noun *officials* fills the AGENT role and the NP *Oslo's penalty* fills the PROCESS role, shown in example (6), below.

    6. [Officials AGENT] {**lifted** Supp [Oslo's penalty PROCESS]}.

---

[5] Given the goal of this work, while recognizing the metaphor, we provide no analysis for *dirt nap*, or further information about its being a compound noun.

Also, in the definitions of LUs that only evoke the frame with certain dependents, e.g. *lift.v* here, FN records the semantic type Support_only_LU. At present, no automatic NLP method captures the complexity of information that FN characterizes. As such, in conjunction with automated semantic parsing (Das et al. 2014), FN holds great potential for use in NLP tasks that depend on processing support verb constructions, as one type of MWE.

5 Conclusion

This paper has provided a brief overview of multiword expressions in FrameNet focusing on one type of such expression, namely support verb constructions. In addition, the present work has achieved its goals of motivating, presenting, and illustrating FrameNet's current policy and newly consistent practice of representing support verb construction. Importantly, the paper also shows that FrameNet offers crucial information about the **meaning** of support verb constructions. Statistical approaches, which tend to focus on the identification of MWEs in text, do not provide such information.

Acknowledgments

FrameNet's treatment of multiword expressions, including support verbs, draws significantly upon Fillmore (2006).

The authors are grateful to the FrameNet team for the numerous discussions about the ideas and annotation conventions presented in this work.

References

C. Bannard. 2005. Learning about the meaning of verb particle constructions from corpora. *Computer Speech and Language Special Issue on MWEs* 19(4): 467–478.

M. Bouveret and C. J. Fillmore. 2008. Matching Verbo-nominal Constructions in FrameNet with Lexical Functions in MTT. In E. Bernal and J. DeCesaris (Eds.). *Proceedings of the 13th EURALEX International Congress*, pp. 297-308.

P. Cook and S. Stevenson. 2006. Classifying Particle Semantics in English Verb-Particle Constructions. In *Proceedings of the Workshop on Multiword Expressions: Identifying and Exploiting Underlying Properties*. ACL: Sydney, 45–53.

D. Das, D. Chen, A. F. T. Martins, N. Schneider, and N. A. Smith. 2014. Frame-semantic parsing. *Computational Linguistics* 40.1: 9–56

C. J. Fillmore. 1985. Frames and the semantics of understanding. *Quaderni di Semantica*, 6.2: 222-254.

C. J. Fillmore. 2006. Multiword Expressions: An Extremist Approach, Unpublished PPT. ICSI and University of California, Berkeley, CA.

C. J. Fillmore. 2012. Encounters with Language. *Computational Linguistics*. 38.4: 701-718.

C. J. Fillmore and C. Baker. 2010. A Frames Approach to Semantic Analysis. In B. Heine and H. Narrog (eds.), *The Oxford Handbook of Linguistic Analysis*. Oxford: OUP, pp. 791-816.

I. A. Mel'čuk, I. 1996. Lexical Functions: A Tool for the Description of Lexical Relations in a Lexicon. In L. Wanner (ed.), Lexical functions in lexicography and natural language processing, Amsterdam: John Benjamins, pp. 37-102.

P. Nakov. 2013. On the interpretation of noun compounds: Syntax, semantics, and entailment, *Natural Language Engineering* 19.3: 291-330.

P. Nakov and M. A. Hearst. 2013. Semantic Interpretation of Noun Compounds Using Verbal and Other Paraphrases, *ACM Transactions on Speech and Language Processing*, special issue on Multiword Expressions, 10.3, Article 13.

M. R. L. Petruck and G. de Melo. 2012. Precedes: A Semantic Relation in FrameNet, *Proceedings of the Workshop on Language Resources for Public Security Applications* at the 8th Conference on International Language Resources and Evaluation (LREC), Istanbul, Turkey, pp. 45-49.

J. Ruppenhofer, M. Ellsworth, M. R. L. Petruck, C. R. Johnson, and J. Scheffczyk. 2010. *FrameNet II: Extended Theory and Practice*. Web Publication: framenet.icsi.berkeley.edu/book.

I. A. Sag, T. Baldwin, F. Bond, A. Copestake, and D. Flickinger. 2002. Multiword expressions: A pain in the neck for NLP. In *Proceedings of the 3rd International Conference on Intelligent Text Processing and Computational Linguistics* (CICLing-2002), Berlin: Springer, pp.1-15.

B. Salehi, P. Cook, and T. Baldwin. 2015. A Word Embedding Approach to Predicting the Compositionality of Multiword Expressions. In *Proceedings of the Annual Conference of the North American Association for Computational Linguistics*, Denver, pp. 977–983.

A. Villavicencio, V. Kordoni, Y. Zhang, M. Idiart, and C. Ramisch. 2007. Validation and evaluation of automatically acquired multiword expressions for grammar engineering. In *Proceedings of the 2007 Joint Conference on Empirical Methods in Natural Language Processing and Computational Natural Language Learning*, pp. 1034–1043, Prague: ACL.

Inherently Pronominal Verbs in Czech:
Description and Conversion Based on Treebank Annotation

Zdeňka Urešová   **Eduard Bejček**   **Jan Hajič**
Charles University in Prague, Faculty of Mathematics and Physics
Institute of Formal and Applied Linguistics
Malostranské nám. 25
11800 Prague 1, Czech Republic
{uresova,bejcek,hajic}@ufal.mff.cuni.cz

Abstract

This paper describes results of a study related to the PARSEME Shared Task on automatic detection of verbal Multi-Word Expressions (MWEs) which focuses on their identification in running texts in many languages. The Shared Task's organizers have provided basic annotation guidelines where four basic types of verbal MWEs are defined including some specific subtypes. Czech is among the twenty languages selected for the task. We will contribute to the Shared Task dataset, a multilingual open resource, by converting data from the Prague Dependency Treebank (PDT) to the Shared Task format. The question to answer is to which extent this can be done automatically. In this paper, we concentrate on one of the relevant MWE categories, namely on the quasi-universal category called "Inherently Pronominal Verbs" (IPronV) and describe its annotation in the Prague Dependency Treebank. After comparing it to the Shared Task guidelines, we can conclude that the PDT and the associated valency lexicon, PDT-Vallex, contain sufficient information for the conversion, even if some specific instances will have to be checked. As a side effect, we have identified certain errors in PDT annotation which can now be automatically corrected.

1 Introduction

Although Multi-Word Expressions (MWEs) attract the attention of more and more NLP researchers, as stated in Rosén et al. (2015), there is no consensus both on MWEs annotation and on what constitutes a MWE. This complicates the research of MWEs based on annotated corpora and language resources. To remedy this situation, the COST network PARSEME[1] (Savary et al., 2015) concentrates on the study of MWEs and their annotation in treebanks aiming at building a set of standardized annotation principles, corpora and evaluation metrics.

In the framework of PARSEME, a Shared Task on automatic detection of verbal Multi-Word Expressions was established in order to provide a multilingual open resource to be available to the NLP community. This initiative runs from 2015 to 2017. There are about twenty corpus contributors to the Shared Task. The task covers languages of different language families. Languages are divided into four language groups of comparable sizes: Germanic, Romance, Slavic and other. Common standardized annotation guidelines have been developed which try to define common principles of verbal MWE annotation, while also taking language specifics into account (Vincze et al., 2016). The guidelines summarize the properties of verbal MWEs and provide basic annotation rules for them. Various types of verbal MWEs as identified by previous research have been classified into seven groups: light verb constructions (LVC), idioms (ID), and then possibly verb particle combinations (VPC), inherently pronominal verbs (IPronV) and inherently prepositional verbs (IPrepV) if these three quasi-universal categories are applicable in the language, possibly other language specific category, and other verbal MWEs (OTH).

In our paper, we concentrate on the inherently pronominal verbs (IPronV) category. The paper is structured as follows: In Section 2, the Czech data (PDT) and the valency lexicon PDT-Vallex are presented. In Section 3, the category of inherently pronominal verbs (IPronV) is described focusing on Czech language specifics. In Section 4, we focus on the relation of the specification of the IPronV category for the Shared Task and the PDT-Vallex and PDT annotation, which then forms the starting point for the conversion procedure into the format of the PARSEME Shared Task. Section 5 concludes the paper.

2 Czech data and lexicon

For our study, we use data from the Czech annotated corpus, the PDT, as described in Sect. 2.1, and from the Czech valency lexicon PDT-Vallex (Sect. 2.2).

---

[1] http://typo.uni-konstanz.de/parseme

Proceedings of the 12th Workshop on Multiword Expressions, pages 78–83,
Berlin, Germany, August 7-12, 2016. ©2016 Association for Computational Linguistics

2.1 The Prague Dependency Treebank

The Prague Dependency Treebank 2.0 (Hajič et al., 2006) published by the Linguistic Data Consortium[2] contains Czech written texts with complex and interlinked morphological, syntactic and complex semantic annotation.[3] Its annotation scheme is based on the formal framework called Functional Generative Description (FGD) (Sgall et al., 1986), which is dependency-based with a "stratificational" (layered) approach to a systematic description of a language. The annotation contains interlinked surface dependency trees and deep syntactic/semantic (*tectogrammatical*) trees. Valency is one of the core FGD concepts, used on the deep layer (Panevová, 1974; Panevová, 1994). We shall note that each verb occurrence at the tectogrammatical level of annotation contains a manually assigned link (in a form of a unique frame ID) to the corresponding valency frame in the valency lexicon (Sect. 2.2).

The PDT has been extended in its versions PDT 2.5 (Bejček et al., 2012) and subsequently in PDT 3.0[4] by adding, e.g., extensive MWE annotation. However, since we are focusing on IPronV in this paper, we have in fact not used this extension, which concerns other (mostly nominal) types of MWEs.

2.2 PDT-Vallex – Czech valency lexicon

The Czech valency lexicon, called PDT-Vallex is publicly available[5] as a part of the PDT family of treebanks; for details, see Urešová (2011), Dušek et al. (2014) and Urešová et al. (2016), which we very briefly summarize here. As such, it has been designed in close connection with the specification of the treebank annotation. Each verb occurrence in the PDT is linked to a specific verb valency frame in the valency lexicon.

Each valency entry in the lexicon contains a headword, according to which the valency frames are grouped, indexed, and sorted. The valency frame consists of valency frame members (slots) and their labels, the obligatoriness feature for each member and the required surface form of valency frame members. Any specific lexical realization of a particular valency frame is exempli-

fied by an understandable fragment of a Czech sentence. Valency frame members are labeled by *functors* based on the FGD theory (ACT for Actor, or first argument, PAT for Patient or 2nd argument, ADDRessee, EFFect and ORIGin for the remaining core argument, and any other functor if deemed obligatory). Notes help to delimit the meaning (verb sense) of the individual valency frames within one valency lexicon entry. In the notes, synonyms, antonyms and aspectual counterparts are often found as additional hints to distinguish among the individual valency frame senses. An example of a valency lexicon entry for *tolerovat* (lit. *tolerate*) is in Fig. 1.

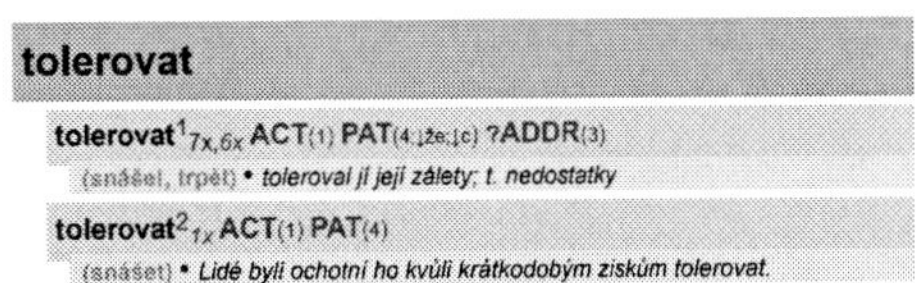

Figure 1: A simple PDT-Vallex entry with two senses (lit. *tolerate*): to tolerate[1] *sth*.PAT to *sb*.ADDR, to tolerate[2] *sb*.PAT

PDT-Vallex 2.0 which we have used in our work contains 11,933 valency frames for 7,121 verbs.

3 Inherently pronominal verbs

The PARSEME Shared Task general guidelines (Vincze et al., 2016) define the IPronV category as a specific quasi-universal[6] verbal MWE category.

We use the guidelines for IPronV identification (Candito and Ramisch, 2016) where the basic rules are described. The guidelines divide verbs with a pronominal clitic into several groups. The first group of IPronV never occurs without the clitic – the clitic must co-occur with the verb, such as:

- cs: *bát se* (lit. *be afraid*)
- fr: *s'évanouir* (lit. *faint*)
- pl: *dowiedzieć się* (lit. *find out*)
- pt: *queixar-se* (lit. *complain*)

The second group of IPronV contains such verbs that might occur without the clitic, but with a different meaning:

---

[2]http://www.ldc.upenn.edu/LDC2006T01
[3]https://ufal.mff.cuni.cz/pdt2.0
[4]http://hdl.handle.net/11858/
00-097C-0000-0023-1AAF-3
[5]http://hdl.handle.net/11858/
00-097C-0000-0023-4338-F

[6]*quasi-universal* = not found / defined for all languages, as opposed to *light verb constructions* (LVC) and *idioms* (ID), which are universal for all languages within the PARSEME Shared Task.

- cs: *hledět si* (lit. *mind sth*) vs. *hledět* (lit. *watch*)
- fr: *s'agir* (lit. *be*) vs. *agir* (lit. *act*)
- pl: *radzić sobie* (lit. *manage*) vs. *radzić* (lit. *advise*)
- pt: *encontrar-se* (lit. *be*) vs. *encontrar* (lit. *meet*)

The guidelines also list several other groups of pronominal verbs defined by an occurrence in a predominantly different syntactic behavior (reciprocals, reflexives, possessive reflexives, synthetic passives, impersonal and inchoative), which are *NOT* considered verbal MWEs (IPronV) unless their meaning has shifted substantially.

Given the complexity of this kind of verbal MWEs, the guidelines for the annotation of IPronV contain a detailed suit of tests for the proper annotation of IPronV. These tests are in the form of a binary decision tree that shows how to apply the tests in order to distinguish which pronominal verb occurrence has to be annotated as verbal MWEs and which should not. For example, test No. 8 distinguishes between a reciprocal use with plural subject and a real inherently pronominal construction:

> *Is it possible to remove the reflective particle and replace the coordinated subject (A and B) or plural subject (A.PL) by a singular subject (A or A.PL) and a singular object, often introduced by* to/with *(B or A.PL), without changing the pronominal verb's meaning? If yes, it is not* IPronV.[7]

3.1 Czech verbs with reflexive particles

The issue of Czech reflexives has been described by many scholars, e.g., Štícha (1981), Panevová (1999) or Panevová (2007), from diverse point of views. For example, in Kettnerová and Lopatková (2014) Czech reflexive verbs are dealt from the lexicographic point of view and a proposal for their lexicographic representation is formulated. Although reflexives are the topic of Czech theoretical (Panevová and Mikulová, 2007; Oliva, 2001) as well as computational linguistic papers (Petkevič, 2013; Oliva, 2003), as far as we know, there is no unified theoretical description of this language phenomenon. We believe the reason is the complexity of this ambiguous phenomenon since the Czech reflexive particle *se* or *si* can be used

both as formal morphological means for word-formation (e.g., reflexivization) and as syntactic means for specific syntactic structures (reflexifity, reciprocity, diatheses). Specifically, *se* is (a) a short (clitic) form of the pronoun *sebe* (lit. all of *itself, myself, yourself, herself, himself, ourselves, yourselves, themselves*) in accusative case, or (b) a reflexive particle for regular formation of passive constructions, particle for "frozen" constructions where it diachronically became part of the verb lexeme (except it is not written together with the verb form; it can be placed quite far from it in a sentence), as well as (c) the reflexivization particle for certain additional types of constructions, such as medio-passive construction of disposition *it reads well* which is expressed in Czech by adding this particle to the verb form (*čte se to dobře*).[8]

3.2 Inherently pronominal verbs in the PDT-Vallex and in the PDT

As has been already mentioned, we are investigating whether the information present in the PDT-Vallex (and in the PDT) can be used for determining the IPronV class. Although the detailed information about specific types of pronominal verbs is not explicitly captured in the PDT-Vallex, it does contain information related to the use of reflexive particles *se* or *si* in Czech. Moreover, the lexicon is linked to the PDT, so each corpus occurrence can be related to the lexicon (and vice versa).

The formal indicator that has been used in the PDT-Vallex to denote "reflexivization" (in the sense used in the PDT and PDT-Vallex annotation, see Mikulová et al. (2006)) is the addition of the particle *se* or *si* to the lemma (entry headword). Therefore, there might be up to three different headwords for each verb lemma in the PDT-Vallex: one without any such particle, one with *se* and one with *si*.[9]

Pronominal *se/si* is the only case of MWE captured in the PDT-Vallex as a headword, which illustrates its specificity in Czech. Czech does not display other similar phenomena such as phrasal verbs in English (*look up, run away* etc.).[10]

---

[7]Candito and Ramisch (2016), page 7

[8]Moreover, *se* is also a vocalized preposition used with the instrumental case, corresponding to English *with*.

[9]Just for completeness, there can never be both particles at the same time.

[10]However, LVCs and IDs do exist in Czech and they can also be identified in PDT-Vallex; see Fig. 2 and its description at the end of this section.

In addition and to our advantage here, PDT-Vallex stores different verb senses separately, as different valency frames under the same headword.[11]

When we applied the specific tests for annotation of IPronV and went through the suggested decision tree step by step, we have determined that the first three questions (inherent reflexives, i.e., reflexives tantum), inherent reflexives due to different senses (i.e., derived reflexives), and inherent reflexives with a different subcategorization than the verb without the particle (i.e., derived reflexives) are easily answered by simply testing the existence of the *se* or *si* particle in the headword of a particular valency frame. In other words, *all* valency frames the headword of which contains the *se* or *si* particle will be marked as IPronV.

We have then analyzed the follow-up tests in the guidelines. These tests, similarly to the Plural/Coordination test shown earlier, test whether the occurrence of the verb construction is rather of a syntactic nature (deagentives etc.), and if YES, it disallows to annotate it as IPronV. However, it was found that since PDT-Vallex abstracts from—or generalizes over—such constructions, keeping only the basic (canonical, active voice) valency frame, we can in fact rely on the *se* or *si* indicators at the headword also for these special cases. In other words, diatheses are not explicitly present in the PDT-Vallex, they are assumed to be formed by regular derivation processes (such as reflexive or periphrastic passivization, reciprocalization, etc.) on the basis of the canonical valency frame as recorded in PDT-Vallex. Since the links from the PDT corpus to the individual valency frames in PDT-Vallex also abstract from such diathetical transformations, we do not have to apply such tests to the PDT-Vallex entries when distinguishing IPronV.

To summarize, we have determined that due to the way PDT-Vallex is structured and linked to the corpus, the only necessary indication that the phrase should be marked as IPronV is that the valency frame it is linked to has a headword with the *se* or *si* particle. In other words, albeit without knowing it, the annotators and creators of PDT-Vallex have already built in the IPronV MWE type in the lexicon using the *se*/*si* indicator.

Statistics for 1580 inherently pronominal verbs as found in the PDT-Vallex are given in Table 1.

| | Particle | |
Type of IPronV	*se*	*si*
reflexive tantum verbs	587	98
derived reflexives	743	152

Table 1: Statistics on 1580 inherently pronominal verbs in PDT-Vallex. Reflexive tantum verbs: clitic is compulsory; derived reflexives: absence of the clitic changes the sense.

Table 2 shows numbers for 72 verbs (headwords in PDT-Vallex) where we expect the annotation to contain overlapping labels IPronV and one of ID or LVC for at least one frame. The number of all ID/LVC frames belonging to pronominal verbs (headwords) is 172.

Type of overlap	No. of headwords
ID only	58
LVC only	9
LVC and ID	5

Table 2: Statistics on verbs potentially overlapping IPronV and ID/LVC annotation.

An example of valency lexicon entry for the verb (headword) *dělat si* with all its valency frames (senses) is displayed in Fig. 2. The first and last frame describes a MWE of inherently pronominal verb meaning, and each occurrence in the corpus can be thus labeled IPronV. All the other frames are examples of an embedded MWE, since on top of being an IPronV, they are also of the LVC category (those having one of the arguments labeled CPHR) or of the ID (idiom) category (those having one of the arguments labeled DPHR). In these seven cases two embedded MWE can be labeled at once: IPronV and either ID or LVC.

4 Conversion of Czech data

Based on the results of the investigation described in Sect. 3.2, we can conclude that the category of IPronV as defined in the guidelines for the PARSEME Shared Task corresponds to such verbs in the PDT whose tectogrammatical lemma contains *se* or *si* in a form of a "word with spaces".

---

¹¹The valency frames for different verb senses for each headword have often different syntactic and semantic description—such as the number of arguments, their surface realization etc.—but they might be identical.

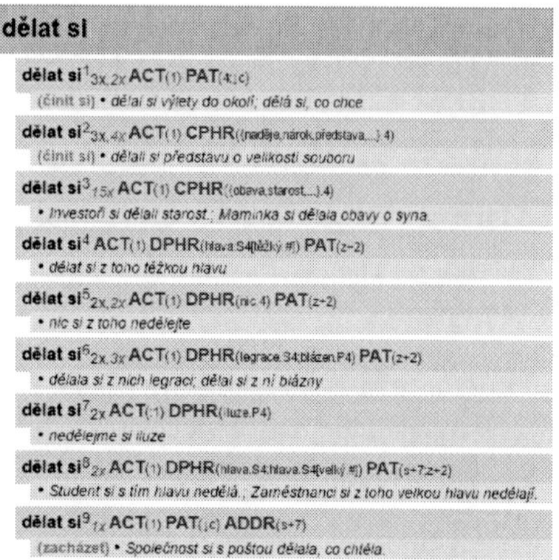

Figure 2: An example of PDT-Vallex entry with several senses of the verb *dělat* (lit. *do/make*) in which the particle *si* has to co-occur.

Translation of Czech examples:

*dělat si*¹: *he's making short trips in the neighborhood; he does whatever he wants*

*dělat si*² (*představu*=image): *they were imagining the size of the file*

*dělat si*³ (*starost*=worry): *the investors were worried; mother was worried about son*

*dělat si*⁴ (*těžkou hlavu*=heavy head): *he did worry*

*dělat si*⁵ (*ne- nic z*=not nothing out-of): *don't worry about it*

*dělat si*⁶ (*legraci, blázny*=fun, fools): *she was making fun of them; he was making monkey out of her*

*dělat si*⁷ (*ne- iluze*=not illusions): *let's don't delude ourselves*

*dělat si*⁸ (*velkou hlavu*=big head): *student is not worried about it; employees do not worry much about it*

*dělat si*⁹ (*s*=with): *the company did whatever they liked with the mail*

However, having the tectogrammatical annotation of the PDT linked to the surface dependencies, we have also checked the lexicon annotation against the corpus not only through the reference linking the PDT's tectogrammatical annotation to PDT-Vallex, but also against the surface dependency annotation.

We worked with a hypothesis that all the IPronV should be linked to a surface verb and a separate node for the particle (*se* or *si*), and that the syntactic function of the *se* or *si* node should be labeled as AuxT. Analytical function AuxT is assigned to the particles *se* or *si* in case the verb sense without them does not exist, which to a large extent also corresponds to the IPronV property at the surface syntactic level (Hajič et al., 2004).[12] We found that in 93.1% of the occurrences, this is indeed the case, but there are more than 700 cases where the syntactic relation was different (not AuxT). After investigating a sample of those, we found that they were errors (such as holding the Adv, Obj, AuxO or AuxR label) in the surface dependency annotation. These cases will not be used for the conversion to the PARSEME Shared Task dataset, unless further investigation can prove that they are indeed all just surface annotation errors in the original data.

5 Conclusions

We have compared the annotation of verbal entries in the PDT (and PDT-Vallex) with the PARSEME Shared Task guidelines for inherently pronominal verbs. The main conclusion is that albeit annotated independently, the PDT/PDT-Vallex annotation covers all IPronV categories relevant for Czech as defined in the guidelines.

By a relatively simple conversion process we have also checked the annotation at the surface syntactic dependency annotation level of the PDT and found a few mismatches. At this time, these mismatches seem to be mostly errors of the surface dependency level annotation in the PDT.[13]

Acknowledgements

The work described herein has been supported by the grant GP13-03351P of the Grant Agency of the Czech Republic, by the grant LD14117 of the Ministry of Education, Youth and Sports of the Czech Republic (MEYSCR) and by the LIN-DAT/CLARIN Research Infrastructure projects, LM2010013 and LM2015071 funded by the MEYSCR. The project also accepted support from the COST Action No. IC1207 "PARSEME", funded by the European Commission. It has also been using language resources developed and distributed by the LINDAT/CLARIN project LM2015071 (http://lindat.cz).

---

[12]Except it might be elided, shared among several verb tokens in coordination etc., so that it is not that "reliable" indicator as the presence of the reflexive particle in the PDT-Vallex headword; for details, see Hajič (1998).

[13]The conversion process should be finished (including all other types of verbal MWEs as defined by the PARSEME Shared Task guidelines, which will be described in a followup publication) by the time of the workshop and we will provide full statistics.

References

Eduard Bejček, Jarmila Panevová, Jan Popelka, Pavel Straňák, Magda Ševčíková, Jan Štěpánek, and Zdeněk Žabokrtský. 2012. Prague dependency treebank 2.5 – a revisited version of PDT 2.0. In Martin Kay and Christian Boitet, editors, *Proceedings of the 24th International Conference on Computational Linguistics (Coling 2012)*, pages 231–246, Mumbai, India. IIT Bombay, Coling 2012 Organizing Committee.

Marie Candito and Carlos Ramisch. 2016. Annotation guidelines for inherently pronominal verbs (PARSEME shared task on automatic detection of verbal MultiWord Expressions), http://typo.uni-konstanz.de/parseme/images/shared-task/guidelines/PARSEME-ST-annotation-guidelines-ipronv.pdf.

Ondřej Dušek, Jan Hajič, and Zdeňka Urešová. 2014. Verbal valency frame detection and selection in Czech and English. In *The 2nd Workshop on EVENTS: Definition, Detection, Coreference, and Representation*, pages 6–11, Stroudsburg, PA, USA. Association for Computational Linguistics.

Jan Hajič, Jarmila Panevová, Eva Buráňová, Zdeňka Urešová, Alevtina Bémová, Jan štěpánek, Petr Pajas, and Jiří Kárník. 2004. Anotace na analytické rovině. Návod pro anotátory. Technical Report TR-2004-23, ÚFAL/CKL MFF UK, Prague.

Jan Hajič, 1998. *Building a Syntactically Annotated Corpus: The Prague Dependency Treebank.* Karolinum, Charles University Press, Prague.

Jan Hajič, Jarmila Panevová, Eva Hajičová, Petr Sgall, Petr Pajas, Jan Štěpánek, Jiří Havelka, Marie Mikulová, Zdeněk Žabokrtský, Magda Ševčíková Razímová, and Zdeňka Urešová. 2006. *Prague Dependency Treebank 2.0.* Number LDC2006T01. LDC, Philadelphia, PA, USA.

Václava Kettnerová and Markéta Lopatková. 2014. Reflexive verbs in a valency lexicon: The case of czech reflexive morphemes. In Andrea Abel, Chiara Vettori, and Natascia Ralli, editors, *Proceedings of the XVI EURALEX International Congress: The User in Focus*, pages 1007–1023, Bolzano/Bozen, Italy. EURAC research, EURAC research.

Marie Mikulová, Alevtina Bémová, Jan Hajič, Eva Hajičová, Jiří Havelka, Veronika Kolářová, Lucie Kučová, Markéta Lopatková, Petr Pajas, Jarmila Panevová, Magda Razímová, Petr Sgall, Jan Štěpánek, Zdeňka Urešová, Kateřina Veselá, and Zdeněk Žabokrtský. 2006. Annotation on the tectogrammatical level in the Prague Dependency Treebank. Annotation manual. Technical Report 30, Prague, Czech Rep.

Karel Oliva. 2001. Reflexe reflexivity reflexiv. *Slovo a slovesnost*, 62(3):200–207.

Karel Oliva. 2003. Linguistics-based PoS-tagging of Czech: disambiguation of se as a test. In *Contributions of the 4th European Conference on Formal Description of Slavic Languages*, pages 299–314. Postdam University, Germany.

Jarmila Panevová and Marie Mikulová. 2007. On reciprocity. *The Prague Bulletin of Mathematical Linguistics*, (87):27–40.

Jarmila Panevová. 1974. On verbal Frames in Functional Generative Description. *Prague Bulletin of Mathematical Linguistics*, 22:3–40.

Jarmila Panevová. 1994. Valency frames and the meaning of the sentence. *The Prague School of Structural and Functional Linguistics*, 41:223–243.

Jarmila Panevová. 1999. Česká reciproční zájmena a slovesná valence. *Slovo a slovesnost*, 60:91–100.

Jarmila Panevová. 2007. Znovu o reciprocitě. *Slovo a slovesnost*, 68:269–275.

Vladimír Petkevič. 2013. Formal (morpho)syntactic properties of reflexive particles se, si as free morphemes in contemporary Czech. In *Proceedings of the 7th International Conference SLOVKO 2013*, pages 206–216. Slovenska akademia vied, Slovakia.

Victoria Rosén, Gyri Losnegaard, Koenraad De Smedt, Eduard Bejček, Agata Savary, Adam Przepiórkowski, Petya Osenova, and Verginica Mititelu. 2015. A survey of multiword expressions in treebanks. In *14th International Workshop on Treebanks and Linguistic Theories (TLT 2015)*, pages 179–193, Warszawa, Poland. IPIPAN, IPIPAN.

Agata Savary, Manfred Sailer, Yannick Parmentier, Michael Rosner, Victoria Rosén, Adam Przepiórkowski, Cvetana Krstev, Veronika Vincze, Beata Wójtowicz, Gyri Smørdal Losnegaard, Carla Parra Escartín, Jakub Waszczuk, Matthieu Constant, Petya Osenova, and Federico Sangati. 2015. PARSEME – PARSing and Multiword Expressions within a European multilingual network. In *7th Language & Technology Conference: Human Language Technologies as a Challenge for Computer Science and Linguistics (LTC 2015)*, Poznań, Poland, November.

Petr Sgall, Eva Hajičová, and Jarmila Panevová. 1986. *The meaning of the sentence in its semantic and pragmatic aspects.* D. Reidel, Dordrecht.

Zdeňka Urešová, Eva Fučíková, and Jana Šindlerová. 2016. Czengvallex: a bilingual czech-english valency lexicon. *The Prague Bulletin of Mathematical Linguistics*, 105:17–50.

Zdeňka Urešová. 2011. *Valenční slovník Pražského závislostního korpusu (PDT-Vallex).* Studies in Computational and Theoretical Linguistics. Ústav formální a aplikované lingvistiky, Praha, Czechia.

Veronika Vincze, Agata Savary, Marie Candito, and Carlos Ramisch. 2016. Annotation guidelines for the PARSEME shared task on automatic detection of verbal Multi-Word Expressions, version 5.0, http://typo.uni-konstanz.de/parseme/images/shared-task/guidelines/PARSEME-ST-annotation-guidelines-v5.pdf.

František Štícha. 1981. K syntakticko-sémantické konkurenci aktivních, participiálních a reflexívních konstrukcí. *Slovo a slovesnost*, 42:183–192.

Using collocational features to improve automated scoring of EFL texts

Yves Bestgen
Centre for English Corpus Linguistics
Université catholique de Louvain
10 Place du Cardinal Mercier
Louvain-la-Neuve, 1348, Belgium
`yves.bestgen@uclouvain.be`

Abstract

This study aims at determining whether collocational features automatically extracted from EFL (English as a foreign language) texts are useful for quality scoring, and allow the improvement of a competitive baseline based on, amongst other factors, bigram frequencies. The collocational features were gathered by assigning to each bigram in an EFL text eight association scores computed on the basis of a native reference corpus. The distribution of the association scores were then summarized by a few global statistical features and by a discretizing procedure. An experiment conducted on a publicly available dataset confirmed the effectiveness of these features and the benefit brought by using several discretized association scores.

1 Introduction

The importance of preformed units in language use is well established (Pawley and Syder, 1983; Schmitt, 2004; Sinclair, 1991). If some of these sequences belong to the traditional phraseological approach, signalled by their syntactic fixedness and semantic non-compositionality, the vast majority of them are conventional word combinations that display statistical idiomaticity (Baldwin and Kim, 2010; Smiskova et al., 2012). This phraseological dimension of language has important implications for learning a foreign language, as shown by many studies in applied linguistics. It not only distinguishes native speakers from nonnative ones, but the number of phraseological units in a learner text is related to the overall level of proficiency in the learned language (e.g., Forsberg, 2010; Levitzky-Aviad and Laufer, 2013; Santos et al., 2012; Verspoor et al., 2012). In these studies, a limited number of expressions were analysed in a small number of texts, giving a very detailed, but also very punctual, view of the phenomenon. In addition, the phraseological nature of a lexical sequence was determined manually using dictionaries or by asking native speakers, making the analysis of numerous texts difficult.

These limitations were overcome by Durrant and Schmitt (2009), who proposed[1] assigning to the bigrams present in an EFL text two association scores (ASs), computed on the basis of a large native reference corpus: (pointwise) Mutual Information (*MI*), which favours bigrams made up of low-frequency words, and the *t*-score, which highlights those composed of high-frequency words. They observed that, compared to native speakers, EFL learners tend to underuse collocations with high *MI* scores while overusing those with high *t*-scores. More recently, Bestgen and Granger (2014, 2015) and Granger and Bestgen (2014) showed that these ASs distinguish advanced learners from intermediate learners, and that the average *MI* score and the proportion of bigrams in the text that are absent from the reference corpus were good predictors of text quality, but that the average *t*-score was much less successful. These studies have a major drawback: the effectiveness of phraseological indices was not compared to that of other features known to be effective predictors. It is therefore impossible to determine whether the phraseological indices are really effective and if they can improve the prediction when combined with other indices. This limitation is probably partly due to the fact that these analyses were not conducted in the field of automatic scoring, but in applied linguistics.

In automatic scoring, phraseological expres-

---

[1] See Bernardini (2007) for an earlier use of this approach in translation studies.

Proceedings of the 12th Workshop on Multiword Expressions, pages 84–90,
Berlin, Germany, August 7-12, 2016. ©2016 Association for Computational Linguistics

sions have long been used almost exclusively for detecting errors, a task for which they have been very useful (e.g., Chodorow and Leacock, 2000; Futagi et al., 2008; Wu et al., 2010). It is noteworthy that a feature tracking the correct use of collocations was considered for inclusion in e-Rater, but its usefulness for predicting text quality seems rather limited (Higgins et al., 2015). Very recently, however, Somasundaran and Chodorow (2014) and Somasundaran et al. (2015) demonstrated the benefit brought by collocation measures, amongst other linguistic features, for automatically scoring spoken picture-based narration tasks. Like Durrant and Schmitt (2009), they used a large corpus to obtain the *MI* scores of every bigram and trigram in the responses and derived a series of collocational features: the maximum, minimum and the median *MI*, and the proportion of bigrams' and trigrams' *MI* scores falling into eight bins, such as [-inf,-20],]-20,-10],]-10,-1] or]20, +inf]. They found that these features were very effective for scoring the responses, even when compared to a competitive baseline system that uses state-of-the-art speech-based features.

Even if these results were extremely promising, they leave a number of questions unanswered. First, they were obtained by studying short oral responses. Can they be generalized to longer written texts, a situation that allows the learner to spend much more time on its production? Then one can wonder whether the use of *MI* is sufficient, or if additional benefits can be obtained by taking into account other associational measures for collocations. In this context, extracting richer features than the mean scores, as done by Somasundaran and Chodorow (2014), seems particularly promising, because Granger and Bestgen (2014) found that the best learner texts contain more middle-level *t*-score bigrams and fewer low and high-level *t*-score bigrams. This observation may be related to the fact that the low *t*-score bigrams are often erroneous combinations of words, while high scores indicate extremely common bigrams in the language, which are easy to learn. It is therefore far from obvious that there is a simple linear or monotonic relationship between the distribution of the association scores (ASs) in a text and its quality. Finally, it would be interesting to determine whether using ASs extracted from a corpus of native texts enables a better prediction than that obtained by using the simple frequency of the uni-

grams and bigrams (Yannakoudakis et al., 2011).

This study attempts to answer these questions by extracting from the bigrams in EFL texts richer features from several association measures as described in Section 2, and by comparing the effectiveness of these collocational features to that of lexical features (Section 3). The conclusion proposes several paths for further research.

2 Extracting Collocation Features

Somasundaran and Chodorow (2014) used only one AS, while Durrant and Schmitt (2009) used two, but there are many other ASs (Pecina, 2010). Evert (2009) recommends a heuristic approach by testing a series of ASs to keep the one that is most appropriate for the task at hand, while Pecina recommends using several ASs simultaneously. These recommendations were followed here by comparing the performance of eight ASs and by combining them (i.e., using simultaneously all of them in the feature set). In addition to *MI* and *t*-score (Church et al., 1991), the six following ASs were evaluated:

1. *MI3* (Daille, 1994), a heuristic modification of *MI*, proposed to reduce its tendency to assign inflated scores to rare words that occur together,

2. *z* (Berry-Rogghe, 1973), the signed square-root of the cell contribution to the Pearson Chi-square for a 2x2 contingency table,

3. *simple-ll* (Evert, 2009), the signed cell contribution to the log-likelihood Chi-square test recommended by Dunning (1993),

4. *Fisher*'s exact test (Pedersen et al., 1996), which corresponds to the probability of observing, under the null hypothesis of independence, at least as many collocations as the number actually observed,

5. Mutual rank ratio (*mrr*, Dean, 2005), a non-parametric measure that has been successful in detecting collocation errors in EFL texts (Futagi et al., 2008),

6. *logDice* (Rychly, 2008), a logarithmic transformation of the Dice coefficient used in the Sketch Engine (Kilgarriff et al., 2014).

In order to extract more information from the distribution of the ASs in each text than the mean or the median, Durrant and Schmitt (2009) and So-masundaran et al. (2015) used a standard procedure in descriptive statistics and automatic information processing known as discretization, binning or quantization (Garcia et al., 2013). It divides a continuous variable into bins and counts the proportion of scores that fall into each bin. In their analyses, the boundaries of the bins were manually and arbitrarily defined. This approach can be used for any AS, but it makes the comparison of the effectiveness of them difficult because a weaker performance may come from a less effective AS or from poorly chosen bin boundaries. To reduce the potential impact of the choice of boundaries, a very simple and completely automatic discretization procedure was used: the Equal Frequency Discretizer, which divides the sorted values into k intervals so that each interval contains approximately the same number of values (Dougherty et al., 1995). It is unsupervised and depends on only one parameter (i.e., the number of bins). In the present study, it was applied separately for each AS, to every bigram present in the learners' texts and consists of two steps:

1. Partitioning the distribution of scores in bins containing the same number of bigrams,

2. Computing for each text the proportion of bigrams whose AS falls into each bin, using as a denominator the total number of bigrams in the text.

3 Experiment

To assess the benefits of relying on collocational features to predict an EFL text's quality, an experiment was conducted. This section describes the corpus used, as well as the procedures for extracting the collocational and baseline features and for scoring the texts.

3.1 Experiment Setup

Dataset: The analyses were conducted on the First Certificate in English (FCE) ESOL examination scripts described in Yannakoudakis et al. (2011, 2012). Extracted from the Cambridge Learner Corpus, this dataset consists of 1238 texts of between 200 and 400 words, to which an overall mark has been assigned. As in Yannakoudakis et al. (2011), the 1141 texts from the year 2000 were used for training, while the 97 texts from the year 2001 were used for testing.

Collocational Features: The global statistical features in Somasundaran et al. (2015) and Bestgen and Granger (2014) were used: the mean, the median, the maximum and the minimum of the ASs, and the proportion of bigrams that are present in the learner text but absent from the reference corpus. Because the best number of bins for discretizing the distributions was not known, the following ones were compared: 3, 5, 8, 10, 15, 20, 25, 33, 50, 75 and 100. To get all these features, each learner text was tokenized and POS-tagged by means of CLAWS7[2] and all bigrams were extracted. Punctuation marks and any sequence of characters that did not correspond to a word interrupt the bigram extraction. Each bigram was then looked up in the 100 million word British National Corpus (BNC[3]) and, if found, assigned its ASs. The collocational features were then computed on the basis of all the different bigrams present in each text (types) to give more weight to their diversity (Durrant and Schmitt, 2009).

Lexical Features: As a benchmark for comparison, the lexical features that were showed to be good predictors of the quality of the texts in this dataset (Yannakoudakis et al., 2011) were chosen. They consist of the frequency of the word unigrams and bigrams. This baseline is particularly relevant because it includes the lexical bigrams that are the basis of the collocational features. These features were extracted as described in Yannakoudakis et al. (2011); the only difference is that they used the RASP tagger and not the CLAWS tagger.

Supervised Learning Approach and Evaluation: As in Yannakoudakis et al. (2011), the automated scoring task was treated as a rank-preference learning problem by means of the SVM-Rank package (Joachims, 2006), which is a much faster version of the SVM-Light package used by Yannakoudakis et al. (2011). The procedure was identical to that described in their study. Since the quality ratings are distributed on a zero to 40 scale, I chose Pearson's correlation coefficient, also used by Yannakoudakis et al. (2011), as the measure of performance.

4 Results

Initial analyses focused on the interest of discretizing the ASs by assessing the benefits obtained

---

[2]http://ucrel.lancs.ac.uk/claws/
[3]http://www.natcorp.ox.ac.uk/corpus/

Nbin	MI	t	MI3	z	simple-ll	fisher	mrr	logDice	All
0	0.57	0.51	0.47	0.49	0.52	**0.62**	0.49	0.47	0.51
3	0.59	0.58	0.53	0.53	0.57	**0.62**	0.53	0.50	0.59
5	0.61	0.64	0.54	0.61	0.63	***0.65***	0.57	*0.51*	0.64
8	0.61	**0.63**	0.54	0.61	0.61	**0.63**	0.58	0.50	0.63
10	0.61	**0.63**	0.53	0.62	**0.63**	**0.63**	0.57	*0.51*	0.64
15	0.61	**0.64**	0.55	0.63	*0.64*	0.63	0.57	0.50	0.64
20	0.61	**0.64**	0.56	0.63	*0.64*	**0.64**	0.58	0.49	0.65
25	0.60	**0.64**	0.56	0.63	0.63	0.63	0.58	0.48	0.64
33	0.61	0.64	*0.57*	***0.65***	*0.64*	0.63	*0.59*	0.50	0.65
50	0.61	***0.65***	*0.57*	0.62	*0.64*	0.63	*0.59*	0.49	0.65
75	*0.62*	0.63	0.56	**0.64**	0.62	0.63	*0.59*	*0.51*	0.65
100	*0.62*	**0.63**	0.54	**0.63**	0.62	**0.63**	*0.59*	0.50	0.65
Mean	0.61	**0.63**	0.55	0.62	0.62	**0.63**	0.57	0.50	0.64

Table 1: Correlations for the collocational features. Note: The global statistical features are always used. The highest value on each line, ignoring the All column, is in bold type. The highest value in each column is italicized. The mean row values were computed for the different numbers of bins, disregarding the 0-bin row.

when these features were added to the global statistical features. Collocational features were then compared to the lexical features and added to them to determine the maximum level of performance that could be achieved.

4.1 Collocational Features

When no discretization procedure was used (the 0 row), *Fisher* was far more effective than the other ASs, followed by *MI*. Adding the discretized features led to far better performances (except for *logDice*), as shown by the *Mean* row. For a small number of bins, *Fisher* remained the best, but for an intermediate number, the best were *t* and *simple-ll*, and for a large number, *z* became competitive. Still, the differences between the best ASs were quite small. From eight bins and beyond, using all the ASs gave the best result, but the gain was relatively small. Regarding the number of bins, at least five seems necessary, but using many more did not harm performance. It is noteworthy that all the correlations reported in table 1 are much larger that the correlation of a baseline system based purely on length ($r = 0.27$).

To determine if the automatic procedure for discretizing the ASs is at least as effective as the bin boundaries manually set by Somasundaran et al. (2015), I used them instead of the automatic bins for the model with eight bins based on *MI*. The correlation obtained was 0.60, a value slightly lower than that reported in Table 1 (0.61).

4.2 Collocational and Baseline Features

The lexical features used alone allowed a 0.68 correlation[4]. These features are thus more effective

than the best combinations of collocational features reported in Table 1, but, as shown in Table 2, adding the collocational features to the lexical ones produces far better performances. Steiner's t-test (Howell, 2008, p. 269-271) for comparing two non-independent correlations showed that collocational features significantly improve the prediction when compared to the baseline (all *ps* <0.005). If *MI* is always one of the best performing ASs, the differences between the ASs are quite low. For all numbers of bins, using all the ASs allows the best performance.

To get an idea of how well the collocational and lexical features perform, the correlations in Table 2 can be compared to the average correlation between the Examiners' scores reported by Yannakoudakis et al. (2011), which give an upper bound of 0.80 while the *All* models with more than three bins obtain a correlation of at least 0.75. Adding collocational features to lexical ones thus reduces by 58% the difference between the lexical features alone and the upper bound. However, the most difficult part of the work is still to be done.

5 Conclusion and Future Work

Following on from Durrant and Schmitt (2009), Somasundaran and Chodorow (2014) and Bestgen and Granger (2014), this study confirms the benefits conferred by collocational features for the automated scoring of EFL texts. It also shows that these features improve a competitive baseline, based among other factors on the bigram frequen-

---

[4]This value is higher by 0.05 than that reported by Yannakoudakis et al. (2011). As I used exactly the same procedure, the difference probably comes from the SVM-Rank/SVM-Light parameters. The SVM-Rank default settings were used except for the squared slacks for the L-norm (i.e., -p 2) because it provided a high performance without having to optimize other parameters such as C.

Nbin	MI	t	MI3	z	simple-ll	fisher	mrr	logDice	All
0	0.70	0.70	0.70	0.70	0.70	**0.71**	0.70	0.70	0.72
3	**0.72**	0.71	0.71	0.71	0.71	0.71	0.71	0.70	0.74
5	**0.72**	0.71	0.71	0.71	0.71	*0.72*	**0.72**	*0.71*	0.76
8	**0.72**	0.71	0.71	0.71	0.71	*0.72*	**0.72**	*0.71*	0.75
10	**0.72**	0.71	0.71	0.71	0.71	*0.72*	**0.72**	*0.71*	0.75
15	**0.72**	*0.72*	*0.72*	0.71	0.71	*0.72*	**0.72**	*0.71*	0.75
20	**0.72**	*0.72*	*0.72*	0.71	0.71	*0.72*	**0.72**	*0.71*	0.76
25	*0.73*	0.72	0.72	0.71	0.71	*0.72*	0.72	0.70	0.75
33	*0.73*	0.72	0.72	0.72	0.71	*0.72*	0.72	0.70	0.75
50	*0.73*	0.72	0.72	0.71	0.72	*0.72*	0.72	0.70	0.76
75	*0.73*	0.71	0.72	0.71	0.71	*0.72*	0.72	0.70	0.75
100	*0.73*	0.72	0.72	0.71	0.71	*0.72*	*0.73*	*0.71*	0.75
Mean	**0.72**	0.71	0.71	0.71	0.71	**0.72**	**0.72**	0.70	0.75

Table 2: Correlations for the collocational and lexical features. See the notes below Table 1.

cies in the texts. As proposed by Somasundaran and Chodorow (2014), binning the AS distributions improves the efficiency and, as proposed by Durrant and Schmitt (2009), considering several ASs also gives extra efficiency. Compared to Bestgen and Granger (2014), the binning allows t to be as effective as the *MI*. This result suggests that it might be interesting to analyse more thoroughly the complex relationship between the AS distributions in a text and its quality.

It must be kept in mind that these observations result from the analysis of a single dataset and replications are more than desirable. It is also necessary to determine whether the collocational features can improve not only the baseline used here, but also a predictive model that includes many other features known for their effectiveness. Further developments are worth mentioning. Unlike Somasundaran et al. (2015), I only used bigrams' collocational features. Whether adding trigrams would further improve the performance is an open question. Trying to answer it requires a thorough study of the association measures for n-grams longer than two words since they have received much less attention (Bestgen, 2014; Gries, 2010). It might also be interesting to evaluate other techniques to discretize the AS distributions, since this study rests on one of the simplest techniques. Further studies are also needed to better understand the impact of the combination of ASs. On the one hand, it is likely that some ASs are partially redundant and that keeping only one might be enough. On the other hand, it would be interesting to determine whether, rather than combining the AS bin proportions independently, it would be better to create the bins on the simultaneous basis of two or more ASs, such as one bin for the bigrams with high *MI* scores and medium t-scores.

Acknowledgments

This work was supported by the Fonds de la Recherche Scientifique - FNRS under Grant J.0025.16. The author is a Research Associate of this institution.

References

Timothy Baldwin and Su N. Kim. 2010. Multiword expressions. In Nitin Indurkhya and Fred J. Damerau, editors, *Handbook of Natural Language Processing*, pages 267–292. CRC Press.

Silvia Bernardini. 2007. Collocations in translated language. combining parallel, comparable and reference corpora. In *Proceedings of the Corpus Linguistics Conference*, pages 1–16.

Godelieve L. M. Berry-Rogghe. 1973. The computation of collocations and their relevance in lexical studies. In Adam J Aitken, Richard W. Bailey, and Neil Hamilton-Smith, editors, *The Computer and Literary Studies*. Edinburgh University Press.

Yves Bestgen and Sylviane Granger. 2014. Quantifying the development of phraseological competence in L2 English writing: An automated approach. *Journal of Second Language Writing*, 26:28–41.

Yves Bestgen and Sylviane Granger. 2015. Tracking L2 writers' phraseological development using collgrams: Evidence from a longitudinal EFL corpus. ICAME 36, Trier, May.

Yves Bestgen. 2014. Extraction automatique de collocations : Peut-on étendre le test exact de Fisher à des séquences de plus de 2 mots? In *Actes de JADT 2014*, pages 79–90.

Martin Chodorow and Claudia Leacock. 2000. An unsupervised method for detecting grammatical errors. In *Proceedings of the Conference of the North American Chapter of the Association of Computational Linguistics (NAACL)*, pages 140–147.

Kenneth Church, William A. Gale, Patrick Hanks, and Donald Hindle. 1991. Using statistics in lexical analysis. In Uri Zernik, editor, *Lexical Acquisition: Using On-line Resources to Build a Lexicon*, pages 115–164. Lawrence Erlbaum.

Paul Deane. 2005. A nonparametric method for extraction of candidate phrasal terms. In *Proceedings of the 43rd Annual Meeting of the Association for Computational Linguistics*, pages 605–613.

James Dougherty, Ron Kohavi, and Mehran Sahami. 1995. Supervised and unsupervised discretization of continuous features. In *Proceedings of 12th International Conference of Machine Learning (ICML)*, pages 194–202.

Ted E. Dunning. 1993. Accurate methods for the statistics of surprise and coincidence. *Computational Linguistics*, 19:61–74.

Philip Durrant and Norbert Schmitt. 2009. To what extent do native and non-native writers make use of collocations? *International Review of Applied Linguistics in Language Teaching*, 47:157–177.

Stefan Evert. 2009. Corpora and collocations. In Anke Lüdeling and Merja Kytö, editors, *Corpus Linguistics. An International Handbook*, pages 1211–1248. Mouton de Gruyter.

Fanny Forsberg. 2010. Using conventional sequences in L2 French. *International Review of Applied Linguistics in Language Teaching*, pages 25–50.

Yoko Futagi, Paul Deane, Martin Chodorow, and Joel Tetreault. 2008. A computational approach to detecting collocation errors in the writing of non-native speakers of English. *Computer Assisted Language Learning*, 21:353–367.

Salvador García, Julian Luengo, José A. Sáez, Victoria López, and Francisco Herrera. 2013. A survey of discretization techniques: Taxonomy and empirical analysis in supervised learning. *IEEE Transactions on Knowledge and Data Engineering*, 25:734–750.

Sylviane Granger and Yves Bestgen. 2014. The use of collocations by intermediate vs. advanced non-native writers: A bigram-based study. *International Review of Applied Linguistics in Language Teaching*, 52:229–252.

Stefan Th. Gries. 2010. Useful statistics for corpus linguistics. In Aquilino Sánchez and Moisés Almela, editors, *A Mosaic of Corpus Linguistics: Selected Approaches*, pages 269–291. Peter Lang, Frankfurt au Main, Germany.

Derrick Higgins, Chaitanya Ramineni, and Klaus Zechner. 2015. Learner corpora and automated scoring. In Sylviane Granger, Gaëtanelle Gilquin, and Fanny Meunier, editors, *Cambridge Handbook of Learner Corpus Research*. Cambridge University Press.

Thorsten Joachims. 2006. Training linear SVMs in linear time. In *Proceedings of the ACM Conference on Knowledge Discovery and Data Mining (KDD)*.

Adam Kilgarriff, Vít Baisa, Jan Bušta, Miloš Jakubíček, Vojtěch Kovář, Jan Michelfeit, Pavel Rychlý, and Vít Suchomel. 2014. The Sketch Engine: ten years on. *Lexicography*, 1(1):7–36.

Tami Levitzky-Aviad and Batia Laufer. 2013. Lexical properties in the writing of foreign language learners over eight years of study: single words and collocations. In Camilla Bardel, Christina Lindqvist, and Batia Laufer, editors, *L2 Vocabulary Acquisition, Knowledge and Use: New Perspectives on Assessment and Corpus Analysis*. Eurosla Monographs Series 2.

Andrew Pawley and Frances H. Syder. 1983. Two puzzles for linguistic theory: nativelike selection and nativelike fluency. In Jack C. Richards and Richard W. Schmidt, editors, *Language and Communication*. Longman.

Pavel Pecina. 2010. Lexical association measures and collocation extraction. *Language Resources & Evaluation*, 44:137–158.

Ted Pedersen, Mehmet Kayaalp, and Rebecca Bruce. 1996. Significant lexical relationships. In *Proceedings of the 13th National Conference on Artificial Intelligence*, pages 455–460.

Pavel Rychlý. 2008. A lexicographer-friendly association score. In *Proceedings of Recent Advances in Slavonic Natural Language Processing*, pages 6–9, Brno. Masarykova Univerzita.

Victor Santos, Marjolijn Verspoo, and John Nerbonne. 2012. Identifying important factors in essay grading using machine learning. In Dina Sagari, Salomi Papadima-Sophocleous, and Sophie Ioannou-Georgiou, editors, *International Experiences in Language Testing and Assessment—Selected Papers in Memory of Pavlos Pavlou*, pages 295–309. Peter Lang, Frankfurt au Main, Germany.

Norbert Schmitt. 2004. *Formulaic sequences: Acquisition, processing and use*. Benjamins.

John Sinclair. 1991. *Corpus, Concordance, Collocation*. Oxford University Press.

Hanna Smiskova, Marjolijn Verspoor, and Wander Lowie. 2012. Conventionalized ways of saying things (CWOSTs) and L2 development. *Dutch Journal of Applied Linguistics*, 1:125–142.

Swapna Somasundaran and Martin Chodorow. 2014. Automated measures of specific vocabulary knowledge from constructed responses (use these words to write a sentence based on this picture). In *Proceedings of the Ninth Workshop on Innovative Use of NLP for Building Educational Applications*, pages 1–11.

Swapna Somasundaran, Chong M. Lee, Martin Chodorow, and Xinhao Wang. 2015. Automated scoring of picture-based story narration. In *Proceedings of the Tenth Workshop on Innovative Use of NLP for Building Educational Applications*, pages 42–48.

Marjolijn Verspoor, Monika S. Schmid, and Xiauyan Xu. 2012. A dynamic usage based perspective on l2 writing. *Journal of Second Language Writing*, pages 239–263.

Jian-Cheng Wu, Yuchia C. Chang, Teruko Mitamura, and Jason S. Chang. 2010. Automatic collocation suggestion in academic writing. In *Proceedings of the Association for Computational Linguistics Conference*, pages 115–119.

Helen Yannakoudakis and Ted Briscoe. 2012. Modeling coherence in ESOL learner texts. In *Proceedings of the 7th Workshop on the Innovative Use of NLP for Building Educational Applications*, pages 33–43.

Helen Yannakoudakis, Ted Briscoe, and Ben Medlock. 2011. A new dataset and method for automatically grading ESOL texts. In *The 49th Annual Meeting of the Association for Computational Linguistics: Human Language Technologies*, pages 180–189.

A study on the production of collocations
by European Portuguese learners

Ângela Costa
INESC-ID
CLUNL
Portugal
angela@l2f.inesc-id.pt

Luísa Coheur
INESC-ID
IST - Universidade de Lisboa
Portugal
luisa.coheur@inesc-id.pt

Teresa Lino
FCSH
CLUNL
Portugal
tlino@fcsh.unl.pt

Abstract

In this paper we present a study on the production of collocations by students of European Portuguese as a foreign language. We start by gathering several corpora written by students, and identify the correct and incorrect collocations. We annotate the latter considering several different aspects, such as the error location, description and explanation. Then, taking these elements into consideration, we compare the performance of students considering their levels of proficiency, their mother tongue and, also, other languages they know. Finally, we correct all the students productions and contribute with a corpus of everyday language collocations that can be helpful in Portuguese classes.

1 Introduction

Collocations are stable and mostly non-idiomatic combinations that fall under the category of multiword expressions. They are usually constituted by two or more words, in which one (the base) determines the other (the collocate) (Hausmann, 2004). For instance, in the collocation *strong coffee*, *coffee* is the base and *strong* is the collocate. Collocations can be seen as pre-fabricated blocks (Corpas Pastor, 1996), available as units on the minds of the speakers of a language, and used in oral and written production in the same way single words are. They are highly frequent in languages, and, thus, assume an important role in the teaching/learning process of a foreign language. However, if most non-native speakers of a given language are able to understand the meaning of a collocation, as these are relatively transparent structures, their production can be challenging, as the relation between their elements is, in most of the cases, arbitrary (Cruse, 2000). As an example, and considering the study of English as a foreign language, there is no way to know *a priori*, that a coffee with too much water is a *weak coffee* and not a **faint coffee* (Mackin, 1978).

In their study concerning the production of multiword expressions by European Portuguese learners, Antunes and Mendes (2015) concluded that collocations are the type of multiword expressions that had the largest number of inaccuracies, independently of the mother tongue. According to the authors, "collocations are particularly difficult for learners of Portuguese L2, because they pose degrees of restrictions that are not easily acquired". Considering that there is little information available in Portuguese dictionaries, compared with resources for English (Antunes and Mendes, 2015), lists of everyday language collocations can be a useful tool for these students. By the same token, documenting their errors when producing collocations, like done by Ramos et al. (2010) and Konecny et al. (2015), can help to identify specific difficulties students may have.

In this paper, we study the collocational performance of students of European Portuguese as a foreign language. We start by gathering a corpus with texts written by Spanish, French, English and German students learning European Portuguese (Section 3). Then (Section 4), we identify their production of collocations, and annotate the incorrect ones with information such as the location of the error, its description and a possible explanation. For the latter cases, we follow an adapted version of the taxonomy suggested in (Ramos et al., 2010). We analyse the attained data (Section 5) and identify the main difficulties. Although most of the results are in line with what can be found in the literature, some are, somehow, unexpected. Our last contribution is a corpus of 549 everyday language collocations, which

Proceedings of the 12th Workshop on Multiword Expressions, pages 91–95,
Berlin, Germany, August 7-12, 2016. ©2016 Association for Computational Linguistics

resulted from correcting the whole set of collocations provided by the students.

2   Related work

As a linguistic phenomenon, collocations have been the subject of numerous studies (Sinclair, 1991; Tutin, 2004; Hausmann, 2004); also, they have proven to be an extremely fruitful thematic of research in language technology (Smadja, 1993; Seretan, 2011; Wehrli, 2014).

Considering the Portuguese language, we detach the work of Leiria (2006), and Antunes and Mendes (2015). The former concerns lexical acquisition by students learning Portuguese as Foreign Language (L2). The author analysed a corpus of written material produced by French, German, Swedish and Chinese students, where she found "privileged co-occurrences" with a certain degree of fixedness, like *velhos amigos* "old friends" or *gastar dinheiro* "spend money", which matches our definition of collocation. However, each one of these elements was evaluated based mostly on the criteria of whether a native speaker would have used it or not (similarly to the work described in (Konecny et al., 2015)), which is different from the evaluation that we will conduct in this work.

Concerning the work of Antunes and Mendes (2015), it focuses on the multiword expressions found on a subset of a learner corpus of Portuguese[1]. The authors identify different types of multiword expressions (including collocations) produced by foreign students, and characterise the errors found according with a taxonomy they propose. In this work, we opted to follow (and extend) the taxonomy proposed by Ramos et al. (2010), as it was specifically tailored to collocations. In fact, having noticed that no theoretically-motivated collocation error tag set was available, and, in many corpora, collocation errors were simply tagged as "lexical errors", the aforementioned authors created a fine-grained three-dimensional typology of collocation errors. The first dimension captures if the error concerns the collocation as a whole or one of its elements (error location); the second dimension captures the language-oriented error analysis (error description); the third dimension exemplifies the interpretative error analysis (error explanation). Ramos and her team annotated the collocational errors on a learner corpus composed by texts produced by foreign students of Spanish that had English as their mother tongue. In this paper, we annotate erroneous productions of Portuguese collocations by using the lexical level of this taxonomy, to which we felt the need to add some categories.

3   Corpora

We gathered a corpus with students productions of collocations in European Portuguese, by considering four corpora, namely: a) *Corpus de Produções Escritas de Aprendentes de PL2 from Centro de Estudos de Linguística Geral e Aplicada* (CELGA) (Pereira, 2014); b) *Recolha de Dados de Aprendizagem de Português Língua Estrangeira* collected by Centro de Linguística da Universidade de Lisboa (CLUL)[2]; c) two other corpora collected by the authors while teaching at Ciberescola da Língua Portuguesa[3], and at Faculdade de Ciências Sociais e Humanas (FCSH)[4].

CELGA and FCSH corpus were collected in the classroom, and the Ciberescola corpus in online classes. Data from CLUL was collected in Portuguese courses given in 18 universities from different countries (Austria, Bulgaria, South Korea, Spain, USA, etc.). Students that participated in CELGA and CLUL corpus were presented with the same stimuli, divided in three main topics: the individual, the society and the environment. Students from FCSH and Ciberescola had more diversified topics, such as description of their house, their last holidays, their city or their hobbies, among others. From these corpora we selected all texts from students that had Spanish, French, English and German as their native language, and organize them in three levels: Level 1 for A1 and A2 students, Level 2 for B1 and B2 students, and Level 3 for C1 and C2 students.

4   Annotation process

We manually annotated all the correct and incorrect productions of collocations in the collected corpus. We followed Tutin and Grossman (2002) definition of collocation: a "privileged lexical co-occurrence of two (or more) linguistic elements that together establish a syntactic relationship".

---

[1]`http://www.clul.ul.pt/research-teams/`
`547`

[2]`http://www.clul.ul.pt/pt/recursos/`
`314-corpora-of-ple`
[3]`http://www.ciberescola.com/`
[4]`http://www.fcsh.unl.pt/clcp/`

Each incorrect collocation was associated with its correct production and the respective syntactic form, as well as with information concerning the student mother tongue and other foreign languages that the student may know. Then, we annotated the incorrect collocations considering: a) its location (base, collocate, or whole collocation); b) its description and c) its explanation, based on an adapted version of the lexical level of Ramos et al. (2010) taxonomy, as previously mentioned.

In what concerns the description of the error, two new error types were added: preposition and better choice. The first is used when the learner selects the wrong preposition, adds or elides it[5] (*apanhar do avião* for *apanhar o avião* ("take the plane")). Better choice is used when the collocation is not wrong, but there is a better choice (*cozinhar uma receita* for *fazer uma receita* ("make a recipe")). The remaining types are a subset of the ones described in (Ramos et al., 2010): a) Substitution captures the incorrect replacement of a collocate or a base by another existing word (*cabelos vermelhos* for *cabelos ruivos* ("red hair")); b) Creation is used when a student creates a word that does not exist, in this case, in the Portuguese lexicon, which is the case of the word *tiempo* in *passar o tiempo* for *passar tempo* ("spend time"); c) Synthesis is applied when a language unit is used instead of a collocation (*descripção* for *fazer uma descrição* ("to make a description")); d) Analysis covers the case in which the learner creates a new expression with the structure of a collocation instead of using a single word (*tomei o almoço* for *almoçar* ("to have lunch")); e) Different sense is used when the learner uses a correct collocation, but with a different meaning from the intended one (*ter uma escolha* for *fazer uma escolha* ("make a choice")).

Regarding the explanation of the error, we add an extra type to Ramos' taxonomy, in order to cover the situation in which the student mixes European and Brazilian Portuguese (*fazer regime* for *fazer dieta* ("to be on a diet")). The remaining types are the following ones: a) Importation deals with the case in which a collocation is created from an expression in another language known by the student (*fazia a merenda* for *lanchar* ("have a snack")), which shows an importation from Italian ("fare merenda"); b) Extension is used when the learner extends the meaning of an existing word in Portuguese (*faz chuva* for *chover* ("to rain")). A more specific case of this type, that we also use in this work is extension – spelling, which should be used when spelling is influenced by the pronunciation of the misspelled word, as in *loungar um carro* for *alugar um carro* ("rent a car"); c) Erroneous derivation addresses the case when the leaner produces an inexistent form in L2 as a result of a process of erroneous derivation, in many cases by analogy with another form in L2 (*modelos teoréticos* for *modelos teóricos* ("theoretical models')')); d) Overgeneralization handles the scenario in which the learner selects a vaguer or more generic word than required (*fazer sms* for *mandar um sms* ("send a message")); e) Erroneous choice is used when the student selects a wrong word without a clear reason and without intervention of the L1 or another L2 (*memória de pula* for *memória de peixe* ("short memory")).

5 Data analysis

Studies like the one presented by Nesselhauf (2005) state that: a) a higher proficiency level in a language is usually characterised by a higher rate in the use of collocations; b) this quantitative gain does not mean a qualitative improvement. Our results, shown in Table 1, do not corroborate the first statement as students from higher levels did not produce collocations in a higher rate. However, the second statement is in line with our results, as only for English students collocational knowledge seems to improve with higher levels of proficiency (that is, considering the total number of produced collocations, the percentage of incorrect collocations decreases with the level).

In our study, 16.53% of the errors concern the base, 74.25% the collocate, and 9.21% the whole collocation (this tendency is observed in all levels and all mother tongues), which is in accordance with Ramos et al. (2010).

Among the deviant collocations, the syntactic form most used by the students was V + N. In fact, that is the most studied sequence in learner corpus research, as students have difficulties selecting the correct verb not only inside a collocation, but also in free sequences of V + N. In Nesselhauf (2005) study with German students of English, one third of the V + N combinations analysed were not acceptable, mainly due to a wrong choice of the verb, which is also in accordance with what we have ob-

---

[5]This type of mistake could have been considered a subtype of Substitution, but in that case additions and elisions would not have been taken into account.

L1	l	Txt	Wds	Corr	Incorr
es	1	148	18002	495/83%	98/17%
	2	92	19615	350/84%	66/16%
	3	7	1354	30/83%	6/17%
fr	1	24	2992	76/87%	11/13%
	2	29	8117	135/93%	10/7%
	3	3	896	12/86%	2/14%
en	1	29	4371	49/69%	22/31%
	2	57	14774	236/82%	52/18%
	3	10	2079	26/90%	3/10%
de	1	64	8174	167/83%	34/17%
	2	73	20304	353/84%	65/16%
	3	1	523	10/100%	0/0%

Table 1: Texts, words, correct (Corr) and incorrect (Incorr) collocations and the corresponding percentage, by L1 and level (l).

L1	l	1	2	3
es	1	26/27%	25/26%	15/15%
	2	25/38%	14/21%	2/3%
	3	1/17%	1/17%	0/0%
fr	1	4/36%	3/27%	0/0%
	2	3/30%	3/30%	0/0%
	3	2/1%	0/0%	0/0%
en	1	8/36%	11/50%	0/0%
	2	16/31%	10/19%	2/4%
	3	3/100%	0/0%	0/0%
de	1	19/56%	9/26%	2/6%
	2	25/38%	9/14%	1/2%
	3	0/0%	0/0%	0/0%

Table 2: Substitutions (1), creations (2), analysis (3) by L1 and level (l).

L1	l	4	5	6	7
es	1	1/1%	11/11%	10/10%	10/10%
	2	3/5%	10/15%	3/5%	9/14%
	3	1/17%	1/17%	0/0%	2/33%
fr	1	0/0%	2/18%	2/18%	0/0%
	2	0/0%	3/30%	0/0%	1/10%
	3	0/0%	0/0%	0/0%	0/0%
en	1	0/0%	1/5%	2/9%	0/0%
	2	2/4%	6/12%	7/13%	9/17%
	3	0/0%	0/0%	0/0%	0/0%
de	1	2/6%	0/0%	2/6%	0/0%
	2	3/5%	11/17%	10/15%	6/9%
	3	0/0%	0/0%	0/0%	0/0%

Table 3: Synthesis (4), different sense (5), preposition (7) and better choice (8) by L1 and level (l).

served. Collocations that include adjectives and adverbs seem to be less frequent. A possible explanation is that learners master nouns and verbs before they get to master adjectives and adverbs whose presence augments at higher proficiency levels (Palapanidi and Llach, 2014).

In what concerns description and explanation of the errors, on Table 2 and 3, substitution was the most common error in all the three levels and for all mother tongues (*música forte* for *música alta* ("loud music") or *cabello largo* for *cabelo comprido* ("long hair")). Creation is the second most common error type also for the three levels and four languages. In the following example, *coger um táxi* for *apanhar um táxi* ("take a taxi"), the word *coger* was created, as it does not exist in Portuguese.

In addition, we verify that Level 1 students mostly use importation from L1 or another L2 (Table 4). In Level 2, importation and extension have similar proportions, and represent 40% of the errors. Level 3 errors have their origin mostly in extensions. This may show that lower level students tend to rely more on other languages, while higher level students use more sophisticated mechanisms, like extending the meaning of a known word. An example is the extension of the delexical verb *fazer* in *fazer uma photo* for *tirar uma foto* ("take a picture"). In line with Leiria (2006), who observed that, regarding combinations of words, the majority of the students use their mother tongue when they are lacking the correct expression, we also conclude that students use their mother tongue as their first support, being the Spanish students the ones that do it the most (46.47%), and English students the ones that do it the least (25.97%). Spanish and French students also use Italian and English, and German students rely in Spanish. Other than German, no other students use German as support language. From this we can conclude that the closest the students native language is to Portuguese, more the language will be used as support, and students clearly are aware of this distance.

6 Conclusions and future work

In this paper we presented a study on the production of collocations by foreign students of European Portuguese. This corpus was annotated, analysed and then corrected, resulting in a corpus of

L1	l	fr	es	it	en	de
es	1	0	52	1	1	0
	2	1	27	6	1	0
	3	0	0	0	2	0
fr	1	5	1	1	0	0
	2	1	0	1	0	0
	3	0	0	0	0	0
en	1	2	11	0	4	0
	2	0	7	0	16	0
	3	0	0	0	0	0
de	1	0	4	0	2	2
	2	0	3	0	2	14
	3	0	0	0	0	0

Table 4: Collocations imported by L1 and level (l).

colocations. As future work, we want to enlarge our corpus, especially with Level 3 students, but also with texts produced by students with other native languages, like Italian. We also intend to study the production of collocations by native speakers of Portuguese. Finally, we want to ask a second annotator to use the same error categories so that we are able to calculate an inter-annotator agreement.

Acknowledgments

This work was partially supported by national funds through FCT - Fundação para a Ciência e a Tecnologia, under project UID/CEC/50021/2013 and under project LAW-TRAIN with reference H2020-EU.3.7. – 653587. Ângela Costa is supported by a PhD fellowship from FCT (SFRH/BD/85737/2012).

References

Sandra Antunes and Amália Mendes. 2015. Portuguese multiword expressions: Data from a learner corpus. In *Third Learner Corpus Research Conference*, Radboud University Nijmegen, September.

Gloria Corpas Pastor. 1996. *Manual de fraseología española*. Biblioteca Románica Hispánica, Madrid.

David Alan Cruse. 2000. *Meaning in Language. An Introduction to Semantics and Pragmatics*. Oxford: Oxford University Press.

Franz Josef Hausmann. 2004. Was sind eigentlich kollokationen? In Kathrin (Hrsg.) Steyer, editor, *Wortverbindungen ? mehr oder weniger fest.*, pages 309–334. Institut fr Deutsche Sprache, Berlin/New York.

Christine Konecny, Erica Autelli, and Andrea Abel. 2015. Identification, classification and analysis of phrasemes in an l2 learner corpus of italian. In Gloria Corpas Pastor, Miriam Buendía Castro, and Rut Gutiérrez Florido, editors, *Europhras2015: Computerised and Corpus-based Approaches to Phraseology: Monolingual and Multilingual Perspectives*, Malaga, Spain, july. EUROPHRAS.

Isabel Leiria. 2006. *Léxico, Aquisição e Ensino do Português Europeu língua não materna*. Fundação Calouste Gulbenkian/ Fundação para a Ciência e a Tecnologia, Lisboa.

Ronald Mackin. 1978. On collocations. words shall be known by the company they keep. In Peter (ed.) Strevens, editor, *In Honour of A. S. Hornby.*, pages 149–165. Oxford University Press, Oxford.

Nadja Nesselhauf. 2005. *Collocations in a Learner Corpus*. Amsterdam and Philadelphia: Benjamins.

Kiriakí Palapanidi and María Pilar Agustín Llach. 2014. Can lexical errors inform about word class acquisition in fl?: evidence from greek learners of spanish as a foreign language. *Revista de Lingüística y Lenguas Aplicadas*, 9(1):67–78.

Isabel Pereira. 2014. Ensino de português língua estrangeira e investigação em pl2 na fluc. In Graça Rio-Torto (ed), editor, *90 Anos de Ensino de Língua e Cultura Portuguesas para Estrangeiros na Faculdade de Letras da Universidade de Coimbra*, pages 39–47. Imprensa da Universidade de Coimbra, Coimbra.

Margarita Alonso Ramos, Leo Wanner, Orsolya Vincze, Gerard Casamayor del Bosque, Nancy Vzquez Veiga, Estela Mosqueira Surez, and Sabela Prieto Gonzlez. 2010. Towards a motivated annotation schema of collocation errors in learner corpora. In Nicoletta Calzolari (Conference Chair), Khalid Choukri, Bente Maegaard, Joseph Mariani, Jan Odijk, Stelios Piperidis, Mike Rosner, and Daniel Tapias, editors, *Proceedings of the Seventh International Conference on Language Resources and Evaluation (LREC'10)*, Valletta, Malta, may. European Language Resources Association (ELRA).

Agnès Tutin and Francis Grossmann. 2002. Collocations régulières et irrégulières: esquisse de typologie du phénomène collocatif. *Revue française de linguistique appliquée*, 7(1):7–25.

Extraction and Recognition of Polish Multiword Expressions using Wikipedia and Finite-State Automata

Paweł Chrząszcz
Computational Linguistics Department, Jagiellonian University
Gołębia 24, 31-007 Kraków, Poland
p.chrzaszcz@uj.edu.pl

Abstract

Linguistic resources for Polish are often missing multiword expressions (MWEs) – idioms, compound nouns and other expressions which have their own distinct meaning as a whole. This paper describes an effort to extract and recognize nominal MWEs in Polish text using Wikipedia, inflection dictionaries and finite-state automata. Wikipedia is used as a lexicon of MWEs and as a corpus annotated with links to articles. Incoming links for each article are used to determine the inflection pattern of the headword – this approach helps eliminate invalid inflected forms. The goal is to recognize known MWEs as well as to find more expressions sharing similar grammatical structure and occurring in similar context.

1 Introduction

Natural language processing often involves feature extraction from text. Extracted features include statistical measures and morphosyntatic tags – the latter are especially important for inflecting languages like Polish. For example, analyzing the word "psem" in the sentence "Wyszedłem z psem na spacer" (*I went for a walk with my dog*) results in recognition of the lemma "pies" (*dog*) and grammatical features: *masculine animate non-personal noun, instrumental case*. To obtain such information, one could use the Polish Inflection Dictionary SFJP (Lubaszewski et al., 2001) with the CLP library (Gajęcki, 2009), Morfeusz (Woliński, 2006) or Morfologik[1]. For recognition of rare words and

feature disambiguation these tools can be augmented with statistical taggers using e.g. SVM, HMM or CRF classifiers. Their current accuracy for Polish reaches 90% (Waszczuk, 2012; Pohl and Ziółko, 2013).

Syntactic features are often insufficient. For example, when searching for sentences about animals, we would not find the sentence "Wyszedłem z psem na spacer" (*I went for a walk with my dog*) as the relation between the words *animal* and *dog* is semantic. Processing text semantics is a difficult task, so we often resort to manually crafted taxonomies based on paradigmatic relations like synonymy and hyponymy. Examples of such resources include WordNet (Fellbaum, 1998) and ontologies like CYC (Matuszek et al., 2006). They usually lack syntagmatic relations, which depend on the semantic roles in the particular utterance – this issue has been addressed in projects like FrameNet (Ruppenhofer et al., 2006). Unfortunately most of such resources are incomplete for English and simply not available for Polish[2].

The resources mentioned above are missing multiword expressions (MWE) which consist of multiple tokens that have their own, distinct meaning, e.g. terms ("tlenek węgla" – *carbon oxide*), idioms ("panna młoda" – *bride*), proper names ("Polski Związek Wędkarski" – *Polish Fishing Association*, "Lech Wałęsa"). Their own meaning, which cannot be inferred from their constituents, is the root cause for including them in syntactic and semantic resources for Polish. Their syntactic features can be extracted from their occurrences in corpora – their inflected forms may be used to build inflection patterns. Semantic features are more difficult

---

[1] Stemming library including precompiled dictionaries, https://github.com/morfologik/morfologik-stemming

[2] Except WordNet, for which there is Polish equivalent (Maziarz et al., 2012).

Proceedings of the 12th Workshop on Multiword Expressions, pages 96–106,
Berlin, Germany, August 7-12, 2016. ©2016 Association for Computational Linguistics

to extract – one could start with assigning simple semantic labels to Wikipedia headwords, like "city" for "Bielsko-Biała" (Chrząszcz, 2012).

2 Problem analysis

Simplest methods for MWE recognition use statistical measures and yield rather poor results (Ramisch et al., 2008; Zhang et al., 2006; Pecina, 2008; Ramisch et al., 2010). To increase result quality, MWE lexicons and tagged corpora are needed (Constant and Sigogne, 2011; Constant et al., 2012). The main issue with Polish is the lack of such resources – the main motivation for this work is to fill in this gap. The work is exploratory as there are no previous attempts to solve the general problem of recognition and extraction of MWEs from Polish text. One of the main assumptions of this work is to avoid the need to create lexical resources or rules by hand and use automatic methods instead – manual refinements or other improvements including e.g. supervised learning could be applied later. The results of this work should become the baseline for more advanced solutions in the future as well as provide linguistic resources (dictionaries) with MWEs.

Semantic resources such as WordNet can often be replaced with Wikipedia – although its content often lacks the quality and formal structure provided by ontologies and WordNet, its large and diverse data collection seems enough to make up for these issues. Wikipedia content can be used in many ways, e.g. to extract words and MWEs (from page titles), semantic labels describing meaning (from article content), semantic relations between concepts (from redirections, links and categories) and as an annotated corpus to train statistical algorithms. It has been successfully used for named entity (NE) recognition (NER), e.g. the category of the entity can be inferred from the definition itself (Kazama and Torisawa, 2007) and links between articles can be considered tags marking NE occurrences in text (Mihalcea and Csomai, 2007; Nothman et al., 2009). There is also some evidence that e.g. semantic relatedness for word pairs can be computed more accurately using Wikipedia than with WordNet or other resources (Gabrilovich and Markovitch, 2007). MWE recognition and extraction using Wikipedia is less common, but there are some attempts of classifying Wikipedia head-

words using e.g. manual rules (Bekavac and Tadic, 2008) or cross-lingual correspondence asymmetries in interwiki links (Attia et al., 2010). Vincze et al. tagged 50 articles of the English Wikipedia to create a corpus with marked MWE occurrences and used a CRF classifier to recognize MWEs and NEs in text with F-measure (F_1) of 63% (Vincze et al., 2011). These examples are enough to let us consider Wikipedia as the primary linguistic resource for MWE recognition and extraction. Together with an inflection dictionary it can be used to extract Polish MWEs using various methods. This work focuses on design and implementation of such methods. However, the first step is to formulate the definition of a Polish MWE that would narrow down the scope of the problem.

3 Definition of a Nominal MWE

The most widely used definition of an MWE is the one by Sag et al.: "idiosyncratic interpretations that cross word boundaries (or spaces)" (Sag et al., 2002). The authors distinguish four different categories of MWEs for which we could find Polish equivalents:

1. Fixed expressions – they have a fixed meaning and structure and are uninflected, e.g.: "ad hoc", "mimo wszystko" (*regardless*), "ani mru-mru" (*not a dicky bird*).

2. Semi-fixed expressions – they are mostly nominal expressions that have a fixed meaning and are inflected. Examples include "panna młoda" (*bride*, literally: *young maiden*), "biały kruk" (*rarity*, literally: *white crow*). Verbal idioms like "mówić trzy po trzy" (*to speak nonsense*) as well as proper names also belong to this category.

3. Syntactically-flexible expressions – they also have a fixed meaning, but their syntactic structure is loose, allowing changes like inserting new tokens or changing their order. They are often verbal templates that can be filled with nouns to make complete sentences, e.g. "działać jak płachta na byka" (*to irritate sb.*, literally *to be like a red rag to a bull*), "gotów na czyjeś każde skinienie" (*to be at one's beck and call*).

4. Institutionalized phrases – their meaning and syntactic structure can be inferred from the in-

Table 1: Examples of nominal MWEs that are the concern of this research. Inflected tokens are <u>underlined</u>.

Category	Examples
Personal names	<u>Józef Piłsudski</u>, <u>Szymon</u> z Wilkowa (*Simon from Wilków*)
Other proper names	<u>Lazurowa Grota</u> (*Azure Cave*), <u>Polski Związek Wędkarski</u> (*Polish Fishing Association*)
Expressions including names	<u>rzeka</u> Carron (*River Carron*), <u>jezioro</u> Michigan (*Lake Michigan*), <u>premier</u> Polski (*Prime Minister of Poland*)
Common words, semantically non-decomposable	<u>panna młoda</u> (*bride*), <u>świnka morska</u> (*guinea pig*), <u>czarna dziura</u> (*black hole*)
Common words, semantically partially decomposable	<u>chlorek</u> sodu (*sodium chloride*), <u>baza wojskowa</u> (*military base*), <u>lampa naftowa</u> (*kerosene lamp*), <u>zaimek względny</u> (*relative pronoun*)

dividual tokens. The complete expression can be considered an MWE only because of its frequent use. Examples include "czyste powietrze" (*clean air*), "dookoła świata" (*around the world*), "ciężka praca" (*hard labour*).

A decision was made to choose only the **second** category from the list above, further limited to the **nominal** expressions. The main motivation for these restrictions is that this category is the most well-defined one and vast majority of MWEs used in Polish text are nominal. What is more, this limitation helps avoid issues with classifying the word as an MWE (Pecina, 2008) as well as non-continuous expressions (Graliński et al., 2010; Kurc et al., 2012). As a consequence, Polish multiword expressions can be defined in this paper as inflected nominal expressions that have a fixed meaning which is not fully decomposable and have a well-defined, strict inflection pattern. An MWE is thus a sequence of tokens (words, numbers and punctuation marks), which fall into two main categories:

- **Inflected tokens** build the main part of the MWE. They can be nouns, adjectives, numerals or adjectival participles. Their case and number have to agree with the corresponding

features of the whole expression. In the base form all inflected tokens are nominative and singular (except *pluralia tantum*). Inflected tokens need not have the same gender, e.g. "kobieta kot" (*cat-woman*), but they cannot change gender through inflection.

- **Uninflected tokens** are all the remaining tokens that remain fixed when the whole expression is inflected, e.g. words, numbers, punctuation marks or other segments (e.g. "K2").

Examples of such MWEs are presented in tab. 1.

4   A system for MWE processing

After defining Polish nominal MWEs, the next goal was to develop a system for automatic extraction and recognition of such expressions. The architecture of the implemented system is shown in fig. 1. The first step is the extraction of data from Polish Wikipedia[3]. To do this, Wikimedia dumps[4] were used. Extracted data included article content, redirections, links between pages, templates and page categories. The Wiktionary[5] was also considered

---

[3] http://pl.wikipedia.org
[4] http://dumps.wikimedia.org
[5] http://pl.wiktionary.org

as a potential data source, but it turned out that the number of MWEs it contained was very low – only 1118 (Wikipedia dump contained about 973 thousand MWEs).

It was decided that all the extracted MWEs should contain at least one inflected token that would be recognized by Polish dictionaries. The main morphosyntactic resource used for token recognition and grammatical feature extraction was the Polish Inflection Dictionary SFJP (Lubaszewski et al., 2001) with the CLP library. Its content was extended with other Polish resources: Morfeusz (Woliński, 2006) and Morfologik. SFJP is a dictionary where each entry has its unique identifier and a vector of forms while the latter two dictionaries use a completely different data format (morphosyntactic tags), so the data needed to be merged using a new format – the resulting dictionary was called CLPM. The content of this dictionary was stored using LMDB[6] – a database optimized for the lowest possible read time. The following example presents the result (**dictionary tag**) returned for the token "wola" found in text:

$$\{(\texttt{ADA-wola}, \{1\}),$$
$$(\texttt{AEA-wole}, \{2, 8, 11, 14\}),$$
$$(\texttt{CC-woli}, \{15, 21\})\}$$

The result is ambiguous. There are three possible recognized lexemes:

- `ADA-wola` – feminine noun "wola" (*will*), singular nominative (1),
- `AEA-wole` – neuter noun "wole" (*craw*), singular genitive (2) or plural: nominative, accusative or vocative (8, 11, 14),
- `CC-woli` – adjective "woli" (*bovine*), plural feminine, nominative or vocative (15, 21).

These ambiguities could be limited by using statistical or rule-based taggers or parsers, but this would introduce a significant error rate – approximately 10% for Polish (Pohl and Ziółko, 2013). It is worth noting that the dictionary tag format presented above is less verbose and repetitive than the morphosyntactic tag format used by Morfeusz and Morfologik. It can also distinguish between fixed and inflected grammatical categories. The main downside is that it is slightly less human-readable.

[6]Symas Lightning Memory-Mapped Database, `http://symas.com/mdb`

4.1 DM Method

DM (Dictionary Matching) is the first proposed method that uses the set of Wikipedia headwords as a lexicon of MWEs. It can be considered both a baseline with which better algorithms could be compared and a building block for compound methods. The main issue with using such a lexicon is that we have no knowledge of the inflection pattern of the headwords – tokens can be inflected or not, have ambiguous form etc. For each headword we create a **dictionary pattern** that includes all the possible variants for each token. For example, while processing the headword "Droga wojewódzka nr 485" (*Provincial road no. 485*) several ambiguities are encountered:

- The token "Droga" (*Road*) can be capitalized or not as all Wikipedia headwords are capitalized and the token itself is a common word.

- The token "Droga" (*Road*) can be inflected or not. Similarly, the token "wojewódzka" (*provincial*) can be inflected or not. The only thing we know is that at least one of these tokens has to be inflected for the expression to be a nominal MWE.

- The token "Droga" (*Road*) can actually also be a feminine adjective meaning *expensive*.

A simple textual format was used to store all possible ambiguous variants for each token (fig. 1, transition 1a). As there could be multiple ambiguities for a single sequence of input tokens and the number of possible variants grows exponentially with the number of ambiguities, it was decided that instead of a flat lexicon with all possible forms, a finite state machine would be used (fig. 1, transition 1b). As the machine outputs the recognized dictionary patterns in each state, it can be defined formally as a **Moore machine**. For this approach to work in case of continuous text, a separate machine has to be started for each token – each instance thus recognizes all possible MWEs starting at that token.

When a sequence of input tokens successfully matches a pattern, the expression is stored in a database with its lemma and disambiguated syntactic features. As an example let us consider the sentence "Rozpoczął się remont drogi wojewódzkiej nr 485." (*Renovation of the provincial road no. 485*

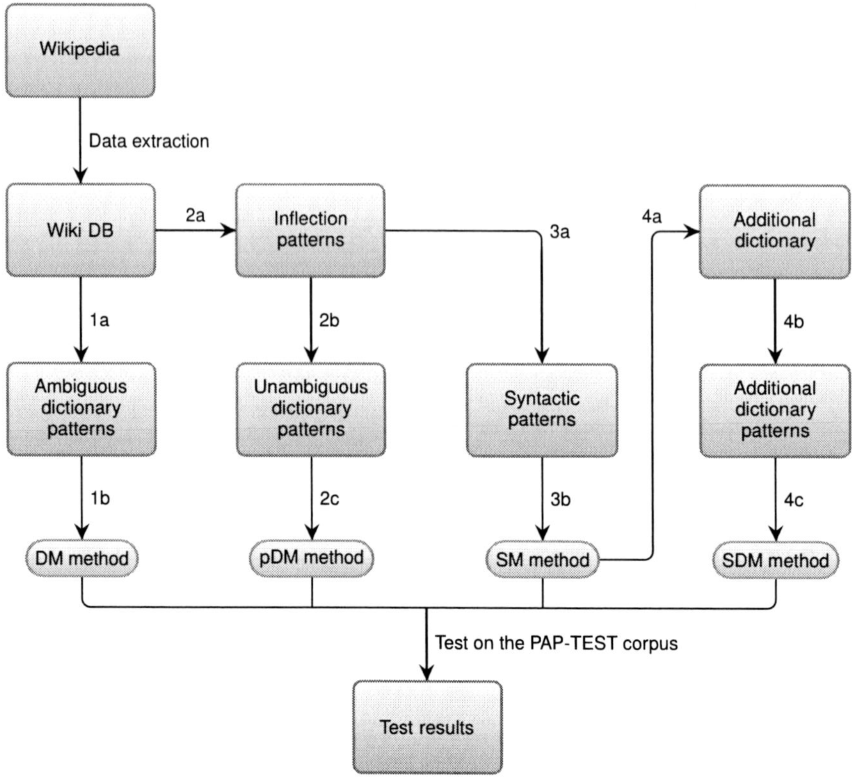

Figure 1: Architecture of the Polish MWE recognition and extraction system.

has started). The sequence "drogi wojewódzkiej nr 485" matches the pattern described above and the whole expression is in the genitive case[7]. The first word is also lowercased. This allows us to not only recognize the MWE, but also disambiguate the pattern and store the disambiguated version in a dictionary of extracted MWEs. Of course this is not always possible – for example the sentence "Droga wojewódzka nr 485 rozpoczyna się w Gdańsku." (*Provincial road no. 485 starts in Gdańsk*) does not allow such disambiguation. Multiple patterns can overlap and the algorithm offers a few different strategies of choosing the best non-contradictory subset of such patterns.

4.2 pDM method

After analysis of the DM method performance it became obvious that there was a need for prior disambiguation of the dictionary patterns. The first

---

attempt to solve this was to use a heuristic disambiguation, but it was limited by the simple finite-state logic it used. To make the method open and not limited by any handcrafted rules, a new approach was chosen. For a given article, it uses incoming links to learn the **inflection pattern** of the headword (fig. 1, transition 2a). For example, the link "czarnej dziury" (genitive case) leads to the headword "Czarna dziura" (*black hole*). This allows us to identify the inflected tokens and determine if the first token is lowercased. For entries that have little or no incoming links, we could either use the original DM method or skip them completely. Another issue is poor quality of the links – some of them are mislabeled, contain incorrect inflected forms or differ from the entry (e.g. are abbreviated or contain additional tokens). This issue is the main reason for designing a quite complex algorithm that determines the inflection pattern for a given Wikipedia headword in the following steps:

1. A statistics of the incoming links is created.

---

[7]Although individual tokens have ambiguous grammatical form, matching them against the dictionary pattern allows to disambiguate it.

Table 2: Elements of the syntactic pattern with context for the link "centralnej **czarnej dziury**."

Pattern element	Content	Description
left context	cc16,cc17,cc20	The label 'cc' means 'adjective' (as the word "centralnej" (*central*) is an adjective), while the numbers 16, 17 and 20 denote the possible cases (genitive, dative or locative) together with the feminine gender.
expression	***cc15 *ad1**	The MWE "czarna dziura" (*black hole*) consists of two inflected tokens, marked with asterisks. The first one is a feminine singular (form number 15) adjective ('cc' label) while the second one is a nominative singular (form number 1) feminine noun ('ad' label). Note: this is the pattern of the MWE in its **base** form.
right context	_p	The full stop following the expression is a punctuation mark ('p' label) without a preceding space ('_' prefix).
grammatical form	{2}	The MWE occurs in the singular genitive form.

2. For each link in the statistics all the possible inflection patterns are generated.

3. An attempt is made to determine if the first token should be capitalized.

4. The largest set of links that have non-contradictory inflection patterns is found.

5. The inflection pattern for the discovered set is saved to the database.

For the entries for which inflection patterns were successfully determined, new unambiguous dictionary patterns are created. They are then used to construct a Moore machine like for the DM method (fig. 1, transitions 2b and 2c). This variant is called **pDM**.

4.3 SM method

The methods of MWE extraction described so far focus on recognition of the Wikipedia entries and extract some new syntactic information. To overcome this limitation, we need to introduce rules or patterns that would allow extraction of new, unknown expressions. Such patterns and rules are often handcrafted (Bekavac and Tadic, 2008; Woźniak, 2011; Buczyński and Przepiórkowski, 2009; Piskorski et al., 2004; Ramisch et al., 2010). However, it turns out that a lot can be achieved using only the existing inflection patterns that we have already created for the pDM method – we could use

them to extract new MWEs that have similar grammatical structure. For example, expressions such as "tlenek węgla" (*carbon oxide*), "siarczan miedzi" (*copper sulfate*) or "wodorotlenek sodu" (*sodium hydroxide*) consist of an inflected masculine nominative noun followed by an uninflected genitive noun. Moreover, the pattern can include the context in which such expressions occur[8], e.g. the mentioned MWEs occur in similar expressions like "...reakcja **siarczanu miedzi** z ..." (...*reaction of copper sulfate with* ...). This observation was the motivation to create a new algorithm that would use the inflection patterns and contexts extracted from links to create **syntactic patterns** describing the syntactic structure of the MWEs as well as the contexts in which they occurred (fig. 1, transition 3a). Different levels of pattern granularity were examined and the final decision was to store the following information:

- For each token of the expression: part of speech, inflection flag (inflected/uninflected), grammatical number and gender for inflected tokens and the case for uninflected ones.

- The context is limited to one token before and after the MWE. The information stored for each token of the context includes token type (word, number, punctuation mark), part

---

[8]Farahmand and Martins also noticed and utilized this fact (Farahmand and Martins, 2014).

Table 3: Examples of syntactic patterns with context created for a few MWEs. There are two unique pattern identifiers: *cpid* identifies the pattern with its context while *pid* identifies the pattern without the context. Form statistics consists of pairs (F, N) where F is a set of grammatical forms in the CLPM format (it has more than one element if the form is ambiguous) and N is the number of occurrences of the MWEs with form set F. A vertical line "|" indicates a sentence boundary while "g" indicates a preposition. The last MWE is a *plurale tantum*.

MWE	*cpid*	*pid*	Pattern with context	Form statistics
ślad macierzy	1	1	`|*ac1 ad2,ad3,ad6,ad7,ad9 cc37`	$(\{1,4\}, 1)$
cząstka elementarna	2	2	`ac1,ac4 *ad1 *cc15 g`	$(\{2,3,6\}, 3), (\{9\}, 8)$
łódź podwodna	2	2	`ac1,ac4 *ad1 *cc15 g`	$(\{9\}, 1)$
łódź podwodna	3	2	`ac1,ac4,ad9 *ad1 *cc15 g`	$(\{9\}, 7)$
wojny syryjskie	4	3	`ac1,ac4 *ad8 *cc36 g`	$(\{9\}, 1)$

of speech, case and for pronouns – the word itself.

For example, the link "centralnej **czarnej dziury**." would result in the pattern `cc16,cc17,cc20 *cc15 *ad1_p`. This example is shown in detail in table 2.

The patterns are saved with their grammatical forms (case and number) in which they occurred in text – this results in a large database of pattern statistics. The next step is to create an automaton similar to the one used for the DM and pDM methods (fig. 1, transition 3b), which is used to recognize expressions matching the patterns and to extract their syntactic features. The resulting method is called **SM** (*Syntactic Matching*). Contrary to pDM, its results are highly ambiguous as each expression could match multiple patterns and yield multiple overlapping results. Choosing the right one requires introducing a function that would assign a quality measure to each result. We decided to use a quantitative measure rs (result score) which sums the numbers of occurrences of the recognized patterns in given forms in the original set of Wikipedia links.

Example. Let us consider the following Wikipedia headwords: "Ślad macierzy" (*matrix trace*), "Cząstka elementarna" (*elementary particle*), "Łódź podwodna" (*submarine*) and "Wojny syryjskie" (*Syrian Wars*). Let us also limit the occurrences of these MWEs to the ones listed in table 3. The table shows that three patterns are created. The second pattern has two different context patterns, hence the four different values of *cpid*. It is also worth noting that the set of forms (F) can have multiple elements in case of ambiguous forms. Such sets cannot be split in the statistics. The patterns from tab. 3 can be used to create the Moore machine shown in fig. 2. This FSM can be then used to recognize MWEs in the following sentence: "Rozwój chmur kłębiastych i lokalnych burz." (*Development of cumulus clouds and local storms*). Table 4 shows the recognized MWE candidates with corresponding values of *cpid*. These results should be now converted into MWEs – this means changing their form to the base one, identifying inflected tokens and the IDs of the tokens in CLPM. As the example is very simple, it turns out that each result yields exactly one MWE candidate and all of them are overlapping. This means that we need to calculate their rs scores. The highest score (16) is achieved by the MWE "chmura kłębiasta" (*cumulus cloud*). This is because the pattern with *cpid*'s 2 and 3 (table 3) has $8 + 1 + 7 = 16$ occurrences for the form sets which intersect $F = \{9\}$. As the remaining candidates (meaning *cumulus clouds* and *cloud development*, respectively) have lower scores (1), they are discarded.

To improve MWE candidate selection, supervised learning was also considered and tested. The training set contained 4000 manually annotated MWE candidates: about 1500 positive and 2500 negative samples. This set was used to train binary classifiers including LDA, SVM with different kernels, Maximum Entropy model, decision trees and finally AdaBoost, which performed best. However, the initial results were only marginally better (within 1%) than the ones given by the rs measure described above. This research is still ongoing.

4.4 SDM method

The results of applying the SM method to a text corpus can be converted to a dictionary format (fig. 1, transition 4a) – this way we would create an additional dictionary resource that could increase the

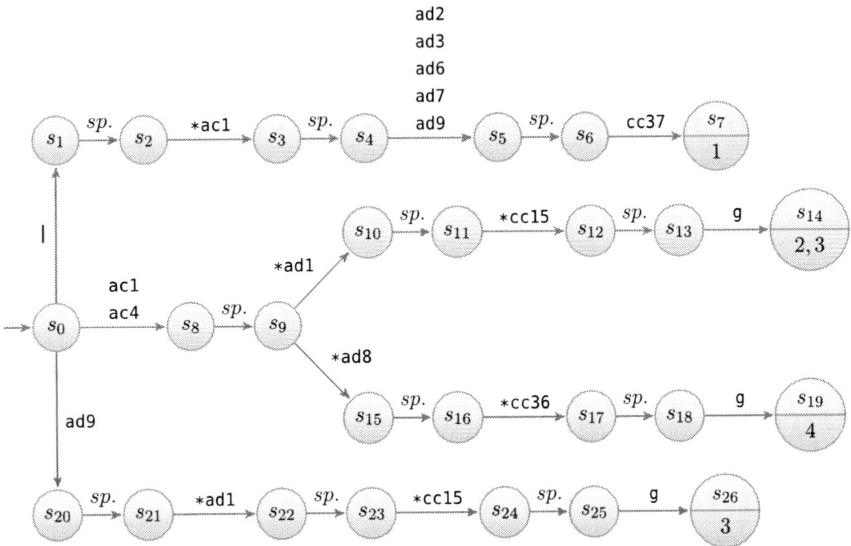

Figure 2: State machine recognizing the patterns from tab. 3. Multiple transitions between the same pair of states are denoted with a single arrow and aligned vertically. The symbol *sp.* means a space. Numbers below the state symbol are *cpid* values of recognized patterns.

Table 4: Results of MWE recognition using the FSM from fig. 2 in the sentence "Rozwój chmur kłębiastych i lokalnych burz.".

$cpid$	Path in the FSM	Forms (F)	Token sequence	MWE (base form)	rs
1		*ac1 ad9 cc37	1, 4	Rozwój chmur	rozwój chmur	1
2, 3	ac1,ac4 *ad1 *cc15 g	9	chmur kłębiastych	chmura kłębiasta	16
4	ac1,ac4 *ad8 *cc36 g	9	chmur kłębiastych	chmury kłębiaste	1

possibilities of the pDM method. Two text corpora were used for this operation:

- PAP-TRAIN – Polish Press Agency (PAP) releases, 3.6 million tokens.

- WIKI – contents of all Wikipedia articles, 202.7 million tokens.

The resulting dictionary was filtered and disambiguated to increase its quality. There is a trade-off between size and quality of the resulting dictionary – the values depend on the threshold rs measure described above. For example, if the target is a dictionary with one million expressions, it would contain about 75% correct MWEs[9]. The remaining steps are similar as for pDM: dictionary patterns are created, followed by the automaton (fig. 1, transitions 4b and 4c). The resulting method is called **SDM**.

____

[9]Tested on a sample of 2000 entries.

5 Tests

The described methods were tested on a random sample of 100 PAP press releases, in which MWEs were manually annotated by two annotators[10]. The test corpus, which contains 572 tagged MWEs, is called PAP-TEST[11]. For each MWE its location was marked and all inflected tokens were also indicated. The test itself consists in choosing one or more methods (**DM, pDM, SM** and **SDM**) with their optimal parameters[12] and re-tagging the PAP-TEST corpus automatically. The resulting automatically tagged corpus, denoted PAP-WW, was then compared with PAP-TEST. As a result, four sets of expressions are determined:

- T_i – correct MWEs present in both corpora

____

[10]Disagreements between annotators were discussed and resolved.

[11]Its content is excluded from PAP-TRAIN.

[12]Two-fold cross validation was performed for parameter optimization.

Table 5: Results of the MWE recognition and extraction tests. The best result in each column is **highlighted**.

Method	Recognition test			Extraction test		
	P_{rec}	R_{rec}	F_{rec}	P_{ext}	R_{ext}	F_{ext}
DM	80.97	42.54	55.78	58.71	30.85	40.44
pDM	**90.12**	38.64	54.09	**86.96**	37.29	52.19
SM	50.46	64.75	56.72	47.82	61.36	53.75
SDM	62.83	64.75	63.77	60.86	62.71	61.77
pDM + SDM + SM	72.27	**70.14**	**71.19**	69.23	**67.19**	**68.19**

with correctly identified inflected tokens.

- T_d – correct MWEs present in both corpora with incorrectly identified inflected tokens.

- F_n – missing MWEs (false negatives, present only in PAP-TEST).

- F_p – incorrect MWEs (false positives, present only in PAP-WW).

Two types of test were performed: the **recognition test** considers T_d elements as correct while the **extraction test** considers them as incorrect. For each test **precision** (P) and **recall** R values are calculated using the following formulas:

$$P_{rec} = \frac{|T_i \cup T_d|}{|T_i \cup T_d \cup F_p|} \qquad R_{rec} = \frac{|T_i \cup T_d|}{|T_i \cup T_d \cup F_n|}$$

$$P_{ext} = \frac{|T_i|}{|T_i \cup T_d \cup F_p|} \qquad R_{ext} = \frac{|T_i|}{|T_i \cup T_d \cup F_n|}$$

For both methods **F-measure** is also calculated: $F_1 = \frac{2PR}{P+R}$, denoted F_{rec} and F_{ext} respectively.

5.1 Test results

The results are shown in table 5. The pDM method is the most precise as it extracts only Wikipedia headwords that have been additionally filtered when creating inflection patterns. The most noticeable difference to DM is in the P_{ext} value. The SM method does not have high precision, but its recall is enough to build a dictionary which enables SDM to reach high results. The last row shows a combined method that merges the results of the three methods: pDM, SDM and SM. The methods are prioritized respectively – this ensures that results of methods with higher recall are preferred. Although the combined method yields good results, there is still a quite large number of errors, whose reasons mostly fall into the following categories:

- Long and complicated expressions, e.g. long school name "V Liceum Ogólnokształcące im. Augusta Witkowskiego" consisting of the short name "V Liceum Ogólnokształcące" and the patron name "August Witkowski", which were recognized separately – this means one false negative and two false positives.

- Missing foreign words (including names) in CLPM, e.g. "Sampras" in "Pete Sampras".

- Spelling and typographical errors like "W.Brytania" (*Great Britain*, missing space), "Białego Domy" (*the White House*, the grammatical form of the tokens does not match).

- Expressions which are not considered MWEs e.g. dates like "stycznia 1921" (January 1921), "grudniu 1981" (December 1981).

To sum up, the results are positive and reflect the quality of the method in a real-word scenario. There are possibilities of future improvement.

6 Conclusions

The results show that it is possible to recognize and extract Polish MWEs using an inflection dictionary and Wikipedia without the need for manually crafted rules or training sets. It is also possible to create a dictionary of Polish MWEs from the results of the extraction process. The main future goal is to clean the resulting dictionary using both manual effort and machine learning algorithms. However, initial research shows that this will be a difficult problem as even a training set of 4000 positive/negative MWE examples used to train various classifiers including AdaBoost was not enough to give improvement in F_{ext} larger than 1%. This research is still ongoing.

References

Mohammed Attia, Lamia Tounsi, Pavel Pecina, Josef van Genabith, and Antonio Toral. 2010. Automatic extraction of arabic multiword expressions. In *23rd International Conference on Computational Linguistics: Proceedings of the Workshop on Multiword Expressions: From Theory to Applications (MWE)*, pages 19–27. Association for Computational Linguistic.

Božo Bekavac and Marko Tadic. 2008. A generic method for multi word extraction from wikipedia. In *30th International Conference on Information Technology Interfaces (ITI)*, pages 663–668. IEEE.

Aleksander Buczyński and Adam Przepiórkowski. 2009. Spejd: A shallow processing and morphological disambiguation tool. In *Human Language Technology. Challenges of the Information Society*, pages 131–141. Springer.

Paweł Chrząszcz. 2012. Enrichment of inflection dictionaries: automatic extraction of semantic labels from encyclopedic definitions. In *Proceedings of the 9th International Workshop on Natural Language Processing and Cognitive Science (NLPCS, ICEIS)*, pages 106–119. SciTePress.

Matthieu Constant and Anthony Sigogne. 2011. Mwu-aware part-of-speech tagging with a crf model and lexical resources. In *Proceedings of the Workshop on Multiword Expressions: from Parsing and Generation to the Real World*, pages 49–56. Association for Computational Linguistics.

Matthieu Constant, Anthony Sigogne, and Patrick Watrin. 2012. Discriminative strategies to integrate multiword expression recognition and parsing. In *Proceedings of the 50th Annual Meeting of the Association for Computational Linguistics: Long Papers – Volume 1*, pages 204–212. Association for Computational Linguistics.

Meghdad Farahmand and Ronaldo Martins. 2014. A supervised model for extraction of multiword expressions based on statistical context features. In *Proceedings of the 10th Workshop on Multiword Expressions (MWE, EACL)*, pages 10–16. Association for Computational Linguistics.

Christiane Fellbaum. 1998. *WordNet: an electronic lexical database*. MIT Press.

Evgeniy Gabrilovich and Shaul Markovitch. 2007. Computing semantic relatedness using wikipedia-based explicit semantic analysis. In *Proceedings of the 20th International Joint Conference on Artifical Intelligence (IJCAI)*, volume 7, pages 1606–1611. Morgan Kaufmann Publishers Inc.

Marek Gajęcki. 2009. Słownik fleksyjny jako biblioteka języka c. In Wiesław Lubaszewski, editor, *Słowniki komputerowe i automatyczna ekstrakcja informacji z tekstu*. AGH Press, Kraków.

Filip Graliński, Agata Savary, Monika Czerepowicka, and Filip Makowiecki. 2010. Computational lexicography of multi-word units: how efficient can it be? In *Proceedings of the Workshop on Multiword Expressions: from Theory to Applications (MWE)*, pages 1–9. Association for Computational Linguistics.

Jun'ichi Kazama and Kentaro Torisawa. 2007. Exploiting wikipedia as external knowledge for named entity recognition. In *Joint Conference on Empirical Methods in Natural Language Processing and Computational Natural Language Learning (EMNLP-CoNLL)*, pages 698–707. ACL.

Roman Kurc, Maciej Piasecki, and Bartosz Broda. 2012. Constraint based description of polish multiword expressions. In *Proceedings of the 8th International Conference on Language Resources and Evaluation (LREC)*, pages 2408–2413. European Language Resources Association.

Wiesław Lubaszewski, H. Wróbel, M. Gajęcki, B. Moskal, A. Orzechowska, P. Pietras, P. Pisarek, and T. Rokicka. 2001. *Słownik Fleksyjny Języka Polskiego*. Computational Linguistics Group, Department of Computer Science, AGH UST and Department of Computational Linguistics, Jagiellonian University, Kraków.

Cynthia Matuszek, John Cabral, Michael J. Witbrock, and John DeOliveira. 2006. An introduction to the syntax and content of cyc. In *AAAI Spring Symposium: Formalizing and Compiling Background Knowledge and Its Applications to Knowledge Representation and Question Answering*, pages 44–49.

Marek Maziarz, Maciej Piasecki, and Stanisław Szpakowicz. 2012. Approaching plWordNet 2.0. In *Proceedings of the 6th Global Wordnet Conference*. Global WordNet Association.

Rada Mihalcea and Andras Csomai. 2007. Wikify!: linking documents to encyclopedic knowledge. In *Proceedings of the 16th Conference on Information and Knowledge Management (CIKM)*, pages 233–242. Association for Computing Machinery.

Joel Nothman, Tara Murphy, and James R Curran. 2009. Analysing wikipedia and gold-standard corpora for ner training. In *Proceedings of the 12th Conference of the European Chapter of the Association for Computational Linguistics*, pages 612–620. Association for Computational Linguistics.

Pavel Pecina. 2008. A machine learning approach to multiword expression extraction. In *Proceedings of the LREC Workshop – Towards a Shared Task for Multiword Expressions (MWE)*, pages 54–61. European Language Resources Association.

Jakub Piskorski, Peter Homola, Małgorzata Marciniak, Agnieszka Mykowiecka, Adam Przepiórkowski, and Marcin Woliński. 2004. Information extraction for polish using the sprout platform. In *Intelligent Information Processing and Web Mining*, volume 25 of *Advances in Soft Computing*, pages 227–236. Springer Berlin Heidelberg.

Aleksander Pohl and Bartosz Ziółko. 2013. A comparison of polish taggers in the application for automatic speech recognition. In *Proceedings of the 6th Language and Technology Conference (LTC)*, pages 294–298.

Carlos Ramisch, Paulo Schreiner, Marco Idiart, and Aline Villavicencio. 2008. An evaluation of methods for the extraction of multiword expressions. In *Proceedings of the LREC Workshop – Towards a Shared Task for Multiword Expressions (MWE)*, pages 50–53. European Language Resources Association.

Carlos Ramisch, Aline Villavicencio, and Christian Boitet. 2010. Mwetoolkit: a framework for multiword expression identification. In *Proceedings of the 7th International Conference on Language Resources and Evaluation (LREC)*, pages 662–669. European Language Resources Association.

Josef Ruppenhofer, Michael Ellsworth, Miriam R.L. Petruck, Christopher R. Johnson, and Jan Scheffczyk. 2006. *FrameNet II: Extended theory and practice*. International Computer Science Institute, Berkeley, CA.

Ivan A. Sag, Timothy Baldwin, Francis Bond, Ann Copestake, and Dan Flickinger. 2002. Multiword expressions: a pain in the neck for nlp. In *Computational Linguistics and Intelligent Text Processing*, volume 2276 of *Lecture Notes in Computer Science*, pages 1–15. Springer Berlin Heidelberg.

Veronika Vincze, István Nagy, and Gábor Berend. 2011. Multiword expressions and named entities in wikipedia articles. In *Proceedings of the International Conference on Recent Advances in Natural Language Processing (RANLP)*, pages 289–295.

Jakub Waszczuk. 2012. Harnessing the crf complexity with domain-specific constraints. the case of morphosyntactic tagging of a highly inflected language. In *Proceedings of the 24th International Conference on Computational Linguistics (COLING)*, pages 2789–2804.

Marcin Woliński. 2006. Morfeusz — a practical tool for the morphological analysis of polish. *Advances in Soft Computing*, 26(6):503–512.

Michał Woźniak. 2011. Automatic extraction of multiword lexical units from polish text. In *5th Language and Technology Conference (LTC)*.

Yi Zhang, Valia Kordoni, Aline Villavicencio, and Marco Idiart. 2006. Automated multiword expression prediction for grammar engineering. In *Proceedings of the Workshop on Multiword Expressions: Identifying and Exploiting Underlying Properties*, pages 36–44. Association for Computational Linguistics.

Impact of MWE Resources on Multiword Recognition

Martin Riedl and **Chris Biemann**
Language Technology
Computer Science Department
Technische Universität Darmstadt
{riedl,biem}@cs.tu-darmstadt.de

Abstract

In this paper, we demonstrate the impact of Multiword Expression (MWE) resources in the task of MWE recognition in text. We present results based on the Wiki50 corpus for MWE resources, generated using unsupervised methods from raw text and resources that are extracted using manual text markup and lexical resources. We show that resources acquired from manual annotation yield the best MWE tagging performance. However, a more fine-grained analysis that differentiates MWEs according to their part of speech (POS) reveals that automatically acquired MWE lists outperform the resources generated from human knowledge for three out of four classes.

1 Introduction

Identifying MWEs in text is related to the task of Named Entity Recognition (NER). However, the task of MWE recognition mostly considers the detection of word sequences that form MWEs and are not Named Entities (NEs). For both tasks mostly sequence tagging algorithms, e.g. Hidden Markov Model (HMM) or Conditional Random Fields (CRF), are trained and then applied to previously unseen text. In order to tackle the recognition of MWEs, most approaches (e.g. (Schneider et al., 2014; Constant and Sigogne, 2011)) use resources containing MWEs. These are mostly extracted from lexical resources (e.g. WordNet) or from markup in text (e.g. Wikipedia, Wiktionary). While these approaches work well, they require respective resources and markup. This might not be the case for special domains or under-resourced languages.

On the contrary, methods have been developed that rank word sequences according to their multiwordness automatically using information from corpora, mostly relying on frequencies. Many of these methods (e.g. C/NC-Value (Frantzi et al., 1998), GM-MF (Nakagawa and Mori, 2002)) require previous filters, which are based on Part-of-Speech (POS) sequences. Such sequences, (e.g. Frantzi et al. (1998)) need to be defined and mostly do not cover all POS types of MWE.

In this work we do not want to restrict to specific MWE types and thus will use DRUID (Riedl and Biemann, 2015) and the Student's t-test as multiword ranking methods, which do not require any previous filtering. This paper focuses on the following research question: how do such lists generated from raw text compete against manually generated resources? Furthermore, we want to examine whether a combination of resources yields better performance.

2 Related Work

There is a considerable amount of research that copes with the recognition of word sequences, be it NE or MWE. The field of NER can be considered as subtask from the recognition of MWE. However, in NER additionally, single-worded names need to be recognized.

The experiments proposed in our paper are related to the ones performed by Nagy T. et al. (2011). Their paper focuses on the introduction of the Wiki50 dataset and demonstrates how the performance of the system can be improved by combining classifiers for NE and MWE. Here, we focus on the impact of different MWE resources.

An extensive evaluation of different measures for ranking word sequences regarding their multiwordness has been done before. Korkontzelos (2010) performs a comparative evaluation of MWE measures that all rely on POS filtering.

Proceedings of the 12th Workshop on Multiword Expressions, pages 107–111,
Berlin, Germany, August 7-12, 2016. ©2016 Association for Computational Linguistics

Riedl and Biemann (2015), in contrast, introduced a measure, relying on distributional similarities, that does not require a pre-filtering of candidate words by their POS tag. It is shown to compare favorably to an adaption of the t-test, which only relies on filtering of frequent words.

3 Datasets

For the evaluation we use the Wikipedia-based Wiki50 (Nagy T. et al., 2011) dataset. This dataset comprises of annotations for both NEs and MWEs as shown in Table 1.

MWE/NE	type	count
MWE	noun compound	2931
MWE	verb-particle construction	447
MWE	light-verb construction	368
MWE	adjective compound	78
MWE	other	21
MWE	idiom	19
NE	person	4099
NE	misc.	1827
NE	location	1562
NE	organization	1499

Table 1: Frequency of MWE types in the Wiki50 dataset.

The dataset primarily consists of annotations for NEs, especially for the person label. The annotated MWEs are dominated by noun compounds followed by verb-particle constructions, light-verb constructions and adjective compounds. Idioms and other MWEs occur only rarely.

4 Method

For detecting MWEs and NEs we use the CRF sequence-labeling algorithm (Lafferty et al., 2001). As basic features, we use a mixture of features used in previous work (Schneider et al., 2014; Constant and Sigogne, 2011). The variable i indicates the current token postion:

- token_j with $j \in \{i-2, i-1, i, i+1, i+2\}$

- token_j & token_{j+1} with $j \in \{i-2, i-1, i, i+1, i+2\}$

- word shape of token_i, as used by Constant and Sigogne (2011)

- has token_i digits

- has token_i alphanumeric characters

- suffix of token_i with length $l \in \{1, 2, 3, 4\}$

- prefix of token_i with length $l \in \{1, 2, 3, 4\}$

- POS of token_j with $j \in \{i-2, i-1, i, i+1, i+2\}$

- POS(token_j) & POS(token_{j+1}) with $j \in \{i-2, i-1, i, i+1, i+2\}$

- POS(token_j) & token_j with $j \in \{i-2, i-1, i, i+1, i+2\}$

- lemma of token_i

- lemma of token_j and lemma of token_{j+1} with $j \in \{i-1, i\}$

For showing the impact of a MWE resource mr, we featurize the resource as follows:

- number of times token_i occurs in mr

- token bigram: token_j token_{j+1} contained in mr with $j \in \{i-1, i\}$

- token trigram: token_j token_{j+1} token_{j+2} occurence in mr with $j \in \{i-2, i-1, i\}$

- token 4-gram: token_j token_{j+1} token_{j+2} token_{j+3} occur in mr with $j \in \{i-3, i-2, i-1, i\}$

5 Multiword Expression Resources

For generating features from MWE resources, we distinguish between resources that are extracted from manually generated/annotated content[1] and resources that can be automatically computed based on raw text. First, we describe the resources extracted from manually annotated corpora or resources.

- **EnWikt**: This resource consists of 82,175 MWEs extracted from Wiktionary.

- **WordNet**: The WordNet resource is a list of 64,188 MWEs that are extracted from Word-Net (Miller, 1995).

- **WikiMe**: WikiMe (Hartmann et al., 2012) is a resource extracted from Wikipedia that consists of 356,467 MWEs from length two to four that have been extracted using markup information.

---

[1] For this, we rely on the MWE resources that are provided here: `http://www.cs.cmu.edu/~ark/LexSem/mwelex-1.0.zip`.

- **SemCor**: This dataset consists of 16,512 MWE and was generated from the Semantic Concordance corpus (Miller et al., 1993).

Additionally, we select the best-performing measures for ranking word sequences according to their multiwordness as described in (Riedl and Biemann, 2015) that do not require any POS filtering:

- **DRUID**: We use the DRUID implementation[2], which is based on a distributional thesaurus (DT) and does not rely on any linguistic processing (e.g. POS tagging).

- **t-test**: The Student's t-test is a statistical test that can be used to compute the significance of the co-occurrence of tokens. For this it relies on the frequency of the single terms as well as the word sequence. As this measure favors to rank word sequences highest that begin and end with stopwords, we remove word sequences that begin and end with stopwords. As stopwords, we select the 100 most frequent words from the Wikipedia corpus.

6 Experimental Setting

We perform the evaluation, using a 10-fold cross validation and use the `crfsuite`[3] implementation of CRF as classifier. For retrieving POS tags, we apply the OpenNLP POS tagger[4]. The lemmatization is performed using the `WordNetLemmatizer`, contained in `nltk` (Loper and Bird, 2002).[5]

For the computation of automatically generated MWEs lists, we use the raw text from an English Wikipedia dump, without considering any markup and annotations. For applying them as resources, we only consider word sequences in the resource that are also contained in the Wiki50 dataset, both training and test data. Based on these candidates, we select the n highest ranked MWE candidates. The previous filtering does not influence the performance of the algorithm but enables an easier filtering parameter.

[2] http://jobimtext.org/jobimtext/components/DRUID/

[3] http://www.chokkan.org/software/crfsuite

[4] We use the version 1.6 available from: https://opennlp.apache.org.

[5] An implementation of the complete system is available at http://maggie.lt.informatik.tu-darmstadt.de/files/mwe/MWE_TAGGER.tar.gz.

7 Results

First, we show the overall performance for the Wiki50 dataset for recognizing labeled MWE and NE spans. We show the performance for training classifiers to predict solely NEs and MWEs and also the combination without the usage of any MWE resource. As can be observed (see Table 2), the detection of NE reaches higher scores than learning to predict MWE.

	precision	recall	F1
MWE +NE	80.83	75.29	77.96
MWE	77.51	57.89	66.28
NE	83.76	82.58	83.16

Table 2: Performance for predicting labels for MWE and NE without using MWE resources.

Comparing the performance between classifying solely NEs and MWEs, we observe low recall for predicting MWE. Next, we will conduct experiments for learning to predict MWE with the use of MWE resources.

In Table 3 we present results for the overall labeled performance for MWEs in the Wiki50 dataset. Using MWE resources, we observe consistent improvements over the baseline approach, which does not rely on any MWE resource (*None*). For manually constructed MWE resources, improvements of up to 3 points F1-measure on MWE labeling are observed, the most useful resource being WikiMe. The combination of manual resources does not yield improvements.

	precision	recall	F1
None	77.51	57.89	66.28
SemCor	78.28	59.78	67.79
WordNet	78.48	60.04	68.04
EnWikt	79.16	60.56	68.62
WikiMe	**79.35**	**61.54**	**69.32**
All resources	78.90	61.44	69.08
t-test 1,000	78.14	59.65	67.65
t-test 10,000	78.60	60.53	68.39
DRUID 1,000	78.42	60.30	68.18
DRUID 10,000	78.56	60.58	68.41
DRUID & t-test 10,000	78.56	60.30	68.23
All	79.06	60.79	68.73

Table 3: Overall performance on the labels for different MWE resources applied solely to the MWEs annotated in the Wiki50 dataset.

Using the top 1000 ranked word sequences that are contained in the Wiki50 corpus, we already obtain improvements for both unsupervised rank-

MWE Resource	Noun Comp.			Verb-part. constr.			light-verb constr.			adj. comp.		
	P	R	F1	P	R	F1	P	R	F1	P	R	F1
None	76.64	63.46	69.43	86.64	59.51	70.56	73.13	26.63	39.04	72.22	16.67	27.08
Semcor	77.25	65.23	70.74	86.83	61.97	72.32	76.34	27.17	40.08	78.26	23.08	35.64
WordNet	77.44	65.47	70.96	88.05	62.64	73.20	75.37	27.45	40.24	73.91	21.79	33.66
EnWikt	78.18	65.88	71.51	86.46	62.86	72.80	79.26	29.08	42.54	78.26	23.08	35.64
WikiMe	**78.41**	**67.28**	**72.42**	87.42	62.19	72.68	77.14	29.35	42.52	80.95	21.79	34.34
All resources	77.94	67.25	72.20	87.16	63.76	73.64	76.19	26.09	38.87	79.17	24.36	37.25
t-test 1,000	77.07	65.03	70.54	87.11	61.97	72.42	76.12	27.72	40.64	77.27	21.79	34.00
t-test 10,000	77.36	65.51	70.94	**88.20**	63.53	73.86	77.55	**30.98**	**44.27**	**81.82**	23.08	36.00
DRUID 1,000	77.30	65.64	71.00	87.97	62.19	72.87	77.37	28.80	41.98	74.07	**25.64**	**38.10**
DRUID 10,000	77.42	65.64	71.05	86.31	**64.88**	**74.07**	**79.70**	28.80	42.32	78.26	23.08	35.64
DRUID & t-test 10,000	77.60	65.37	70.96	86.50	63.09	72.96	76.55	30.16	43.27	78.26	23.08	35.64

Table 4: Detailed performance in terms of precision (P), recall (R) and F1-measure (F1) for the different MWE types. The experiments have been performed only on the MWE annotations.

ing measures. Whereas we observe improvements by around 1 points F1 for the t-test, we gain improvements of almost 2 points for DRUID. When extracting the top 10,000 MWEs, additional improvements can be obtained, which are close to the performances using the markup-based MWE resources. Here, using DRUID with the top 10,000 highest ranked MWEs achieves the third best improvements in comparison to all resources. Using more than the top 10,000 ranked word sequences does not result in any further performance improvement. Surprisingly, using MWE resources as features for MWE recognition improves the performance only marginally.

We assume that each resource focuses on different kinds of MWEs. Thus, we also show results for the four most frequent MWE types in Table 4. Inspecting the results using MWE lists, that are generated using human knowledge, we obtain the best performance for noun compounds using WikiMe. Verb-particle constructions seem to be better covered by the WordNet-based resource. For light-verb constructions the highest F1 measures are observed using EnWikt and WikiMe and for adjective compounds EnWikt achieves the highest improvements. We omit presenting results for the MWE classes other and idiom as only few annotations are available in the Wiki50 dataset.

Inspecting results for the t-test and DRUID, we obtain slightly higher F1 measures for noun-compounds using DRUID. Whereas for verb-particle constructions the t-test achieves the overall highest precision, recall and F1 measure of DRUID are higher. However, t-test achieves better results for light-verb constructions and using DRUID yields the highest F1 measure for adjective compounds.

Overall, only for noun compounds the best results are obtained using MWE lists that are generated from lexical resources or text annotations. For all remaining labels, the best performance is obtained using MWE lists that can be generated in an unsupervised fashion. However, as noun compounds constitutes the largest class, using unsupervised lists does not result to the best overall performance.

In addition, we performed the classification task of MWEs without labels, as shown in Table 5. In contrast to the overall labeled results (see Table 3) the performance drops. Whereas one might expect higher results for the unlabeled dataset, the labels help the classifier in order to use features according to the label. This is in accordance with the previous findings shown in Table 4.

	P	R	F1
None	74.47	58.20	65.34
SemCor	75.01	59.50	66.36
WordNet	75.32	59.47	66.46
EnWikt	**76.04**	60.35	**67.29**
WikiMe	75.78	**60.48**	67.27
All resources	76.07	61.44	67.97
t-test 1,000	74.89	58.59	65.75
t-test 10,000	75.81	60.20	67.11
DRUID 1,000	75.42	59.78	66.70
DRUID 10,000	75.17	**60.48**	67.03
DRUID & t-test 10,000	75.81	60.35	67.20
All	76.39	60.79	67.70

Table 5: Unlabeled results for MWEs recognition.

Furthermore, in this evaluation highest improvements are achieved with the EnWikt. Using MWE lists that are generated in an unsupervised fashion results in comparable scores to the EnWikt. Again, these resources have the third-

highest performance of all lists and outperform
SemCor and WordNet.

8 Conclusion

In this paper, we have investigated whether unsu-
pervisedly acquired MWE resources are comparable with knowledge-based or manual-annotation-
based MWE resources for the task of MWE tagging in context. The highest overall performance,
both for the labeled and unlabeled tagging task,
is achieved using lists extracted from Wikipedia
(WikiMe) and Wiktionary (EnWikt). However, for
three out of four MWE types, resources that are
extracted using unsupervised methods achieve the
highest scores. In summary, using MWE lists for
MWE recognition with sequence tagging is a feature that adds a few points in F-measure. In the
case that high quality MWE resources exist, these
should be used. If not, it is possible to replace
them with unsupervised extraction methods such
as the t-test or DRUID.

References

Matthieu Constant and Anthony Sigogne. 2011.
MWU-Aware Part-of-Speech Tagging with a CRF
Model and Lexical Resources. In *Proceedings of the
Workshop on Multiword Expressions: from Parsing
and Generation to the Real World held in conjunc-
tion with ACL-2011*, pages 49–56, Portland, OR,
USA.

Katerina T. Frantzi, Sophia Ananiadou, and Jun-ichi
Tsujii. 1998. The C-value/NC-value Method of
Automatic Recognition for Multi-Word Terms. In
*Proceedings of the Second European Conference on
Research and Advanced Technology for Digital Li-
braries*, ECDL 1998, pages 585–604, Heraklion,
Greece.

Silvana Hartmann, György Szarvas, and Iryna
Gurevych. 2012. Mining multiword terms from
wikipedia. In *Semi-Automatic Ontology Development: Processes and Resources*, pages 226–258. IGI
Global, Hershey, PA, USA.

Ioannis Korkontzelos. 2010. *Unsupervised Learning
of Multiword Expressions*. Ph.D. thesis, University
of York, UK.

John D. Lafferty, Andrew McCallum, and Fernando
C. N. Pereira. 2001. Conditional Random Fields:
Probabilistic Models for Segmenting and Labeling Sequence Data. In *Proceedings of the Eigh-
teenth International Conference on Machine Learning*, ICML 2001, pages 282–289, Williams College,
Williamstown, MA, USA.

Edward Loper and Steven Bird. 2002. NLTK: The
Natural Language Toolkit. In *Proceedings of the
ACL-02 Workshop on Effective Tools and Method-
ologies for Teaching Natural Language Process-
ing and Computational Linguistics*, pages 63–70,
Philadelphia, PA, USA.

George A. Miller, Claudia Leacock, Randee Tengi, and
Ross T. Bunker. 1993. A semantic concordance. In
*Proceedings of the Workshop on Human Language
Technology*, HLT '93, pages 303–308, Princeton,
New Jersey.

George A. Miller. 1995. Wordnet: A lexical database
for english. *Communications of the ACM*, 38:39–41.

István Nagy T., Gábor Berend, and Veronika Vincze.
2011. Noun Compound and Named Entity Recognition and their Usability in Keyphrase Extraction. In
*Proceedings of the International Conference Recent
Advances in Natural Language Processing 2011*,
pages 162–169, Hissar, Bulgaria.

Hiroshi Nakagawa and Tatsunori Mori. 2002. A
Simple but Powerful Automatic Term Extraction
Method. In *International Workshop on Com-
putational Terminology held in conjunction with
COLING-02*, COMPUTERM 2002, pages 1–7,
Taipei, Taiwan.

Martin Riedl and Chris Biemann. 2015. A Single
Word is not Enough: Ranking Multiword Expressions Using Distributional Semantics. In *Proceedings of the Conference on Empirical Methods in
Natural Language Processing*, EMNLP 2015, pages
2430–2440, Lisboa, Portugal.

Nathan Schneider, Emily Danchik, Chris Dyer, and
Noah Smith. 2014. Discriminative Lexical Semantic Segmentation with Gaps: Running the MWE
Gamut. *Transactions of the Association for Computational Linguistics*, 2:193–206.

A Word Embedding Approach to Identifying Verb–Noun Idiomatic Combinations

Waseem Gharbieh and **Virendra C. Bhavsar** and **Paul Cook**
Faculty of Computer Science, University of New Brunswick
Fredericton, NB E3B 5A3 Canada
{waseem.gharbieh,bhavsar,paul.cook}@unb.ca

Abstract

Verb–noun idiomatic combinations (VNICs) are idioms consisting of a verb with a noun in its direct object position. Usages of these expressions can be ambiguous between an idiomatic usage and a literal combination. In this paper we propose supervised and unsupervised approaches, based on word embeddings, to identifying token instances of VNICs. Our proposed supervised and unsupervised approaches perform better than the supervised and unsupervised approaches of Fazly et al. (2009), respectively.

1 Verb–noun Idiomatic Combinations

Much research on multiword expressions (MWEs) in natural language processing (NLP) has focused on various type-level prediction tasks, e.g., MWE extraction (e.g., Church and Hanks, 1990; Smadja, 1993; Lin, 1999) — i.e., determining which MWE types are present in a given corpus (Baldwin and Kim, 2010) — and compositionality prediction (e.g., McCarthy et al., 2003; Reddy et al., 2011; Salehi et al., 2014). However, word combinations can be ambiguous between literal combinations and MWEs. For example, consider the following two usages of the expression *hit the roof*:

1. I think Paula might <u>hit the roof</u> if you start ironing.

2. When the blood <u>hit the roof</u> of the car I realised it was serious.

The first example of *hit the roof* is an idiomatic usage, while the second is a literal combination.[1] MWE identification is the task of determining

---

[1]These examples, and idiomaticity judgements, are taken from Cook et al. (2008).

which token instances in running text are MWEs (Baldwin and Kim, 2010). Although there has been relatively less work on MWE identification than other type-level MWE prediction tasks, it is nevertheless important for NLP applications such as machine translation that must be able to distinguish MWEs from literal combinations in context.

Some recent work has focused on token-level identification of a wide range of types of MWEs and other multiword units (e.g., Newman et al., 2012; Schneider et al., 2014; Brooke et al., 2014). Many studies, however, have taken a word sense disambiguation–inspired approach to MWE identification (e.g., Birke and Sarkar, 2006; Katz and Giesbrecht, 2006; Li et al., 2010), treating literal combinations and MWEs as different word senses, and have exploited linguistic knowledge of MWEs (e.g., Patrick and Fletcher, 2005; Uchiyama et al., 2005; Hashimoto and Kawahara, 2008; Fazly et al., 2009; Fothergill and Baldwin, 2012).

In this study we focus on English verb–noun idiomatic combinations (VNICs). VNICs are formed from a verb with a noun in its direct object position. They are a common and productive type of English idiom, and occur cross-lingually (Fazly et al., 2009).

VNICs tend to be relatively lexico-syntactically fixed, e.g., whereas *hit the roof* is ambiguous between literal and idiomatic meanings, *hit the roofs* and *a roof was hit* are most likely to be literal usages. Fazly et al. (2009) exploit this property in their unsupervised approach, referred to as CFORM. They define lexico-syntactic patterns for VNIC token instances based on the noun's determiner (e.g., *a*, *the*, or possibly no determiner), the number of the noun (singular or plural), and the verb's voice (active or passive). They propose a statistical method for automatically determining a given VNIC type's canonical idiomatic form, based on the frequency of its usage in these

112

Proceedings of the 12th Workshop on Multiword Expressions, pages 112–118,
Berlin, Germany, August 7-12, 2016. ©2016 Association for Computational Linguistics

patterns in a corpus.[2] They then classify a given token instance of a VNIC as idiomatic if it occurs in its canonical form, and as literal otherwise. Fazly et al. also consider a supervised approach that classifies a given VNIC instance based on the similarity of its context to that of idiomatic and literal instances of the same expression seen during training.

Distributed representations of word meaning in the form of word embeddings (Mikolov et al., 2013) have recently been demonstrated to benefit a wide range of NLP tasks including POS tagging (e.g., Ling et al., 2015), question answering (e.g., Dong et al., 2015), and machine translation (e.g., Zou et al., 2013). Moreover, word embeddings have been shown to improve over count-based models of distributional similarity for predicting MWE compositionality (Salehi et al., 2015).

In this work we first propose a supervised approach to identifying VNIC token instances based on word embeddings that outperforms the supervised method of Fazly et al. (2009). We then propose an unsupervised approach to this task, that combines word embeddings with Fazly et al.'s unsupervised CFORM approach, that improves over CFORM.

2 Models for VNIC Identification Based on Word Embeddings

The following subsections propose supervised and unsupervised approaches to VNIC identification based on word embeddings.

2.1 Supervised VNIC Identification

For the proposed supervised approach, we first extract features based on word embeddings from word2vec representing a token instance of a VNIC in context, and then use these representations of VNIC tokens to train a supervised classifier.

We first form a vector $\vec{e}$ representing a given VNIC token at the type level. $\vec{e}$ is formed by averaging the embeddings of the lemmatized component words forming the VNIC.

We then form a vector $\vec{c}$ representing the context of the VNIC token instance. MWEs, including VNICs, can be discontiguous. We therefore form two vectors, $\vec{c}_{\text{verb}}$ and $\vec{c}_{\text{noun}}$, representing the context of the verb and noun components, respectively, of the VNIC instance, and then average

Original text: *You can <u>see</u> the <u>stars</u>, now, in the city*

Context tokens for verb (*see*): *you, can, the, now*

Context tokens for noun (*stars*): *can, the, now, in*

$$\vec{c}_{\text{verb}} = \frac{vec(you)+vec(can)+vec(the)+vec(now)}{4}$$

$$\vec{c}_{\text{noun}} = \frac{vec(can)+vec(the)+vec(now)+vec(in)}{4}$$

$$\vec{c} = \frac{\vec{c}_{\text{verb}}+\vec{c}_{\text{noun}}}{2}$$

Figure 1: An example of computing $\vec{c}$ for a window size (k) of 2, where $vec(w)$ is the vector for word w obtained from word2vec.

these vectors to form $\vec{c}$. More precisely, $\vec{c}_{\text{verb}}$ and $\vec{c}_{\text{noun}}$ are formed as follows:

$$\vec{c_j} = \frac{1}{2k} \sum_{i=-k, i\neq 0}^{k} w_{t-i}^{j} \tag{1}$$

where k is the window size that the word2vec model was trained on, and w_t^j is the embedding of the word in position t of the input sentence relative to the jth component of the MWE (i.e., either the verb or noun). In forming $\vec{c}_{\text{verb}}$ and $\vec{c}_{\text{noun}}$ the other component token of the VNIC is not considered part of the context. The summation is done over the same window size that the word2vec model was trained on so that $\vec{c_j}$ captures the same information that the word2vec model has learned to capture. After computing $\vec{c}_{\text{verb}}$ and $\vec{c}_{\text{noun}}$ these vectors are averaged to form $\vec{c}$. Figure 1 shows the process for forming $\vec{c}$ for an example sentence.

Finally, to form the feature vector representing a VNIC instance, we subtract $\vec{e}$ from $\vec{c}$, and append to this vector a single binary feature representing whether the VNIC instance occurs in its canonical form, as determined by Fazly et al. (2009). The feature vectors are then used to train a supervised classifier; in our experiments we use the linear SVM implementation from Pedregosa et al. (2011). The motivation for the subtraction is to capture the difference between the context in which a VNIC instance occurs ($\vec{c}$) and a type-level representation of that expression ($\vec{e}$), to potentially represent VNIC instances such that the classifier is able to generalize across expressions (i.e., to generalize to MWE types that are unseen during training). The canonical form feature is included because it is known to be highly informative as to

---

[2]In some cases a VNIC may have a small number of canonical forms, as opposed to just one.

whether an instance is idiomatic or literal.

2.2 Unsupervised VNIC Identification

Our unsupervised approach combines the word embedding–based representation used in the supervised approach (without relying on training a supervised classifier, of course) with the unsupervised CFORM method of Fazly et al. (2009). In this approach, we first represent each token instance of a given VNIC type as a feature vector, using the same representation as in Section 2.1.[3] We then apply k-means clustering to form k clusters of the token instances.[4] All instances in each cluster are then assigned a single class, idiomatic or literal, depending on whether the majority of token instances in a cluster are in that VNIC's canonical form or not, respectively. In the case of ties the method backs off to a most-frequent class (idiomatic) baseline. This method is unsupervised in that it does not rely on any gold standard labels.

3 Materials and Methods

In this section we describe training details for the word embeddings and the dataset used for evaluation.

3.1 Word embeddings

The word embeddings required by our proposed methods were trained using the gensim[5] implementation of the skip gram version of word2vec (Mikolov et al., 2013). The model was trained on a snapshot of English Wikipedia from 1 September 2015. The text was pre-processed using wp2txt[6] to remove markup, and then tokenized with the Stanford tokenizer (Manning et al., 2014). Tokens occurring less than 15 times were removed, and the negative sampling parameter was set to 5.

3.2 VNC-Tokens Dataset

The VNC-Tokens dataset (Cook et al., 2008) contains instances of 53 VNIC types — drawn from the British National Corpus (Burnard, 2007) — that have been manually annotated at the token level for whether they are literal or idiomatic usages. The 53 expressions are divided into three

---

[3]Based on results in preliminary experiments we found that normalizing the feature vectors led to modest improvements in this case.

[4]In our experiments we use the implementation of k-means clustering from Pedregosa et al. (2011).

[5]https://radimrehurek.com/gensim/

[6]https://github.com/yohasebe/wp2txt

Window	Dimensions	Dev	Test
	50	87.3	85.9
1	100	**88.2**	85.5
	300	86.3	**88.3**
	50	86.4	84.2
2	100	86.7	84.2
	300	86.5	86.7
	50	86.0	83.4
5	100	85.9	84.2
	300	87.3	85.7
	50	85.5	84.3
8	100	85.6	85.9
	300	85.8	86.3
Baseline		62.1	61.9
Fazly et al. (2009) CFORM		72.3	73.7
Fazly et al. (2009) Supervised		80.1	82.7

Table 1: Percent accuracy using a linear SVM for different word2vec parameters. Results for a most-frequent class baseline, and the CFORM and supervised methods from Fazly et al. (2009), are also shown.

subsets: DEV, TEST, and SKEWED. SKEWED consists of 25 expressions that are used primarily idiomatically, or primarily literally, while DEV and TEST consist of 14 expressions each that are more balanced between their idiomatic and literal usages. Fazly et al. (2009) focus primarily on DEV and TEST; we therefore only consider these subsets here. DEV and TEST consist of a total of 597 and 613 VNIC tokens, respectively, that are annotated as either literal or idiomatic usages.[7]

4 Experimental Results

In the following subsections we describe the results of experiments using our supervised approach, the ability of this method to generalize across MWE types, and finally the results of the unsupervised approach.

4.1 Supervised Results

Following Fazly et al. (2009), the supervised approach was evaluated using a leave-one-token-out strategy. That is, for each MWE, a single token instance is held out, and the classifier is trained on the remaining instances. The trained model is then used to classify the held out instance. This is

---

[7]Both DEV and TEST also contain instances that are annotated as "unknown"; following Fazly et al. (2009) we exclude these instances from our study.

	CFORM		Oracle	
k	Dev	Test	Dev	Test
2	67.8 ±3.13	64.2 ±2.57	82.6 ±0.65	81.5 ±2.86
3	68.2 ±4.36	71.1 ±2.99	84.2 ±2.94	83.2 ±2.58
4	69.7 ±5.24	**78.1** ±3.30	86.0 ±3.02	85.9 ±2.82
5	**71.8** ±6.58	76.5 ±4.07	86.9 ±3.54	87.9 ±2.36

Table 2: The percent accuracy, and standard deviation, of our unsupervised approach incorporating CFORM (left), and an oracle (right), for differing values of k.

repeated until all the instances of the MWE type have been classified. The idiomatic and literal classes have roughly comparable frequencies in the dataset, therefore, again following Fazly et al., macro-averaged accuracy is reported.[8] Nevertheless, the idiomatic class is more frequent; therefore, also following Fazly et al., we report a most-frequent class baseline that classifies all instances as idiomatic. Results are shown in Table 1 for a variety of settings of window size and number of dimensions for the word embeddings.

The results reveal the general trend that smaller window sizes, and more dimensions, tend to give higher accuracy, although the overall amount of variation is relatively small. The accuracy on DEV and TEST ranges from 85.5%–88.2% and 83.4%–88.3%, respectively. All of these accuracies are higher than those reported by Fazly et al. (2009) for their supervised approach. They are also substantially higher than the most-frequent class baseline, and the unsupervised CFORM method of Fazly et al.

That a window size of just 1 performs well is interesting. A word2vec model with a smaller window size gives more syntactically-oriented word embeddings, whereas a larger window size gives more semantically-oriented embeddings (Trask et al., 2015). The CFORM method of Fazly et al. (2009) is a strong unsupervised benchmark for this task, and relies on the lexico-syntactic pattern in which an MWE token instance occurs. A smaller window size for the word embedding features might be better able to capture similar information to CFORM, which could explain the good performance of the model using a window size of 1.

4.2 Generalization to Unseen VNICs

We do not expect to have substantial amounts of annotated training data for every VNIC. We there-

fore further consider whether the supervised approach is able to generalize to MWE types that are unseen during training. Indeed, this scenario motivated the choice of representation of VNIC token instances in Section 2.1. In these experiments we perform a leave-one-type-out evaluation. In this case, all token instances for a single MWE type are held out, and the token instances of the remaining MWE types (limited to those within either DEV or TEST) are used to train a classifier. The classifier is then used to classify the token instances of the held out MWE type. This process is repeated until all instances of all MWE types have been classified.

For these experiments we consider the setup that performed best on average over DEV and TEST in the previous experiments (i.e., a window size of 1 and 300 dimensional vectors). The macro-averaged accuracy on DEV and TEST is 68.9% and 69.4%, respectively. Although this is a substantial improvement over the most-frequent class baseline, it is well-below the accuracy for the previously-considered leave-one-token-out setup. Moreover, the unsupervised CFORM method of Fazly et al. (2009) gives substantially higher accuracies than this supervised approach. The limited ability of this model to generalize to unseen MWE types further motivates exploring unsupervised approaches to this task.

4.3 Unsupervised Results

The k-means clustering for the unsupervised approach is repeated 100 times with randomly-selected initial centroids, for several values of k. The average accuracy and standard deviation of the unsupervised approach over these 100 runs are shown in the left panel of Table 2. For $k = 4$ and 5 on TEST, this approach surpasses the unsupervised CFORM method of Fazly et al. (2009); however, on DEV this approach does not outperform Fazly et al.'s CFORM approach for any of the val-

---

[8]This is equivalent to macro-averaged recall.

ues of k considered. Analyzing the results on individual expressions indicates that the unsupervised approach gives especially low accuracy for *hit roof* — which is in DEV— as compared to the CFORM method of Fazly et al., which could contribute to the overall lower accuracy of the unsupervised approach on this dataset.

We now consider the upperbound of an unsupervised approach that selects a single label for each cluster of usages. In the right panel of Table 2 we show results for an oracle approach that always selects the best label for each cluster. In this case, as the number of clusters increases, so too will the accuracy.[9] Nevertheless, these results show that, even for relatively small values of k, there is scope for improving the proposed unsupervised method through improved methods for selecting the label for each cluster, and that the performance of such a method could potentially come close to that of the supervised approach. A word's predominant sense is known to be a powerful baseline in word-sense disambiguation, and prior work has addressed automatically identifying predominant word senses (McCarthy et al., 2007; Lau et al., 2014). The findings here suggest that methods for determining whether a set of usages of a VNIC are predominantly literal or idiomatic could be leveraged to give further improvements in unsupervised VNIC identification.

5 Conclusions

In this paper we proposed supervised and unsupervised approaches, based on word embeddings, to identifying token instances of VNICs that performed better than the supervised approach, and unsupervised CFORM approach, of Fazly et al. (2009), respectively. In future work we intend to consider methods for determining the predominant "sense" (i.e., idiomatic or literal) of a set of usages of a VNIC, in an effort to further improve unsupervised VNIC identification.

Acknowledgments

This work is financially supported by the Natural Sciences and Engineering Research Council of Canada, the New Brunswick Innovation Foundation, and the University of New Brunswick.

---

[9]When the number of clusters is equal to the number of instances, the accuracy will be 100%.

References

Timothy Baldwin and Su Nam Kim. 2010. Multiword expressions. In Nitin Indurkhya and Fred J. Damerau, editors, *Handbook of Natural Language Processing*, CRC Press, Boca Raton, USA. 2nd edition.

Julia Birke and Anoop Sarkar. 2006. A clustering approach for nearly unsupervised recognition of nonliteral language. In *Proceedings of the 11th Conference of the European Chapter of the Association for Computational Linguistics (EACL-2006)*. pages 329–336.

Julian Brooke, Vivian Tsang, Graeme Hirst, and Fraser Shein. 2014. Unsupervised multiword segmentation of large corpora using prediction-driven decomposition of n-grams. In *Proceedings of COLING 2014, the 25th International Conference on Computational Linguistics: Technical Papers*. Dublin, Ireland, pages 753–761.

Lou Burnard. 2007. Reference guide for the British National Corpus (XML Edition). Oxford University Computing Services.

Kenneth W. Church and Patrick Hanks. 1990. Word association norms, mutual information, and lexicography. *Computational Linguistics* 16(1):22–29.

Paul Cook, Afsaneh Fazly, and Suzanne Stevenson. 2008. The VNC-Tokens Dataset. In *Proceedings of the LREC Workshop on Towards a Shared Task for Multiword Expressions (MWE 2008)*. Marrakech, Morocco, pages 19–22.

Li Dong, Furu Wei, Ming Zhou, and Ke Xu. 2015. Question answering over freebase with multi-column convolutional neural networks. In *Proceedings of the 53rd Annual Meeting of the Association for Computational Linguistics and the 7th International Joint Conference on Natural Language Processing*. volume 1, pages 260–269.

Afsaneh Fazly, Paul Cook, and Suzanne Stevenson. 2009. Unsupervised type and token identification of idiomatic expressions. *Computational Linguistics* 35(1):61–103.

Richard Fothergill and Timothy Baldwin. 2012. Combining resources for mwe-token classification. In *SEM 2012: The First Joint Conference on Lexical and Computational Semantics – Volume 1: Proceedings of the main conference and the shared task, and Volume 2: Proceedings of the Sixth International Workshop on Semantic Evaluation (SemEval 2012)*. Montréal, Canada, pages 100–104.

Chikara Hashimoto and Daisuke Kawahara. 2008. Construction of an idiom corpus and its application to idiom identification based on WSD incorporating idiom-specific features. In *Proceedings of the 2008 Conference on Empirical Methods in Natural Language Processing*. Honolulu, Hawaii, pages 992–1001.

Graham Katz and Eugenie Giesbrecht. 2006. Automatic identification of non-compositional multi-word expressions using latent semantic analysis. In *Proceedings of the Workshop on Multiword Expressions: Identifying and Exploiting Underlying Properties*. Sydney, Australia, pages 12–19.

Jey Han Lau, Paul Cook, Diana McCarthy, Spandana Gella, and Timothy Baldwin. 2014. Learning word sense distributions, detecting unattested senses and identifying novel senses using topic models. In *Proceedings of the 52nd Annual Meeting of the Association for Computational Linguistics (ACL 2014)*. Baltimore, USA, pages 259–270.

Linlin Li, Benjamin Roth, and Caroline Sporleder. 2010. Topic models for word sense disambiguation and token-based idiom detection. In *Proceedings of the 48th Annual Meeting of the Association for Computational Linguistics*. Uppsala, Sweden, pages 1138–1147.

Dekang Lin. 1999. Automatic identification of non-compositional phrases. In *Proceedings of the 37th Annual Meeting of the Association for Computational Linguistics*. College Park, MD, pages 317–324.

Wang Ling, Yulia Tsvetkov, Silvio Amir, Ramon Fermandez, Chris Dyer, Alan W Black, Isabel Trancoso, and Chu-Cheng Lin. 2015. Not all contexts are created equal: Better word representations with variable attention. In *Proceedings of the 2015 Conference on Empirical Methods in Natural Language Processing*. Lisbon, Portugal, pages 1367–1372.

Christopher Manning, Mihai Surdeanu, John Bauer, Jenny Finkel, Steven Bethard, and David McClosky. 2014. The Stanford CoreNLP Natural Language Processing Toolkit. In *Proceedings of the 52nd Annual Meeting of the Asso-*

ciation for Computational Linguistics: System Demonstrations. Baltimore, USA, pages 55–60.

Diana McCarthy, Bill Keller, and John Carroll. 2003. Detecting a continuum of compositionality in phrasal verbs. In *Proceedings of the ACL-SIGLEX Workshop on Multiword Expressions: Analysis, Acquisition and Treatment*. Sapporo, Japan, pages 73–80.

Diana McCarthy, Rob Koeling, Julie Weeds, and John Carroll. 2007. Unsupervised acquisition of predominant word senses. *Computational Linguistics* 33(4):553–590.

Tomas Mikolov, Kai Chen, Greg Corrado, and Jeffrey Dean. 2013. Efficient estimation of word representations in vector space. In *Proceedings of Workshop at the International Conference on Learning Representations, 2013*. Scottsdale, USA.

David Newman, Nagendra Koilada, Jey Han Lau, and Timothy Baldwin. 2012. Bayesian text segmentation for index term identification and keyphrase extraction. In *Proceedings of the 24th International Conference on Computational Linguistics (COLING 2012)*. Mumbai, India, pages 2077–2092.

Jon Patrick and Jeremy Fletcher. 2005. Classifying verb-particle constructions by verb arguments. In *Proceedings of the Second ACL-SIGSEM Workshop on the Linguistic Dimensions of Prepositions and their use in Computational Linguistics Formalisms and Applications*. Colchester, UK, pages 200–209.

Fabian Pedregosa, Gaël Varoquaux, Alexandre Gramfort, Vincent Michel, Bertrand Thirion, Olivier Grisel, Mathieu Blondel, Peter Prettenhofer, Ron Weiss, Vincent Dubourg, et al. 2011. Scikit-learn: Machine learning in python. *The Journal of Machine Learning Research* 12:2825–2830.

Siva Reddy, Diana McCarthy, and Suresh Manandhar. 2011. An empirical study on compositionality in compound nouns. In *Proceedings of the Fifth International Joint Conference on Natural Language Processing (IJCNLP 2011)*. Chiang Mai, Thailand, pages 210–218.

Bahar Salehi, Paul Cook, and Timothy Baldwin. 2014. Using distributional similarity of multiway translations to predict multiword expression compositionality. In *Proceedings of the*

14th Conference of the EACL (EACL 2014). Gothenburg, Sweden, pages 472–481.

Bahar Salehi, Paul Cook, and Timothy Baldwin. 2015. A word embedding approach to predicting the compositionality of multiword expressions. In *Proceedings of the 2015 Conference of the North American Chapter of the Association for Computational Linguistics: Human Language Technologies*. Denver, Colorado, pages 977–983.

Nathan Schneider, Emily Danchik, Chris Dyer, and Noah A. Smith. 2014. Discriminative lexical semantic segmentation with gaps: Running the mwe gamut. *Transactions of the Association of Computational Linguistics* 2:193–206.

Frank Smadja. 1993. Retrieving collocations from text: Xtract. *Computational Linguistics* 19(1):143–177.

Andrew Trask, David Gilmore, and Matthew Russell. 2015. Modeling order in neural word embeddings at scale. *Journal of Machine Learning Research* 37.

Kiyoko Uchiyama, Timothy Baldwin, and Shun Ishizaki. 2005. Disambiguating Japanese compound verbs. *Computer Speech and Language, Special Issue on Multiword Expressions* 19(4):497–512.

Will Y. Zou, Richard Socher, Daniel Cer, and Christopher D. Manning. 2013. Bilingual word embeddings for phrase-based machine translation. In *Proceedings of the 2013 Conference on Empirical Methods in Natural Language Processing*. Seattle, Washington, USA, pages 1393–1398.

Author Index